THE DAILY STUDY BIBLE

THE LETTERS TO TIMOTHY, TITUS
AND PHILEMON

M—1

THE LETTERS TO TIMOTHY, TITUS and PHILEMON

The Rev. WILLIAM BARCLAY, D.D.

*Professor of Divinity and Biblical Criticism at the
University of Glasgow*

THE SAINT ANDREW PRESS
EDINBURGH

Published by The Saint Andrew Press
121 George Street, Edinburgh
and printed in Scotland by
McCorquodale & Co. Ltd., Glasgow

First Edition	-	May, 1956
Second Edition	-	March, 1960
Second Impression	-	August, 1962
Third Impression	-	1964
Fourth Impression	-	1965
Fifth Impression	-	1970

ISBN 0 7152 0090 9

To

R. G. M.

A GREAT ENCOURAGER

GENERAL INTRODUCTION

IT may truly be said that this series of Daily Bible Studies began almost accidentally. A series which the Church of Scotland was using came to an end, and another series was immediately required. I was asked to write a volume on *Acts*, and, at the moment, had no intention beyond that. But one volume followed another, until the demand for one volume became a plan to write on the whole New Testament.

The translation which is given in each volume claims no special merit. It was included in order that the reader might be able to carry both the text of the New Testament and the comments on it wherever he went, and that he might be able to read it anywhere. While I was making the translation, the translations of Moffatt, Weymouth, and Knox were ever beside me. *The American Revised Standard Version, The Twentieth Century New Testament,* and *The New Testament in Plain English,* by Charles Kingsley Williams, have been in constant use. Since its publication, I have consistently consulted *The Authentic New Testament,* translated by Hugh J. Schonfield.

I cannot see another edition of these books going out to the public without expressing my very deep and sincere gratitude to the Church of Scotland Publications Committee for allowing me the privilege of first beginning, and then continuing, this series. And in particular I wish to express my very great gratitude to the convener, Rev. R. G. Macdonald, O.B.E., M.A., D.D., and to the committee's secretary and manager, Rev. Andrew McCosh, M.A., S.T.M., for constant encouragement and never-failing sympathy and help.

As these volumes went on, the idea of the whole series developed. The aim is to make the results of modern scholarship available to the non-technical reader in a form that it does not require a theological education to understand; and then to seek to make the teaching of the New Testament books revelant to life and work to-day. The whole aim of these books is summed up in Richard of Chichester's famous prayer; they are meant to enable men and women to know Jesus Christ more clearly, to love Him more dearly, and to follow Him more nearly. It is my prayer that they may do something to make that possible.

FOREWORD

I MUST begin this foreword, as I have had to begin all the other forewords in this series of books, by expressing my very sincere gratitude to the Publications Committee of the Church of Scotland for allowing me first to start and then to continue with this series of Daily Bible Readings. In particular I cannot be too grateful to the Rev. R. G. Macdonald, O.B.E., D.D., the Convener of the Committee, and to the Rev. A. McCosh, M.A., S.T.M., the Publications Manager, for their constant patience and encouragement.

This volume seeks to expound I *and* 2 *Timothy* and *Titus*, which are generally known as *The Pastoral Epistles*, and Paul's only surviving private letter, *Philemon*.

The Pastoral Epistles, as I *and* 2 *Timothy* and *Titus* are called, have been undeservedly neglected by ordinary readers of the Bible. They are of the greatest interest, for no letters in the New Testament give such a vivid picture of the growing Church. In them we see the problems of a Church which is a little island of Christianity in a sea of paganism; and in them we see as nowhere else the first beginnings of the ministry of the Church. These letters have an interest all their own; and the more one studies them, the more interesting they become. It has been the fashion to describe them as sub-apostolic, to speak of them as second generation Christianity, to imply or even to say that they fall below the level of the letters written in the great thrilling dawn of the Church. But the fact is that just because they were written when the Church was becoming an institution, they speak most directly to our situation and condition.

As we have said in every volume, the translation claims no special merit. It has indeed only been made and included so that the reader could carry these volumes with him and read them anywhere.

The Pastoral Epistles have been fortunate in their commentaries. There are several notable volumes on the Greek text. That by Walter Lock in the *International Critical Commentary* is a monument of sound and sober scholarship. That by Sir Robert Falconer is slighter, but full of illumination compressed into small compass. The recent commentary by E. K. Simpson is written with verve and with a mastery of Hellenistic Greek words which will ensure it a place among the great commentaries. P. N. Harrison's work on the *Pastoral Epistles* represents a life-time of labour, and for examination of the language of the letters can never be surpassed. On the English text the old commentary by A. E. Humphreys in the Cambridge Bible is still very far from negligible. The quite recent commentary by B. S. Easton is excellent, especially on the meaning of words. The commentary by E. F. Brown in the *Westminster Commentary* is a unique volume. It has always been said that the *Pastoral Epistles* are the most useful of all books for the modern missionary, for they describe the very situation of the younger Churches to-day. E. F. Brown was for many years a missionary in India, and again and again he adduces the most interesting and relevant modern parallels to the situations in the *Pastorals*. Of all commentaries this is the most useful for the preacher. The volume by E. F. Scott in the Moffatt Commentary is consistently useful.

To myself the *Pastoral Epistles* were at least to some extent a new discovery. To work through them has been an absorbing experience; and it is my prayer that this book may do something to bring to life for those who read it the problems and the heroisms of the early Church.

As we have said, *Philemon* is the only one of Paul's personal letters to have survived. Although it is so small a letter it has been blessed in its commentators. Usually it is included in commentaries with one of the longer letters. In the case of J. B. Lightfoot it is included with *Colossians*. In the *International Critical Commentary* it is included with *Philippians,* and the commentary is by M. R. Vincent. In the Moffatt Commentary it is included with *Colossians* and *Ephesians,* and the commentator is E. F. Scott. In the new Cambridge Greek Testament it is included with C. F. D. Moule's commentary on *Colossians*. In every case the charm and loveliness of this letter has brought the best out of its commentators.

The work of E. J. Goodspeed on *Philemon* is of special importance, and can be found in his *Introduction to the New Testament*. Goodspeed's conclusions have been studied and followed by C. L. Mitten. *Philemon among the Letters of Paul,* by John Knox, is also important.

Short as *Philemon* is there is no letter in the New Testament which takes us nearer to the heart of Paul.

It is my hope that by the study of these letters we may gain a new vision of the Church and a new insight into the mind and heart of Paul.

WILLIAM BARCLAY.

CONTENTS

I TIMOTHY

xi

CONTENTS

2 TIMOTHY

CONTENTS

TITUS

PHILEMON

THE LETTERS TO TIMOTHY

THE LETTERS TO TIMOTHY

INTRODUCTION

Personal Letters

1 and 2 *Timothy* and *Titus* have always been regarded as forming a separate group of letters, different from the other letters of Paul. The most obvious difference is that they, along with the little letter to *Philemon*, are written to *persons*, whereas all other Pauline letters are written to *Churches*. The Muratorian Canon, which was the earliest official list of New Testament books, says that they were written " from personal feeling and affection." They are private rather than public letters.

Ecclesiastical Letters

But it very soon began to be seen that, though these are on the face of it personal and private letters, they have a significance and a relevance far beyond a merely personal reference. In 1 *Timothy* 3: 15 the aim of these *A I M* letters is set down. They are written to Timothy " that thou mayest know how thou oughtest to behave thyself in the house of God, which is the Church of the living God." These letters are written to set out the conduct which befits those who live in the household of God. So, then, it came to be seen that these letters have not only a personal significance, but that they have also what one might call an *ecclesiastical* significance. So the Muratorian Canon says of them that, though they are personal letters written out of personal affection, " they are still hallowed in the respect of the Catholic Church, and *in the arrangement of ecclesiastical discipline*." Tertullian said that Paul wrote " two letters to Timothy and one to Titus, which were composed *concerning the state of the Church* (de ecclesiastico statu)." It is not then surprising that the first name which was given to them was *Pontifical Letters*. A pontifical letter is a letter written by the *pontifex*, the priest, the controller of the Church.

Pastoral Letters

But bit by bit they came to acquire the name by which they are still known—*The Pastoral Epistles*. In writing of I *Timothy* Thomas Aquinas, as long ago as 1274, said, "This letter is as it were *a pastoral rule* which the Apostle delivered to Timothy." In his introduction to the second letter, he writes, "In the first letter he gives Timothy instructions concerning ecclesiastical order; in this second letter he deals with a *pastoral care* which should be so great that it will even accept martyrdom for the sake of the care of the flock." But this title, The Pastoral Epistles, really became affixed to these letters from 1726, in which year a great scholar, Paul Anton by name, gave a series of famous lectures on them which he called lectures on The Pastoral Epistles.

These letters then deal with the care and the organization of the Church and of the flock of God; they tell men how to behave within the household of God; they give instructions as to how God's house should be administered, as to what kind of people the leaders and pastors of the Church should be, and as to how the threats which endanger the purity of the Christian faith and life should be dealt with.

The Growing Church

The supreme interest of these letters is that we get in them as nowhere else a picture of the infant Church. In those early days the Church was an island in a sea of paganism. On every side the most perilous of infections threatened it. The people who were in it were only one remove from their heathen background and origin. It would have been so easy for them to slip back and to relapse into the pagan standards from which they had come. The tarnishing atmosphere was all around them. It is a most interesting and significant fact that missionaries tell us that of all letters the Pastoral Epistles speak most directly to the situation of the younger Churches.

THE LETTERS TO TIMOTHY

The situation with which these letters deal is a situation which is being re-enacted in India, in Africa, in China every day. These letters can never lose their interest because in them we see, as nowhere else, the problems which continually beset the growing Church.

The Ecclesiastical Background of the Pastorals

But from the very beginning these letters have presented their problems to New Testament scholars. There are many who have felt that as they stand they cannot have come directly from the hand and pen of Paul. That this is no new feeling may be seen from the fact that Marcion, who, although he was a heretic, was the first man to draw up a list of New Testament books, did not include them among the letters of Paul. Let us then see what makes people doubt their direct Pauline authorship.

In these letters we are confronted with the picture of a Church which has a fairly highly developed ecclesiastical organization. There are *elders* (I *Timothy* 5: 1, 17-19; *Titus* 1: 5-7); there are *bishops*, or superintendents or overseers (I *Timothy* 3: 1-7; *Titus* 1: 7-16); there are *deacons* (I *Timothy* 3: 8-13). From I *Timothy* 5: 17, 18 we learn that by that time elders were even salaried officials. The elders that rule well are to be counted worthy of a double pay, as it should be translated, and the Church is urged to remember that the labourer is worthy of his hire. There is at least the beginning of the order of widows who became so prominent later on in the early Church (I *Timothy* 5: 2-16). There is clearly here a quite elaborate structure within the Church, a structure which, some would claim, is too elaborate for the early days in which Paul lived and worked. It looks as if the Church has taken the first steps towards becoming the highly organized institution which it later became and which it is to-day.

The Days of Creeds

It is even claimed that in these letters we can see the

5

days of creeds emerging. The word *faith* changed its meaning. In the earliest days, in Paul's greatest letters, faith is always *faith in a person*; faith is the most intimate possible personal connection of love and trust and obedience with Jesus Christ. In later days faith became *faith in a creed*; it became the acceptance of certain doctrines. It is said that in the Pastoral Epistles we can see this change emerging. In the later days men will come who will depart from the *faith* and give heed to doctrines of devils (I *Timothy* 4: 1). A good servant of Jesus Christ must be nourished in the words of *faith and good doctrine* (I *Timothy* 4: 6). The heretics are men of corrupt minds, reprobate concerning the *faith* (2 *Timothy* 3: 8). The duty of Titus is to rebuke men that they may be sound in the *faith* (*Titus* 1: 13). This comes out very particularly in an expression which is peculiar to the Pastorals. Timothy is urged to keep hold of " that good thing which has been committed unto thee " (2 *Timothy* 1: 14). The word for *that which has been committed* is *parathēkē*. *Parathēkē* means a *deposit* in the sense of a deposit which has been entrusted to a banker or to someone for safe-keeping. *Parathēkē* is characteristically and essentially something which has been entrusted and which must be handed back or handed on absolutely unaltered and unchanged. That is to say the stress is on *orthodoxy*. Instead of being a close, personal relationship to Jesus Christ, as it was in the thrilling and throbbing days of the early Church, faith has become the acceptance of an orthodox creed. It is even held that in the Pastorals we have the echoes and the fragments of the very earliest creeds.

> " God was made manifest in the flesh;
> Justified in the Spirit;
> Seen of angels;
> Preached unto the Gentiles;
> Believed on in the world;
> Received into glory " (I *Timothy* 3: 16).

That indeed sounds like the fragment of a creed to be recited and repeated.

> " Remember that the Lord Jesus Christ of the seed
> of David was raised from the dead according to
> my gospel " (2 *Timothy* 2: 8).

That indeed sounds like a reminder of a sentence from an
accepted creed.

Within the Pastorals there undoubtedly are indications
that the day of insistence on orthodoxy and acceptance
of a creed has begun, and that the days of the first thrilling
personal discovery of Christ are beginning to fade.

A *Dangerous Heresy*

It is clear that in the forefront of the situation against
which the Pastoral Epistles were written there was a
dangerous heresy which was threatening the welfare of
the Christian Church. If we can distinguish the various
characteristic features of that heresy, we may be able
to go on to identify it.

It was characterized by *speculative intellectualism*. It
produced questions (I *Timothy* I: 4); those involved in
it doted about questions (I *Timothy* 6: 4); it dealt in
foolish and unlearned questions (2 *Timothy* 2: 23); its
foolish questions are to be avoided (*Titus* 3: 9). The word
which in each case is used for *questions* is the word *ekzētēsis*,
which means *speculative discussion*. This heresy was
obviously a heresy which was a playground of the intellectuals, or rather the pseudo-intellectuals of the Church.

It was characterized by *pride*. The heretic is proud,
although in reality he knows nothing (I *Timothy* 6: 4).
There are indications that these intellectuals set themselves
on a plane above the ordinary Christian; in fact they may
well have said that complete salvation was outside the
grasp of the ordinary man and was only open to them.
There are times when the Pastoral Epistles stress the word
all in a most significant way. The grace of God, which
brings salvation, has appeared to *all* men (*Titus* 2: II).
It is God's will that *all* men should be saved and come to a
knowledge of the truth (I *Timothy* 2: 4). The intellectuals

7

tried to make the greatest blessings of Christianity the exclusive possession of a chosen few; and in contradistinction to that exclusiveness the true faith stresses the all-embracing love of God.

There were within that heresy two opposite tendencies. There was a tendency to *asceticism*. The heretics tried to lay down special food laws, forgetting that everything God has made is good (I *Timothy* 4: 4, 5). They listed many things as impure, forgetting that unto the pure all things are pure (*Titus* I: 15). It is not impossible that they regarded sex as something unclean and that they belittled marriage, and even tried to persuade those who were married to renounce marriage, for in *Titus* 2: 4 the simple duties of the married life are stressed as being binding on the Christian. But it is also clear that this heresy issued in *immorality*. The heretics even invaded private houses and led away weak and foolish women in evil lusts and desires (2 *Timothy* 3: 6). They are characterized by lust (2 *Timothy* 4: 3). They profess to know God, but are themselves abominable (*Titus* I: 16). These heretics were out to impose upon people, and to feather their own nests, and to make money out of their false teaching. To them gain is godliness (I *Timothy* 6: 5); they teach and deceive for filthy lucre's sake (*Titus* I: 11). On the one hand this heresy issued in an unchristian asceticism, and on the other it produced an equally unchristian immorality.

This heresy was characterized by *words* and *tales* and *genealogies*. It was full of vain babblings and useless controversies (I *Timothy* 6: 20). It produced endless genealogies (I *Timothy* I: 4; *Titus* 3: 9). It produced myths and fables (I *Timothy* I: 4; *Titus* I: 14).

It was at least in some way and to some extent tied up with *Jewish legalism*. Amongst its devotees are those of the circumcision (*Titus* I: 10). The aim of the heretics is to be teachers of the law (I *Timothy* I: 7). It pressed on men Jewish fables and the commandments of men (*Titus* I: 14).

Finally, these heretics denied *the resurrection of the body*. They said that any resurrection that a man was going to experience had been experienced already (2 *Timothy* 2: 18). This is probably a reference to those who held that there was no resurrection of the body, and that the resurrection which the Christian experienced was the resurrection in a spiritual sense when a man died with Christ and rose again with Him in the experience of baptism (*Romans* 6: 4).

The Beginnings of Gnosticism

Is there then any heresy which fits all this material? There is, and its name was *Gnosticism*. The basic thought of Gnosticism is that all matter is essentially evil and spirit alone is good. That basic belief had certain consequences.

The Gnostic believed that matter is as eternal as God; and that when God created the world He had to use this essentially evil matter. That had very important consequences for thought. It meant that to them God was not and could not be the direct creator of the world. In order to touch this flawed matter God had to send out a series of emanations—they called them æons—each one more and more distant from Himself until at last there came an emanation or æon so distant from God that it could deal with matter and create the world. So between man and God there stretched a ladder and a series of these emanations. Each of these emanations had his name and his genealogy. So Gnosticism very literally had endless fables and endless genealogies. If a man was ever to get to God, he must, as it were, ascend this ladder of emanations; and to do that he needed a very special kind of knowledge including all kinds of passwords to get him past each stage. Only a person of the highest intellectual calibre could hope to acquire this knowledge and know these passwords and so get to God. The ordinary person could never get past the lower stages on the way to God. He was earthbound, and only the intellectual man could master these speculations and acquire that knowledge and climb to God.

Still further, if matter was altogether evil, then the body is altogether evil. From that, two opposite possible consequences spring. Either, the body must be buffeted, subjected, neglected, held down, and so a rigorous asceticism resulted, in which the needs of the body were eliminated as far as possible, and the instincts of the body, especially the sex instinct, were as far as possible destroyed; or, if the body is altogether evil, it may be held that it is of no importance what we do with the body; therefore its instincts and desires and lusts can be glutted and sated and given their way, because the body does not matter. The Gnostic therefore became either an ascetic, or a man to whom morality had ceased to have any relevance at all.

And still further, if the body is evil, then clearly there can be no such thing as the resurrection of the body. It was not the resurrection of the body, but the destruction of the body, to which the Gnostic looked forward.

It is abundantly clear how accurately all this fits the situation of the Pastoral Epistles. In Gnosticism we see the intellectualism, the intellectual arrogance, the fables and the genealogies, the asceticism and the immorality, the refusal to contemplate the possibility of a bodily resurrection, which are all part and parcel of the heresy against which the Pastoral Epistles were written.

One single element in the heresy has not yet been fitted into place—the Judaism and the legalism of which the Pastoral Epistles speak. That too finds its place. Sometimes Gnosticism and Judaism joined hands, and, as it were, entered into an unholy alliance. We have already said that the Gnostics insisted that to climb the ladder to God a very special knowledge was necessary; and that some of them insisted that for the good life a strict asceticism was essential. It was the claim of certain of the Jews that it was precisely the Jewish law and the Jewish food regulations which provided that special knowledge and that necessary asceticism; and so there were times when Judaism and Gnosticism went hand in hand.

It is quite clear that the heresy at the back of the Pastoral Epistles is Gnosticism. And there are some who have used that very fact to try to prove that Paul could have had nothing to do with the writing of them, because, they say, Gnosticism did not emerge until much later than Paul. It is quite true that the great formal systems of Gnosticism, connected with such names as Valentinus and Basilides, did not arise until the second century; but these great figures only systematized what was already there. The basic ideas of Gnosticism were there in the atmosphere which surrounded the early Church, even in the days of Paul. It is easy to see their attraction, and it is also easy to see that, if they had been allowed to flourish and develop unchecked, they could have turned Christianity into a speculative philosophy, and wrecked the Christian religion. It is easy to see that in facing Gnosticism the Church was facing one of the gravest dangers which ever threatened the Christian faith.

The Language of the Pastorals

But the most impressive argument against the direct Pauline origin of the Pastorals is a fact which is quite clear in the Greek, but not so clear in any English translation. The total number of words in the Pastoral Epistles is 902, of which 54 are proper names; and of these 902 words no fewer than 306 never occur in any other of Paul's letters. That is to say 36 per cent, more than a third of the words in the vocabulary of the Pastoral Epistles, are totally absent from the vocabulary of Paul in his other letters. In fact 175 words in the Pastoral Epistles occur nowhere in the New Testament at all. On the other hand, it is only fair to say that there are 50 words in the Pastoral Epistles which occur in Paul's other letters, and nowhere else in the New Testament. Further, it is true that when the other letters of Paul and the Pastorals say the same thing they say it in different ways, using different words and different turns of speech to express the same idea.

Further yet, many of Paul's favourite words are absent entirely from the Pastoral Epistles. The word for the *cross* (stauros) and *to crucify* (stauroun) occur 27 times in Paul's other letters, and never in the Pastorals. *Eleutheria* and the kindred words which have to do with *freedom* occur 29 times in Paul's other letters, and never in the Pastorals. *Huios*, the word for *son*, and *huiothesia*, the word for *adoption*, occur 46 times in Paul's other letters, and never in the Pastorals.

Still further, Greek is a language which has many more little words which are called *particles* and *enclitics* than English has. Sometimes they indicate a tone of voice more than anything else. Every Greek sentence is joined to the sentence which goes before, and these little untranslatable words are the joins. Of these particles, enclitics, pronouns and prepositions there are 112 in Paul's other letters, which he uses altogether 932 times, and they never occur in the Pastorals.

There is clearly something which has to be explained here. On the strength of the vocabulary and of the style, we would find it hard to believe that Paul wrote the Pastoral Epistles in the same sense as he wrote his other letters.

Paul's Activities in the Pastorals

But perhaps the most obvious difficulty of the Pastorals is the simple fact that they show Paul engaged in activities for which there is neither place nor room in his life as we know it from the book of Acts. He has clearly conducted a mission in Crete (*Titus* 1: 5). And he proposes to spend a winter in Nicopolis which is in Epirus (*Titus* 3: 12). Now it is clear that in Paul's life as we know it that particular mission and that particular winter just cannot be fitted in. But it may well be that it is just here that we have stumbled on the whole solution to the problem.

Was Paul released from his Roman Imprisonment?

Let us pause to sum up. We have seen that the Church organization of the Pastorals is more elaborate than in any other Pauline letter. We have seen that the stress on orthodoxy and on keeping what has been delivered as a trust sounds like second or third generation Christianity, when the thrill of the new discovery is wearing off, and when the Church is on the way to becoming an institution. We have seen that Paul is depicted as carrying out a mission or missions which cannot be fitted into the scheme of his life as we have it in *Acts*. But the strange fact about *Acts* is that it leaves it quite uncertain what happened to Paul in Rome. It ends by telling us that Paul lived for two whole years in a kind of semi-captivity preaching the gospel without let or hindrance (*Acts* 28: 30, 31). But *Acts* does not tell us how that captivity ended, or whether it ended in Paul's release or his condemnation and execution. It is true that the general assumption is that it ended in his condemnation and death, but there is a by no means negligible stream of tradition which tells that it ended in his release, his liberty for two or three further years, his re-imprisonment and his final execution about the year A.D. 67.

Let us look at this question, for it is of the greatest interest. We will not be able to attain certainty, but we can at least investigate the question—even if it must remain a question.

First, it is clear that when Paul was in prison in Rome, he did not regard release as impossible; in fact it looks as if he expected it. When he wrote to the Philippians from prison in Rome, he said that he was at the moment sending Timothy to them, and then he goes on, " But I trust in the Lord that I also myself shall come shortly " (*Philippians* 2: 24). When he wrote to Philemon, sending back the runaway Onesimus, he says, " But withal prepare me also a lodging; for I trust that through your prayers

I will be given unto you " (*Philemon* 22). Clearly Paul was prepared for release, whether or not release ever came.

Second, let us remember a plan that was very dear to Paul's heart. Before Paul went to Jerusalem on that journey on which he was arrested, he wrote to the Church at Rome, and in that letter he is planning a visit to Spain. " When I take my journey to Spain," he writes, " I will come to you." " I will come by you," he writes, " into Spain " (*Romans* 15: 24, 28). He was planning at that time to visit Spain, and to visit Rome on the way to Spain. Was that visit ever paid?

Clement of Rome, when he wrote to the Church at Corinth about A.D. 90, said of Paul that he preached the gospel in the East and in the West; that he instructed the whole world (that is, the Roman Empire) in righteousness; and that he went to the extremity (*terma*, the terminus) of the West, before his martyrdom. What did Clement mean by *the extremity of the West*? There are many who argue that Clement meant nothing more than Rome. Now it is true that someone writing away in the East in Asia Minor would probably think of Rome as *the extremity of the West. But Clement was writing from Rome*; and it is difficult to see that for anyone in Rome *the extremity of the West* could be anything else but Spain. It certainly seems that Clement believed that Paul reached Spain.

The greatest of all the early Church historians was Eusebius. In his account of Paul's life Eusebius writes: " Luke who wrote the *Acts of the Apostles*, brought his history to a close at this point, after stating that Paul had spent two whole years at Rome as a prisoner at large, and preached the word of God without constraint. Thus, after he had made his defence, it is said that the Apostle was sent again on the ministry of preaching, and that on coming to the same city a second time he suffered martyrdom " (Eusebius, *Ecclesiastical History*, 2.22.2). Eusebius has nothing to say about Spain, but he did know the story that Paul had been released from his first Roman imprisonment.

The Muratorian Canon, that first list of New Testament books, describes Luke's scheme in writing Acts: " Luke related to Theophilus events of which he was an eye-witness, as also, in a separate place, he evidently declares the martyrdom of Peter (he probably refers to *Luke* 22: 31, 32); but omits the journey of Paul from Rome to Spain." Clearly the Muratorian Canon knew of a journey of Paul to Spain.

In the fifth century two of the great Christian fathers are definite about Paul's journey to Spain. Chrysostom in his sermon on 2 *Timothy* 4: 20 says: " Saint Paul after his residence in Rome departed to Spain." Jerome in his *Catalogue of Writers* says that Paul " was dismissed by Nero that he might preach Christ's gospel in the West."

There is beyond doubt a stream of tradition which held that Paul journeyed to Spain.

This is a matter on which we will have to come to our own decision. The one thing which makes us doubt the historicity of Paul's journey to Spain is that in Spain itself there is not and never was any tradition at all that Paul had worked and preached there; there are no stories about him, and no places connected with his name. It would be indeed strange if the memory of that visit had become totally obliterated. It could well be that the whole story of Paul's release and journey to the west arose simply as a deduction from Paul's expressed intention to visit Spain in *Romans* 15. On the whole it is true to say that most New Testament scholars do not think that Paul was released from his imprisonment; the general consensus of opinion would be that Paul's only release from his Roman imprisonment was by death.

Paul and the Pastoral Epistles

What then shall we say of Paul's connection with these letters? If we can accept the tradition of Paul's release, and of his return to preaching and teaching, and of his death as late as A.D. 67, then we might well believe that the letters as they stand came from his hand. But, if we cannot believe that—and the evidence is on the whole against it—are we to go on to say that the Pastoral Epistles have no connection with Paul at all? We must remember that the ancient world did not think of these things as we do. The ancient world would see nothing wrong in issuing a letter under the name of a great teacher, if it was sure that the letter said the very things that teacher would say under the contemporary circumstances. To the ancient world it was a natural and a seemly thing that a disciple should write in his master's name. No one, either in the world or in the Church, would have seen anything wrong in a disciple of Paul meeting a new and threatening situation with a letter under the name of Paul. To think in terms of forgery is completely to misunderstand the mind of the ancient world. Are we then to swing completely to the other extreme and to say that some disciple of Paul issued these letters in the name of Paul years after Paul was dead, and at a time when the Church was much more highly organized than ever it was during Paul's lifetime?

As we see it, that is precisely what we cannot say. It is quite incredible that any disciple would put into Paul's mouth a claim to be the chief of sinners (I *Timothy* I: 15). A disciple's tendency would be to stress Paul's holiness, and not to talk about his sin. It is quite incredible that anyone writing in the name of Paul would give Timothy the simple, homely advice to drink a little wine for the sake of his health (I *Timothy* 5: 23). The whole of 2 *Timothy* 4 is so personal and so full of intimate, loving details that no one but Paul could have written it.

Wherein then lies the solution? It may well be that something like this happened. It is quite obvious that many letters of Paul went lost. Clearly, apart from his great public letters, Paul must have had a continuous private

correspondence; and of that private correspondence we possess only one letter, the little letter to Philemon. It alone escaped the destruction which is the ultimate fate of all private correspondence. Now it may well be that in the later days there were some fragments of Paul's correspondence in the possession of some Christian teacher. This Christian teacher saw the Church of his day and his locality in Ephesus threatened on every side. It was threatened with heresy from without and from within. It was threatened with a fall away from its own high standards of purity and truth. The quality of its members and the standard of its office-bearers were degenerating. This teacher had in his possession little letters of Paul which said exactly the things that should be said, but, as they stood, they were too short and too fragmentary to publish. So he took them and amplified them and made them supremely relevant to his own situation and sent them out to the Church.

In the Pastoral Epistles we are still hearing the voice of Paul, and often hearing it speak with a unique personal intimacy, but we think that the form of the letters is due to a Christian teacher who summoned the help and the spirit of Paul to his aid, when the Church of his day needed the guidance which only Paul could have given.

I and II TIMOTHY

THE ROYAL COMMAND

I *Timothy* I: I, 2

Paul, an apostle of Christ Jesus, by the royal command of God, our Saviour, and of Jesus Christ, our Hope, writes this letter to Timothy, his true child in the faith. Grace, mercy and peace be to you from our Lord Jesus Christ.

THERE never was a man who magnified his office as Paul did. He did not magnify it in pride; he magnified it in wonder that God had chosen him for a task like that. Twice in the opening words of this letter he lays down the greatness of his privilege.

(i) First he calls himself *an apostle of Christ Jesus*. The word *apostle* is the Greek word *apostolos*, which comes from the verb *apostellein* which means *to send out*. An *apostolos* was *one who was sent out*. As far back as Herodotus *apostolos* means an *envoy*, and *ambassador*, one who is sent out to represent his country and his king. Paul always regarded himself as the envoy and the ambassador of Christ. And, in truth, that is the office of every Christian. It is the first duty of every ambassador to form a liaison between the country to which he is sent and the country from which he is sent. He is the connecting link. And the first duty of every Christian is to be a connecting link between his fellow men and Jesus Christ.

(ii) Second, he says that he is an apostle *by the royal command of God*. The word he uses is *epitagē*. *Epitagē* is the word which Greek uses for the injunctions and obligations which some inviolable law lays on a man; for the royal command which comes to a man from the king; and above all for the instructions which come to a man either directly or by some oracle from God. For instance,

19

a man in an inscription dedicates an altar to the goddess Cybele *kat'epitagēn*, in accordance with the command of the goddess, which, he tells us, had come to him in a dream. Paul thought of himself as a man holding the king's commission. It was by God, by royal command, that he was commissioned to his task. If any man can arrive at this consciousness of being despatched by God, then a new splendour and a new magnificence enters into life. However humble his part may be in it, he is nonetheless on royal service.

> " Life can never be dull again
> When once we've thrown our windows open wide
> And seen the mighty world that lies outside,
> And whispered to ourselves this wondrous thing,
> ' We're wanted for the business of the King! ' "

It is always a privilege to do even the humblest and most menial things for someone whom we love and respect and admire, for someone whom we hero-worship. All his life the Christian can be doing that, for he is always on the business of the King.

Then Paul goes on to give to God and to Jesus two great titles.

He speaks of God our Saviour. This is a new way of speaking. We do not find this title for God in any of Paul's earlier letters. There are two backgrounds from which it comes. (a) It comes from an Old Testament background. It is Moses' charge against Israel that Jeshurun " forsook God which made him, and lightly esteemed *the Rock of his Salvation* " (*Deuteronomy* 32: 15). The Psalmist sings of how the good man will receive righteousness from *the God of his salvation* (*Psalm* 24: 5). It is Mary's song, " My soul doth magnify the Lord, and my spirit hath rejoiced in *God my Saviour* " (*Luke* 1: 46, 47). When Paul called God *Saviour*, he was going back to an idea which had always been dear to Israel. (b) There is a pagan background. It so happened that just at this time the title.

sōtēr, Saviour, was much on the lips of men. Men had always used it. In the old days the Romans had called Scipio, their great general, " our hope and our salvation." But at this very time it was the title which the Greeks gave to Aesculapius, the god of healing. Aesculapius, the Saviour, they called him. And it was one of the titles which Nero, the Roman Emperor, had taken to himself. The Roman Emperor claimed to be governor and Saviour of the world. So in this opening sentence of his letter Paul is taking the title which was much on the lips of a seeking and a wistful world and giving it to the only person to whom it belonged by right.

We must never forget that Paul called God Saviour. It is possible for us to take to ourselves a quite wrong idea of the Atonement and of what Jesus did. Sometimes people speak of the Atonement in a way which indicates that something Jesus did pacified the anger of God. They make us think of an-angry, vengeful God in contradistinction to a gentle, loving Jesus. The idea they give is that God in wrath was bent on our destruction and that somehow God's wrath was turned to love by Jesus. Nowhere in the New Testament is there any support for that. It was because God so *loved* the world that He sent Jesus into the world (*John* 3: 16). It is God who is Saviour. At the back of the whole process there is the love of God. We must never think or preach or teach of a God who had to be pacified and persuaded into loving us, for everything begins from the love of God.

THE HOPE OF THE WORLD

I *Timothy* I: I, 2 (*continued*)

HERE Paul uses one of the titles which was to become one of the great titles of Jesus Christ—" Christ Jesus, our hope." Long ago the Psalmist had demanded of himself: " Why art thou cast down, O my soul? " And he had answered: " Hope in God " (*Psalm* 43: 5). Paul himself speaks of " Christ in you, the hope of glory " (*Colossians* 1: 27). John was to speak of the dazzling prospect which confronted the Christian, the prospect of being like Christ; and then he goes on to say: "Every man that hath this hope in him purifieth himself " (1 *John* 3: 2, 3).

In the early Church this was to become one of the most precious titles of Christ. Ignatius of Antioch, when he was on his way to execution in Rome, writes to the Church in Ephesus: " Be of good cheer in God the Father and in Jesus Christ our common hope " (Ignatius, *To the Ephesians* 21: 2). Polycarp writes: " Let us therefore persevere in our hope and the earnest of our righteousness, who is Jesus Christ " (*Epistle of Polycarp* 8). Men saw in Jesus Christ their hope.

(i) Men found in Christ *the hope of moral victory and of self-conquest.* It was not that the ancient world did not know its sin; it was not that it was not conscious of its moral degradation. Epictetus had spoken wistfully of " our weakness in necessary things." Seneca had said that " we hate our vices and love them at the same time." He said, " We have not stood bravely enough by our good resolutions; despite our will and resistance we have lost our innocence. Nor is it only that we have acted amiss; we shall do so to the end." Persius, the Roman poet, wrote poignantly: " Let the guilty see virtue, and pine that they have lost her for ever." Persius talks of " filthy Natta benumbed by vice." The ancient world knew this moral helplessness only too well; and Christ came, not only telling men what was right, but giving them the power to do it. He came not only with a message of righteousness, but with the gift of the power to conquer sin. Christ gave to men who had lost it the hope of moral victory instead of moral defeat.

(ii) Men found in Christ *the hope of victory over circumstances.* Christianity came into the world in an age of the most terrible personal insecurity. When Tacitus, the Roman historian, came to write the history of that very age in which the Christian Church came into being, he began by saying, " I am entering upon the history of a period rich in disaster, gloomy with wars, rent with seditions; nay, savage in its very hours of peace. Four emperors perished by the sword; there were three civil wars; there were more with foreigners, and some had the character of both at once . . . Rome wasted by fires; its oldest temples burned; the very capitol set in flames by Roman hands; the defilement of sacred rites; adultery in high places; the sea crowded with exiles; island rocks drenched with murder; yet wilder was the frenzy in Rome; nobility, wealth, the refusal of office, its acceptance, everything was a crime, and virtue was the surest way to ruin. Nor were the rewards of the informers less odious than their deeds. One found his spoils in a priesthood or a consulate; another in a provincial governorship, another behind the throne. All was one delirium of hate and terror; slaves were bribed to betray their masters, freedmen their patrons; and he who had no foe was betrayed by his friend." (Tacitus, *Histories* I, 2). As Gilbert Murray said, the whole age was suffering from " the failure of nerve." Men were longing for some ring-wall of defence against " the advancing chaos of the world." It was Christ who in such times gave men the strength to live, and the courage, if need be, to die. In the certainty that nothing on earth could separate them from the love of God in Christ Jesus, men found the conquest of circumstances which the terrors of the age demanded.

(iii) Men found in Christ the hope of *victory over death*. They found the certainty that there was more than simply a tortured life and after that extinction. They found the certainty that life was going somewhere. They found in Christ at one and the same time strength for mortal things, and the immortal hope. Christ, our hope, was—and still should be—the battle-cry of the Church.

TIMOTHY, MY SON

I Timothy I: I, 2 (*continued*)

IT is to Timothy that this letter is sent, and Paul was never able to speak of Timothy without the thrill of affection in his voice.

Timothy was a native of Lystra. Lystra was in the province of Galatia. It was a Roman colony; it called itself "the most brilliant colony of Lystra," but in reality it was a little place at the ends of the civilized earth. Its importance was that there was a Roman garrison quartered there to keep control of the wild tribes of the Isaurian mountains which lay beyond. It was on the first missionary journey that Paul and Barnabas arrived at Lystra (*Acts* 14: 8-21). At that time there is no mention of Timothy; but it has been suggested that, when Paul was in Lystra, he found a lodging in Timothy's home, for Paul knew well the faith and devotion of Timothy's mother Eunice and of his grandmother Lois (2 *Timothy* I: 5). On that first visit Timothy must have been very young, but the Christian faith laid hold upon him, and Paul became his hero. It was at Paul's visit to Lystra on the second missionary journey that life began for Timothy (*Acts* 16: I-3). Young as he was, Timothy had become one of the ornaments of the Christian Church in Lystra. There was such a charm and enthusiasm in the lad that all men spoke well of him. To Paul, Timothy seemed the very man to be his helper and his assistant. Maybe even then Paul had dreams that this lad was the very person whom he might teach and mould and train to take up his work when his day was over. Timothy was the child of a mixed marriage; his mother was a Jewess, and his father was a Greek (*Acts* 16: I). So Paul took him and circumcised him. It was not that Paul was a slave of the law, or that he saw in circumcision any special virtue; but Paul knew well that if Timothy was to work amongst the Jews, there would be an initial prejudice against him if he was uncircumcised; and Paul took this step only as a practical measure whereby Timothy's usefulness as an evangelist would be increased.

From that time forward Timothy was Paul's constant companion. He was left behind at Berea with Silas when Paul escaped to Athens, and later joined Paul there (*Acts* 17: 14, 15). In due time he arrived in Athens (*Acts* 18: 5). He was sent as Paul's emissary to Macedonia (*Acts* 19: 22). He was there when the collection from the Churches was being taken to Jerusalem (*Acts* 20: 4). He was with Paul in Corinth when Paul wrote his letter to Rome (*Romans* 16: 21). He was Paul's emissary to Corinth when there was trouble in that unruly Church (1 *Corinthians* 4: 17; 16: 10). He was with Paul when Paul wrote 2 Corinthians (2 *Corinthians* 1: 1, 19). It was Timothy whom Paul sent to see how things were going in Thessalonica and he was with Paul when Paul wrote his letter to that Church (1 *Thessalonians* 1: 1; 3: 2, 6). He was with Paul in prison when Paul wrote to Philippi, and Paul was planning to send him to Philippi as his representative (*Philippians* 1: 1; 2: 19). He was with Paul when Paul wrote to the Church at Colossae and to Philemon (*Colossians* 1: 1; *Philemon* 1: 1). Constantly Timothy was by Paul's side, and when Paul had a difficult job to do Timothy was the man who was sent to do it.

Over and over again Paul's voice vibrates with love and with affection when he speaks of Timothy. When he is sending him to that sadly divided Church at Corinth, he writes: " I have sent unto you Timothy, who is my beloved son and faithful in the Lord " (1 *Corinthians* 4: 17). When he is planning to send him to Philippi, he writes: " I have no man whose mind is in such harmony with mine. . . . As a son with a father he hath served with me in the gospel " (*Philippians* 2: 20, 22). Here Paul calls Timothy "his true son." The word that he uses for *true* is *gnēsios*. This word has two meanings. It was the normal word for a *legitimate* child in contradistinction to an illegitimate child. It was the word for *genuine, sterling*, as opposed to counterfeit and unreal.

Timothy was the man whom Paul could trust. Timothy was the man whom Paul could send anywhere, knowing that he would go. Happy indeed is the leader who possesses a lieutenant like that. Timothy is our example of how we should serve in the faith. Christ needs servants like Timothy and so does Christ's Church.

GRACE, MERCY AND PEACE

1 *Timothy* 1: 1, 2 (*continued*)

PAUL always began his letters with a blessing (*Romans* 1: 7; 1 *Corinthians* 1: 3; 2 *Corinthians* 2: 2; *Galatians* 1: 3; *Ephesians* 1: 2; *Philippians* 1: 2; *Colossians* 1: 2; 1 *Thessalonians* 1: 1; 2 *Thessalonians* 1: 2; *Philemon* 3). But in all these other letters only two of these words occur—Grace and Peace. It is only in the letters to Timothy and to Titus that this third word Mercy occurs (2 *Timothy* 1: 2; *Titus* 1: 4). Let us look at these three great words.

(i) In the word *Grace* there are always three dominant ideas. (a) In classical Greek the word means outward grace or favour, beauty, attractiveness, winsomeness, sweetness. Usually, although not quite always, it is applied to persons. The English word *charm* comes very near to expressing its meaning. Grace is characteristically a lovely and a winsome thing. (b) In the New Testament there is always the idea of sheer generosity. Grace is something unearned and undeserved, something which could not have been earned and which could not have been deserved. It is opposed to that which is a debt. Paul says that if it is a case of earning things, then the reward is not a matter of grace, but of debt (*Romans* 4: 4). Grace is something which is unearned. It is opposed to works. Paul says that God's election of His chosen people is not the consequence of works, but of grace (*Romans* 11: 6). Grace is something given, not something deserved. (c) In the New Testament there is always the idea of sheer *universality*. Again and again Paul uses the word grace in connection with the reception of the Gentiles into the family of God. He thanks God for the grace of God which is given to the Corinthians in Jesus Christ (I *Corinthians* I: 4). He talks of the grace of God bestowed on the Churches of Macedonia (2 *Corinthians* 8: I). He talks of the Galatians being called into the grace of Christ (*Galatians* I: 6). The hope which came to the Thessalonians came through grace (2 *Thessalonians* 2: I6). It was God's grace which made Paul an apostle to the Gentiles (I *Corinthians* I5: I0). It was by the grace of God that he moved amongst the Corinthians (2 *Corinthians* I: I2). It was by grace that God called him and separated him from his mother's womb (*Galatians* I: I5). It is the grace given to him by God which enables him to write boldly to the Church at Rome (*Romans* I5: I5). To Paul the great demonstration of the grace of God was the reception of the Gentiles into the Church and his apostleship to them. Grace is a lovely thing; grace is a free thing; and grace is a universal thing. As F. J. Hort wrote so beautifully: "Grace is a comprehensive word, gathering up all that may be supposed to be expressed in the smile of a heavenly king, looking down upon His people."

(ii) Normally, the second of the great Pauline words of greeting is the word *Peace*. *Peace* was the normal Jewish word of greeting, and, in Hebrew thought, it expresses, not simply the negative absence of trouble, but "the most comprehensive form of well-being." Peace is everything which makes for a man's highest good. Peace is the state a man is in when he is within the love of God. F. J. Hort writes: "Peace is the antithesis to every kind of conflict and war and molestation, to enmity without and distraction within."

> "Bowed down beneath a load of sin,
>   By Satan sorely pressed,
> By war without and fear within,
>   I come to Thee for rest."

Therein is the longing for peace.

(iii) The word *Mercy* is the new word in the apostolic blessing. In Greek the word is *eleos*, and in Hebrew it is *chesedh*. Now *chesedh* is the word which is often in the Old Testament translated *loving-kindness*. And when Paul prayed for *mercy* on Timothy, he is saying, to put it very simply, " Timothy, may God be good to you." But there is more to it than that. This word *chesedh* is used in the *Psalms* no fewer than one hundred and twenty-seven times. And time and time again it has the meaning of *help in time of need*. It denotes, as Parry puts it, " God's active intervention to help." As Hort puts it, " It is the coming down of the Most High to help the helpless." In *Psalm* 40: 11 the Psalmist rejoices, " Thy loving-kindness and Thy truth shall continually guard me." In *Psalm* 57: 3 he says, " He shall send from heaven and save me . . . God shall send forth His mercy and truth." In *Psalm* 86: 14-16 he thinks of the forces of the evil men which are arrayed against him, and comforts himself with the thought that God is " plenteous in mercy and truth." It is by God's abundant mercy that He has given us the living hope of the resurrection (*I Peter* 1: 3). The Gentiles should glorify God for that mercy which has rescued them from sin and hopelessness (*Romans* 15: 9). God's mercy is God active to save. It may well be that Paul added the word Mercy to his two usual words, Grace and Peace, because Timothy was in a situation when he was up against it, and Paul wanted in one word to tell him that the Most High was the help of the helpless.

ERROR AND HERESY

I *Timothy* 1: 3-7

> I am writing to you now to reinforce the plea that I already made to you, when I urged you to stay in Ephesus while I went to Macedonia, that you might pass on the order to some of the people there, not to teach erroneous novelties, nor to give their attention

to idle tales and endless genealogies, which only succeed in producing empty speculations rather than the effective administration of God's people, which should be based on faith. The instruction which I gave you is designed to produce love which issues from a pure heart, a good conscience and an undissembling faith. But some of these people of whom I am talking have never even tried to find the right road, and have turned aside out of it to empty and useless discussions, in their claim to become teachers of the law, although they do not know what they are talking about, nor do they realize the real meaning of the things about which they dogmatize.

IT is clear that at the back of the Pastoral Epistles there is some heresy which is endangering the Church. And right at the beginning of our study of these letters it will be well to examine this heresy and to try to see what it is. We will therefore collect the facts about it now.

This very passage brings us face to face with two of its great characteristics. It dealt in *idle tales* and *endless genealogies*. These two things were not peculiar to this heresy; they were deeply engrained and rooted into the thought of the ancient world. First, there were the *idle tales*. One of the characteristics of the ancient world was that the poets and even the historians loved to work out romantic and fictitious tales about the foundation of cities and of families. They loved to construct long stories in which they traced the foundation of the city and the beginning of the family right back to the gods. They would tell of how some god came to earth and founded the city, or how some god descended to this world and took in marriage some mortal maid and so founded a line whose origin was divine. The ancient world was full of stories like that. Second, there were the *endless genealogies*. The ancient world had a passion for genealogies. We can see that even in the Old Testament with its chapters of names, and in the New Testament with the genealogies of Jesus with which Matthew and Mark begin their gospels. A man like Alexander the Great had a completely artificial pedigree constructed in which he traced his lineage back, on the one side to Achilles and Andromache, and on the other side to Perseus and Hercules. There was something about genealogies which fascinated the ancient world. It would therefore be the easiest thing in the world for Christianity to go lost in endless, romantic, fabulous stories about origins, and in elaborate and imaginary genealogies. That was a danger which was inherent in the whole situation in which Christian thought was developing and growing up.

That danger was peculiarly threatening from two directions.

It was threatening from the *Jewish direction*. To the Jews there was no book in the world like the Old Testament. Their scholars spent a lifetime studying it and expounding it. In the Old Testament there are many chapters and many sections which are long lists of names, long genealogies. And one of the favourite occupations of the Jewish scholars was to construct an imaginary and edifying biography for every name in the list! We can see at once that such a task was endless. A man could go on for ever doing that; and it may be that that was what was partly in Paul's mind. He may be saying, " When you ought to be working and labouring at the Christian life, you are sitting working out imaginary biographies and genealogies. You are wasting your time on elaborate and elegant fripperies, when you should be getting down to life and living." This may be an always-needed warning to us never to allow Christianity and Christian thinking to get lost and bogged in speculations which do not matter.

THE SPECULATIONS OF THE GREEKS

I *Timothy* I: 3-7 (*continued*)

BUT this danger came with an even greater threat from the Greek side. At this time in history there was developing a Greek line of thought which came to be known as *Gnosticism*. We find it specially in the background of the Pastoral Epistles, the Letter to the Colossians and the Fourth Gospel.

Gnosticism was entirely speculative. It began with the problem of the origin of evil, of sin and of suffering. Where did these things come from? If God is altogether good, He could not have created them. How then did they get into the world? The Gnostic answer was that in the beginning creation was not creation out of nothing; that before time began *matter* existed. They believed that this matter was essentially flawed, that it was imperfect, that it was an evil thing; and they believed that out of this flawed and essentially evil matter the world was created. Thereby they explained the sin and the suffering and the imperfection of the world. But no sooner had they got this length than they ran into another difficulty. If matter is essentially evil and God is essentially good, then God could not Himself have touched and handled and moulded and formed things out of this matter. So they began on another set of speculations. They said that God put out an emanation, and that this emanation put out another emanation, and the third emanation put out a fourth emanation and so on and on until there came into being an emanation who was so distant from God that he could touch and handle matter, and that it was not God but this emanation who created the world. They went even further than that. They held that each successive emanation knew less and less about God; that you came to a stage in the series of emanations at which the emanations were completely ignorant of God; more, that you came to a final stage in the series when the emanations were not only ignorant of God but actively hostile to Him. So they arrived at the thought that the god who created the world was actually quite ignorant of and completely hostile to the real and the true God. Later on they went even further, and they identified the God of the Old Testament with the ignorant and the hostile creating god, and the God of the New

31

Testament with the true and the real God. They further provided each one of the emanations with a complete biography. And so they built up an elaborate mythology of gods and emanations, each with his story and his biography and his genealogy. There is no doubt at all that the ancient world was riddled with that kind of thinking; and that it even entered the Church itself. When it entered the Church it made Jesus the greatest of the emanations, the emanation closest to God. It classed Him as the highest link in the endless chain between God and man. It made Him no longer unique, but only a link in a chain.

Now this Gnostic line of thought had certain characteristics, and these characteristics appear all through the Pastoral Epistles as the characteristics of the heretics whose heresies are threatening the Church and the purity of the faith.

(i) This Gnosticism is obviously highly speculative, and because it was highly speculative, it was intensely intellectually snobbish. It believed that all this intellectual speculation was quite beyond the mental grasp of ordinary simple people, and that this teaching was for an intellectual aristocracy, a chosen few, the elite of the Church. So Timothy is warned against " profane and vain babblings and oppositions of science falsely so called " (I *Timothy* 6: 20). He is warned against a religion of speculative questions instead of humble faith (I *Timothy* I: 4). He is warned against the man who is proud of his intellect, and who yet really knows nothing, but who dotes about questions and about strifes of words (I *Timothy* 6: 4). He is told to shun " profane and vain babblings," for they can only produce ungodliness (2 *Timothy* 2: 16). He is told to avoid " foolish and unlearned questions " which in the end can only engender strife (2 *Timothy* 2: 23). Further, the Pastoral Epistles go out of their way to stress the fact that this idea of an intellectual aristocracy, a chosen elite is quite wrong, for God's love is a universal love. God wants *all* men to be saved and *all* men to come

32

to a knowledge of the truth (I *Timothy* 2: 4). God is the Saviour of *all* men, especially those who believe (I *Timothy* 4: 10). The Christian Church would have nothing to do with any kind of faith which was founded on intellectual speculation, and which set up an arrogant and contemptuous intellectual aristocracy within the Church.

(ii) This Gnosticism was concerned with this long series of emanations. It gave to each of them a biography and a pedigree; it gave to each of them a place and a stage on the way to God, and an importance in the chain between God and men. These gnostics were concerned with " endless genealogies " (I *Timothy* 1: 4). They went in for " old wives' fables " about them (I *Timothy* 4: 7). They turned their ears away from the truth to fables (2 *Timothy* 4: 4). They dealt in fables like the Jewish fables (*Titus* 1: 14). Worst of all, they thought in terms of two gods, and they thought of Jesus as one of a whole series of mediators between God and man; whereas in truth " there is one God, and one mediator between God and man, the man Christ Jesus " (I *Timothy* 2: 5). There is only one King eternal, immortal, invisible, there is only one wise God (I *Timothy* 1: 17). Christianity would have nothing to do with a religion which took the unique place from God and from Jesus Christ.

THE ETHICS OF HERESY

I *Timothy* 1: 3-7 (*continued*)

THE danger of this Gnosticism was not only an intellectual danger. It had certain very serious moral and ethical consequences. We must remember that its basic belief was that matter was essentially flawed and evil, and that spirit alone was good. In actual ethical belief and conduct that issued in two opposite results.

(i) If matter is evil, then the body is evil; and the body must be subjected and despised and held down. Therefore this Gnosticism could and did issue in a rigid asceticism which regarded the body as an unmitigated evil. It forbade men to marry, for the instincts of the body were entirely to be suppressed. It laid down strict food laws, for the needs of the body must as far as possible be eliminated. So the Pastorals speak of those who forbid to marry and who command to abstain from meats (I *Timothy* 4: 3). The answer to these people is that everything which God has created is good, and is to be received with thanksgiving (I *Timothy* 4: 4). The Gnostic looked on creation as an evil thing, created by an evil God. The Christian looks on creation as a noble thing, the handiwork and the gift of a good God. The Gnostic believed that an evil God had made all things badly; the Christian believes that a good God has made all things well. The Christian lives in a world where all things are pure; the Gnostic lives in a world where all things are defiled (*Titus* I: 14).

(ii) But this Gnosticism could issue in precisely the opposite ethical belief. If the body is evil, then it does not matter what a man does with it. The body is of no importance; all that matters is the spirit. Therefore, let a man glut and sate his appetites; these things are of no importance, and therefore a man can use his body in the most licentious and unbridled way and it makes no difference. So the Pastorals speak of those who lead away foolish women until they are laden with sin and the victims of all kinds of lusts (2 *Timothy* 3: 6). Such men profess to know God, but they live lives which are abominable and reprobate (*Titus* I: 16). Such Gnostics believed that since the body was completely unimportant and altogether evil, it did not matter what a man did with it; and so they gave unbridled freedom to their lusts and their passions and their lowest desires. They used their religious beliefs as an excuse for complete immorality.

(iii) This Gnosticism had still another consequence. The Christian believed in the resurrection of the body. That is not to say that the Christian ever believed that we are resurrected with this mortal, human body; but the

Christian always believed that even after the resurrection from the dead a man would have a spiritual body, provided by God. Paul discusses this whole question in I *Corinthians* 15. But the Gnostic held that there was no such thing as the resurrection of the body (2 *Timothy* 2: 18). They believed that after death a man would be a kind of disembodied spirit. The basic difference is that the Gnostic believed in the destruction of the body; the Christian believes in the redemption of the body. The Gnostic believed in what he would call *soul salvation*; the Christian believes in *whole salvation*.

So behind the Pastoral Epistles there are these dangerous heretics; these men who gave their lives to intellectual speculations; these men who saw this as an evil world and the creating God as an evil God; these men who put between the world and man and God an endless series of emanations and lesser gods, and who spent their time equipping each of them with endless fables and genealogies; these men who reduced Jesus Christ to the position of a link in a chain and who took away His uniqueness; these men who lived either in a rigorous asceticism or an unbridled licentiousness; these men who denied the resurrection of the body. It was these dangerous heretical beliefs that the Pastorals were written to counteract and to combat.

THE MIND OF THE HERETIC

I *Timothy* I: 3-7 (*continued*)

IN this passage there is a clear picture of the mind of the dangerous heretic. There is a kind of heresy in which a man differs from orthodox belief because he has honestly thought things out and cannot agree with them. He does not take any pride in being different; he is different, not in order to draw attention to himself, but simply because he has to be. Such a heresy does not affect a man's character;

35

it may in fact make him a lovely character, because he has really and truly thought out his own faith, and is not living on a second-hand and unconsidered orthodoxy. But that is not the heretic whose picture is drawn here. Here there are distinguished five characteristics of the dangerous heretic.

(i) He is driven by the desire for novelty. He is like someone who must be in the latest fashion and who must undergo the latest craze. He despises old things for no better reason than that they are old, and desires new things for no better reason than that they are new. Christianity has always a problem to solve. The problem of presenting truth is the problem of presenting old truth in a new way. It is not the truth that changes, but the presentation of it. It is quite true that every age must find its own way of presenting Christian truth. Every teacher and preacher must talk to men in language and in categories which they understand. But the truth presented remains the same. The new presentation and the old truth go ever hand in hand.

(ii) He exalts the mind at the expense of the heart. His conception of religion is speculation, and not experience. Christianity never demanded that any man should stop thinking for himself, but Christianity does demand that every man's thinking should spring from and be dominated by a personal experience of Jesus Christ.

(iii) He deals in argument instead of action. He is more interested in abstruse discussion than in the effective administration of the household of the faith. He forgets that the truth is not only something which a man accepts with his mind, but is also something which he translates into action in his life. Long ago the distinction between the Greek and the Jew was drawn. The Greek loved argument for the sake of argument; there was nothing that he liked better than to sit with a group of friends and indulge in a series of mental acrobatics and enjoy " the stimulus of a mental hike." But he was not specially interested in reaching conclusions, and in evolving a principle of *action*. He loved argument for nothing beyond the argument, and he loved discussion for discussion's sake. The Jew too liked argument; but he wished every argument and every discussion to reach a conclusion; he wished it to end in a decision which demanded action. There is always a danger of heresy when we fall in love with words and forget deeds, for deeds are the acid test against which every argument must be tested.

(iv) He is moved by arrogance rather than by humility. His desire is to teach rather than to learn. He looks down with a certain contempt on simple-minded people, who cannot follow his flights of intellectual speculation. He regards those who do not reach his own conclusions as ignorant fools. The Christian has somehow to combine an immovable certainty with a gentle humility; the Christian to the end of the day must be ready to learn.

(v) He is guilty of dogmatism without knowledge. He does not really know what he is talking about, and he does not really understand the significance of the things about which he dogmatizes. The strange thing about religious argument is that anyone and everyone thinks that he or she has a right to express a dogmatic opinion. In all other branches of knowledge we demand that a person should have a certain knowledge before he lays down the law. But there are those who dogmatize about the Bible and its teaching although they have never even tried to find out what scholars and experts in language and history have said. It may well be that the Christian cause has suffered more from ignorant dogmatism than from anything else.

When we think of the characteristics of those who were troubling the Church at Ephesus we can see that their descendants are still with us.

THE MIND OF THE CHRISTIAN THINKER

I Timothy I: 3-7 (*continued*)

JUST as this passage draws the picture of the thinker who disturbs the Church, so it also draws the picture of the really Christian thinker. He too has five characteristics.

(i) His thinking is based on *faith*. The effective administration of the household of God must be based on faith. Faith simply means taking God at His word; faith simply means believing that God is as Jesus Christ proclaimed Him to be. That is to say, the Christian thinker begins from the first principle that Jesus Christ has said the last word about God and has given the full revelation of Him. The Christian thinker always thinks on the basis of Jesus Christ.

(ii) His thinking is motivated and dominated by *love*. Paul's whole design is to produce love. To think in love will always save us from certain things. It will save us from *arrogant* thinking. It will save us from *contemptuous* thinking. It will save us from *condemning* either that with which we do not agree, or that which we do not understand. It will save us from expressing our arguments and our views in such a way that we hurt other people. Love saves us from *destructive thinking* and *destructive speaking*. To think in love is always to think in sympathy. The man who argues in love argues not to defeat his opponent, but to win him.

(iii) His thinking comes from a *pure heart*. Here the word that is used is very significant. It is the word *katharos*. Originally this word simply meant *clean* as opposed to *soiled* or *dirty*. But later it came to have certain most suggestive uses. It is used of corn that has been winnowed and cleansed of all chaff. It is used of an army which has been sifted and purified of all cowardly and undisciplined soldiers until there is nothing left but first-class fighting men. It is used of something which is without any soiling or debasing admixture. So, then, a pure heart is a heart whose motives are absolutely pure and absolutely unmixed. In the heart of the Christian thinker there is no thought of self-display, no desire to show how clever he is, no desire to win a purely debating victory, no desire to show up the ignorance of his opponent, no desire to score off the person with whom he is discussing the faith. His only desire is to help and to illumine and to lead nearer to God. The Christian thinker is selfless in his devotion to truth, and his desire to help. He is moved only by love of truth and love for men.

(iv) His thinking comes from a *good conscience.* The Greek word for *conscience* is *suneidēsis*. It literally means *a knowing with*. And the real meaning of conscience is a *knowing with oneself*. To have a good conscience is to be able to look the knowledge which one shares with no one but oneself in the face, and not to be ashamed of anything in it. Emerson said of Seneca that he said the loveliest things if only he had the right to say them. The Christian thinker is the man the thoughts of whose heart, and the deeds of whose life, give him the right to say what he says—and that is the most acid test of all.

(v) The Christian thinker is the man of *undissembling faith*. The phrase literally means the faith *in which there is no hypocrisy*. That simply means that the great characteristic of the Christian thinker is *sincerity*. He is sincere in his desire to find the truth; and he is sincere in his desire to communicate the truth. Both the processes of his thinking and the motives of his teaching must be able to stand the scrutiny of God.

THOSE WHO NEED NO LAW

I *Timothy* I: 8-11

We know that the law is good, if a man uses it legitimately, in the awareness that the law was not instituted to deal with good men, but with the lawless and the undisciplined, the irreverent and the sinners, the impious and the polluted, those who have sunk so low that they strike their fathers and their mothers, murderers, fornicators, homosexuals, slave-dealers and kidnappers, liars, perjurers, and all those who are guilty of anything which is the reverse of sound teaching, that teaching which is in accordance with the glorious gospel of the blessed God, that gospel which has been entrusted to me.

THIS passage begins with a thought which was a favourite thought in the ancient world. The place of the law is to deal with evil-doers. The good man does not need any law to control his actions or to threaten him with punishments; and in a world of good men there would be no need for any laws at all.

Antiphanes, the Greek, had it: " He who does no wrong needs no law." It was the claim of Aristotle that " philosophy enables a man to do without external control that which others do because of fear of the laws." Ambrose, the great Christian bishop, wrote: " The just man has the law of his own mind, of his own equity and of his own justice as his standard; and therefore he is not recalled from fault by terror of punishment, but by the rule of honour." Pagan and Christian alike regarded true goodness as something which had its source in a man's heart; as something which was not dependent on the rewards and punishments of the law.

But in one thing the pagan and the Christian differed. The pagan looked back to an ancient golden time when all things were good and when no law was needed. The ancient peoples believed with all the wistful longing of their hearts in the good old days. Ovid, the Roman poet, drew one of the most famous pictures of that ancient golden time (*Metamorphoses* I: 90-112). " Golden was that first age, which with no one to compel, without a law, of its own will, kept faith and did the right. There was no fear of punishment, no threatening words were to be read on brazen tablets; no suppliant throng gazed fearfully upon the judge's face; but without judges men lived secure. Not yet had the pine tree, felled on its native mountains, descended thence into the watery plain to visit other lands; men knew no shores except their own. Nor yet were cities begirt with steep moats; there were no trumpets of straight, no horns of curving brass, no swords or helmets. There was no need at all of armed men, for nations, secure from war's alarms, passed the years in gentle peace." These were the golden days when none was evil and when none was afraid. Tacitus, the Roman historian, had the same picture (*Annals* 3: 26). " In the earliest times, when men had as yet no evil passions, they led blameless, guiltless lives, without either punishment or restraint. Led by their own nature to pursue none but virtuous ends, they required no rewards; and as they desired nothing contrary to the right, there was no need for pains and penalties." The ancient world looked back and longed for the days that were gone for ever. But it is characteristic of Christianity to look forward and not back. The Christian faith does not look back to a lost golden age; it looks forward to the day when the only law will be the love of Christ within a man's heart, for Christianity is certain that the day of law cannot end until the day of love dawns.

There should be only one controlling factor in the lives of every one of us. Our goodness should come, not from fear of the law, not even from fear of judgment. But from fear to disappoint the love of Christ and to grieve the fatherly heart of God. The Christian's dynamic to right living lies in the fact that he knows that sin is not only breaking God's law, but that sin is also breaking God's heart. It is not the law of God but the love of God which constrains us.

THOSE WHOM THE LAW CONDEMNS

I *Timothy* I: 8-11 (*continued*)

IN an ideal state, when the Kingdom comes, there will be no necessity for any other law than the love of God and good within a man's heart; but as things are, the case is very different. And here Paul sets out a catalogue of sins which the law must control and condemn. The interest of this passage is that it shows us the background against which Christianity grew up. This list of sins and vices is in fact a description of the world in which the early Christians lived and moved and had their being. Nothing shows us so well how the Christian Church was a little island of purity in a vicious and infected world. We talk about it being hard to be a Christian in a modern civilization; we have only to read a passage like this to see how infinitely harder it must have been in the circumstances in which the Church first began. Let us take this terrible list and look at the items on it.

There were the *lawless* (*anomoi*). The lawless are those who know the laws of right and wrong, and who break them deliberately and open-eyed. No one can blame a man for breaking the law if he does not know that such a law exists; but the *lawless* are those who are well aware of the laws and who deliberately violate them in order to satisfy their own ambitions and desires.

There were the *undisciplined* (*anhupotaktoi*). They are the unruly and the insubordinate. These are those who refuse to accept and to obey any authority. They are like soldiers who mutinously disobey the word of command, who rebelliously break their ranks. They are either too proud or too unbridled to accept any discipline or control.

There are the *irreverent* (*asebeis*). The Greek word *asebēs* is a terrible word. It describes not indifference, not the slip and the lapse into sin. It describes " positive and active irreligion," the spirit which deliberately and defiantly withholds from God that which is His right.

42

It describes human nature "in battle array against God."
The *asebēs* is the kind of man who goes his own way and
defies God to do His worst.

There are the sinners (*hamartōloi*). In its commonest
usage this is a word which describes character. It can be
used, for instance, of a slave who is of loose and lax and
useless character. It describes the person who has no
moral standards left.

There were the impious (*anosioi*). The Greek word
hosios is a noble word; it describes, as Trench puts it,
"the everlasting ordinances of right, which no law or
custom of man has constituted, for they are anterior to
all law and custom." The things which are *hosios* are
part of the very constitution of the universe, the everlasting
sanctities. The Greek, for instance, shudderingly declared
that the Egyptian custom where brother could marry
sister, or the Persian custom where son could marry mother,
was *anosion, impious, unholy*. The man who is *anosios* is
worse than a mere lawbreaker. He is the man who violates
the ultimate sanctities and the ultimate decencies of life.

There were the polluted (*bebēloi*). *Bebēlos* is an ugly
word with a queer history. It originally simply meant
that which can be trodden upon in contradistinction to that
which is sacred to some god, and therefore inviolable.
It then came to mean *profane* in opposition to *sacred*.
It then came to mean the man who profanes the sacred
things, the man who desecrates God's day, disobeys God's
laws, belittles God's worship, and soils the life which God
has given him to live. The man who is *bebēlos* soils everything he touches.

There were *those who struck or even killed their parents*
(*patralōai* and *mētralōai*). Under Roman law a son who
struck his parents was liable to nothing less than death.
The words describe a son or daughter who is lost to gratitude,
lost to respect and lost to shame. And it must ever be
remembered that this most cruel of blows can be a blow,
not upon the body, but upon the heart.

There were those who were *murderers* (*androphonoi*), literally *man-slayers*. Paul was thinking of the Ten Commandments and of how breach after breach of them characterized the heathen world. As we read this we must not think that this at least has nothing to do with us, for Jesus widened this commandment so that it includes not only the act of murder, but also the feeling of anger against a brother in the heart.

There were the *fornicators and the homosexuals* (*pornoi* and *arsenokoitai*). It is difficult for us to realize the state of the ancient world in matters of sexual morality. It was riddled with unnatural vice. One of the extraordinary things was the actual connection of immorality and religion. The Temple of Aphrodite at Corinth had a thousand priestesses attached to it who were sacred prostitutes and who at evening came down to the city streets and plied their trade. It is said that Solon was the first law-maker in Athens to legalize prostitution; it is said that he instituted public brothels in Athens, and that with the profits of these brothels a new temple was built to Aphrodite, the goddess of love. E. F. Brown was a missionary in India, and in his commentary on the Pastoral Epistles on this passage he quotes an extraordinary section from the Penal Code of India. There is a section of that code which forbids obscene representations; and then it goes on to say: " This section does not extend to any representation or sculpture, engraved, painted or otherwise represented on or in any temple, or any car used for the conveyance of idols, or kept or used for any religious purpose." One of the extraordinary things is that in the non-Christian religions time and time again immorality and obscenity flourish under the very protection of religion. It has often been said and said truly that chastity was the one completely new virtue which Christianity brought into this world. We may well think of the task of the Christian in the early days who was endeavouring to live according to the Christian ethic in a world like that.

There were the *andrapodistai*. The word may either mean *slave-dealers* or *slave-kidnappers*. Probably both meanings are involved in it here. It is true that slavery was an integral part of the life of the ancient world. It is true that Aristotle declared that civilization was founded on slavery, that certain men and women were born to be hewers of wood and drawers of water, and only existed to perform the menial tasks of life for the convenience of the cultured classes. But even in the ancient world voices were raised against slavery. Philo spoke of slave-dealers as those " who despoil men of their most precious possession, their freedom." But this more probably refers to kidnapper of slaves. Slaves were valuable property. An ordinary slave with no special gifts or talents or crafts fetched from £16 to £20. A specially accomplished slave who was a clever craftsman would fetch three or four times as much. Beautiful youths were in special demand as pages and cupbearers and would fetch as much as between £800 and £900. Marcus Antonius is said to have paid £2,000 for two well-matched youths who were wrongly represented to be twins. In the days when Rome was specially eager to learn the arts of Greece, and when slaves who were skilled in Greek literature and music and art were specially valuable, there is a record of a certain Lutatius Daphnis who was sold for £3,500. The result of all this was that frequently valuable slaves were either seduced to leave their masters or kidnapped. The kidnapping of specially beautiful or specially valuable and accomplished slaves was a common feature of ancient life.

Finally there were liars (*pseustai*) and perjurers (*epiorkoi*), men who did not hesitate to lie and to twist the truth to gain dishonourable ends.

Here is a vivid picture of the atmosphere in which the ancient Church grew up. It was against an infection like that that the writer of the Pastorals sought to protect and guard the Christians in his charge.

THE CLEANSING WORD

I *Timothy* I: 8-11 (*continued*)

INTO this world there came the Christian message, and this passage tells us three things about this message.

(i) It is *sound* teaching. The word which is used for sound (*hugiainein*) literally means *health-giving*. The great characteristic of Christianity is that it is an ethical religion. It demands from a man not only the keeping of certain ritual laws, but the living of a good life. E. F. Brown draws a comparison between Islam and Christianity. A Mohammedan can be regarded as a very holy man if he observes certain ceremonial rituals, although his moral life is quite unclean. If he is careful to fulfil all the ceremonial laws, his blessing will be sought as a man influential with God, even if his moral conduct is degraded and debased. E. F. Brown quotes a recent writer on Morocco: " The great blot on the creed of Islam is that precept and practice are not expected to go together, except as regards the ritual, so that a man may be notoriously wicked yet esteemed religious, having his blessing sought as that of one who has power with God, without the slightest sense of incongruity. The position of things was very well put to me one day by a Moor in Fez, who remarked: ' Dc you want to know what our religion is? We purify ourselves with water while we contemplate adultery; we go to the mosque to pray and as we do so we think how best to cheat our neighbours; we give alms at the door and go back to our shop to rob; we read our Korans and go out to commit unmentionable sins; we fast and go on pilgrimage and yet we lie and kill.' " It must always be remembered that Christianity does not mean observing a ritual, even if that ritual consists of bible-reading and church-going; it means living a good life. Christianity, if it is real Christianity, is health-giving; it is the moral antiseptic which alone can cleanse life.

(ii) It is a *glorious gospel*; that is to say, it is *glorious good news.* It is good news of forgiveness for past sins, and of power to conquer sin in the days to come. It is good news of God's mercy, God's cleansing and God's grace.

(iii) It is good news *which comes from God.* The Christian gospel is not the discovery made by man; it is the good news revealed by God. It is not something which man created or man discovered; it is something which God offers and God supplies. It does not offer only the help of man; it offers nothing less than the power of God.

(iv) That good news *comes through men.* It was good news which was entrusted to Paul to bring to others. God makes His offer and God needs His messengers. And the real Christian is the person who has himself closed with and accepted the offer of God, and who has realized that he cannot keep that good news to himself, but that he must transmit it to and communicate and share it with others who have not yet found it.

SAVED TO SERVE

I *Timothy* I: 12-17

> I give thanks to Jesus Christ, our Lord, who has filled me with His power, that He showed that He believed that He could trust me, by appointing me to His service, although I was formerly an insulter, a persecutor and a man of insolent and brutal violence. But I received mercy from Him, because it was in ignorance that I acted thus, in the days when I did not believe. But the grace of our Lord rose higher than my sin, and I found it in the faith and love of those whose lives are lived in Jesus Christ. This is a saying on which we can rely, and which we are completely bound to accept, that Christ Jesus came into the world to save sinners—of whom I am chief. This was why I received mercy—so that in me Jesus Christ might display all that patience of His, so that I might be the first outline sketch of those who would one day come to believe in Him, that they might find eternal life. To the King, eternal, immortal, invisible, to the only God, be honour and glory for ever and ever. Amen.

THIS passage begins with a very paean of thanksgiving. There were four tremendous things for which Paul wished to thank Jesus Christ.

(i) He thanked Him because He *chose* him. Paul never had the feeling that he had chosen Christ, but that Christ had chosen him. It was as if when he was heading straight for destruction, Jesus Christ had laid His hand upon his shoulder and arrested him in the way. It was as if when he was busy throwing away his life, Jesus Christ had suddenly brought him to his senses. In the days of the war I knew a Polish airman. He had crowded more thrilling hairbreadth escapes from death and from worse than death into a few years than the vast majority of men do into a lifetime. Sometimes he would tell the story of escape from occupied Europe, of parachute descents from the air, of rescue from the sea, and then at the end of this amazing odyssey, he would always say, with a look of wonder in his eyes: " And now I am God's man." That is how Paul felt; he was Christ's man for Christ had chosen him.

(ii) He thanked Him because He *trusted* him. It was to Paul an amazing thing, that he, the arch-persecutor, had been chosen as the missionary and the pioneer of Christ. It was not only that Jesus Christ had forgiven him; it was that Christ had trusted him. Sometimes in human affairs we forgive a man who has committed some mistake or who has been guilty of some sin, but we make it very clear that his past makes it impossible for us to trust him again with any responsibility. But Christ had not only forgiven Paul; He had entrusted him with His work to do. The man who had been the persecutor of Christ had been made the ambassador of Christ.

(iii) He thanked Him because He had *appointed* him. And we must be very careful to note that for which Paul felt himself appointed. He was appointed to *service*. Paul never thought of himself as appointed to honour, to prestige, to authority, to leadership within the Church. His glory was that he was saved to serve. Plutarch tells that when a Spartan won a victory in the games, his reward was that he might stand beside his king in battle. There was a Spartan wrestler at the Olympic games; he was offered a very considerable bribe if he would abandon the struggle; but he refused. Finally after a terrific effort he won his victory. Someone said to him: " Well, Spartan, what have you got out of this costly victory you have won? " He answered: " I have won the privilege of standing in front of my king in battle." His reward was to serve and, if need be, to die for his king. It was for service, not honour, that Paul knew himself to be chosen.

(iv) He thanked Him because He had *empowered* him. Paul was one of those who had long since discovered that Jesus Christ never gives a man a task to do without also giving him the power to do it. Paul would never have said, " See what I have done." He would always have said, " See what Jesus Christ has enabled me to do." No man is good enough, no man is strong enough, no man is pure enough, no man is wise enough to be the servant of Christ. But if a man will give himself to Christ, he will go, not in his own strength, but in the strength of his Lord.

THE MEANS OF CONVERSION

I *Timothy* I: 12-17 (*continued*)

IN this passage there are two further interesting things.

In it Paul's Jewish background comes out. He says that Jesus Christ had mercy on him because he committed his sins against Christ and His Church in the days of his ignorance, before he came to believe. We often think that the Jewish viewpoint was that sacrifice atoned for sin. We think that the course of sacrifice was that a man sinned; that sin offended God and broke his relationship with God; then sacrifice was made and God's anger was appeased and the relationship was restored. It may well have been that that was in fact the popular and the debased view of sacrifice. But the highest Jewish thought insisted on two things. First, it insisted that sacrifice could never atone for deliberate sin, the sin of arrogance, the sin of presumption, the sin of the high hand and the lofty heart. It insisted that sacrifice could only atone for the sins a man committed in ignorance, the sins a man committed, not in deliberate cold blood, but when he was swept away in a moment of passion. Deliberate, defiant, arrogant sin was beyond the power of sacrifice to atone for. Second, the highest Jewish thought insisted that sacrifice could atone for no sin at all unless there was penitence and contrition in the heart of the man who brought the sacrifice. Here Paul is speaking out of his Jewish background. His heart had been broken by the mercy of Christ; his sins had been committed in the days before he knew Christ and His love. And for these reasons he felt that there was still mercy for him.

But in this passage there is a still more interesting matter, which is pointed out by E. F. Brown. Verse 14 is a difficult verse. In the Authorised Version it runs: " The grace of God was exceeding abundant with faith and love which is in Jesus Christ." The first part is not difficult; it simply means that the grace of God rose higher than Paul's sin. But what exactly is the meaning of the phrase " with faith and love which is in Christ Jesus "? E. F. Brown suggests that the meaning is this—that the work of the grace of Christ in Paul's heart was helped and supported by the faith and the love he found in the members of the Christian Church; that the effect of the grace of Christ was aided by the sympathy and the understanding and the kindness he received from men like Ananias, who opened his eyes and who called him brother (*Acts* 9: 10-19), and like Barnabas, who stood by him when the rest of the Church regarded him with bleak suspicion (*Acts* 9: 26-28). The idea is that the gift of the grace of Christ was helped by the Christian charity of certain members of the Church who lived in Christ. That is a very lovely idea. And if that be so, we can see that there are three factors which co-operate in the conversion of any man.

(i) First, there is God. It was the prayer of Jeremiah: " Turn Thou us unto Thee, O Lord " (*Lamentations* 5: 21). Unless the Spirit of God works in a man's heart, he cannot even begin to desire God. As Augustine had it, we would never even have begun to seek for God unless God had already found us. The prime mover is God; at the back of a man's first desire for goodness there is the seeking love of God.

(ii) There is a man's own self. The Authorised Version renders *Matthew* 18: 3 entirely passively: " Except ye *be converted* and become as little children, ye shall not enter into the Kingdom of Heaven." The Revised Version gives a much more active rendering: " Except ye *turn* and become as little children, ye shall not enter into the Kingdom of Heaven." This much is certain—there must be human response to divine appeal. God gave men free will and men can use that free will either to accept or to refuse the offer of God. A man must himself make that essential act of submission to God.

(iii) There is the human agency of some Christian person. It is Paul's conviction that he is sent " to open the eyes of the Gentiles, and to turn them from darkness to light, and from the power of Satan unto God, that they may receive forgiveness of sins " (*Acts* 26: 18). It is James's belief that any man who converts the sinner from the error of his way " shall save a soul from death and shall hide a multitude of sins " (*James* 5: 19, 20). So then there is a double duty laid upon us. It has been said that a saint is someone who makes it easier to believe in God, and that a saint is someone in whom Christ lives again. We must give thanks for those who showed us Christ, and whose words and example brought us to Him; and we must strive to be the influence, the sign-post, the light which brings others to God. In this matter of conversion the initiative of God, the response of man, and the influence of the Christian all combine.

THE UNFORGOTTEN SHAME AND THE UNDYING INSPIRATION

1 *Timothy* 1: 12-17 (*continued*)

THE thing which stands out above all in this passage is Paul's insistence upon remembering his own sin. He heaps up a very climax of words to show what he did to Christ and the Church. He was an *insulter* of the Church; he had flung his hot and angry words at the Christians, accusing them of crimes against God, while it was he himself who was the criminal. He was a *persecutor*; he had taken every means which was open to him under the Jewish law to annihilate the Christian Church. Then there comes the terrible word; he had been *a man of insolent and brutal violence.* The word in Greek is *hubristēs*. It indicates a kind of arrogant sadism; it describes the man who is out to inflict pain and injury for the sheer joy of inflicting it. The corresponding abstract noun is *hubris*. Aristotle defines it like this: " *Hubris* means to hurt and to grieve people, in such a way that shame comes to the man who is hurt and grieved, and that not that the person who inflicts the hurt and injury may gain anything else in addition to what he already possesses, but simply that he may find delight in his own cruelty and in the suffering of the other person." In this word there is a sadistic delight in inflicting pain. That is what Paul was once like in regard to the Christian Church. Not content with words of insult, he went to the limit of legal persecution. Not content with legal persecution, he went to the limit of sadistic brutality in his attempt to stamp out the Christian faith. Paul remembered that; and to the end of the day Paul regarded himself as the chief of sinners. It is not that he *was* the chief of sinners; he still *is* the chief of sinners. True, he could never forget that he was a forgiven sinner; but equally true, he could never forget that he was a sinner. Why then should Paul remember his own sin with such vividness?

(i) The memory of his sin was the surest way to keep him from all pride. There could be no such thing as spiritual pride for a man who had done the things that he had done. John Newton was one of the great preachers and the supreme hymn-writers of the Church; but there was a time when John Newton had been guilty of every sin, and when he had sunk to the lowest depths to which a man can sink. In the days when he had sailed the seas in the slave-trader's ship, John Newton had plumbed the depths. So when John Newton became a converted man and a preacher of the gospel, he wrote a text in great letters, and fastened it above the mantlepiece of his study where he could not fail to see it: " Thou shalt remember that thou wast a bondman in the land of Egypt and the Lord thy God redeemed thee." John Newton composed his own epitaph and it ran: " John Newton, Clerk, once an Infidel and Libertine, a Servant of Slaves in Africa, was by the Mercy of our Lord and Saviour Jesus Christ, Preserved, Restored, Pardoned, and Appointed to Preach the Faith he had so long laboured to destroy." John Newton never forgot that he was a forgiven sinner; neither did Paul. Neither must we. It does a man good to remember his sins, for it saves him from spiritual pride.

(ii) The memory of his sin was the surest way to keep his gratitude aflame. To remember that for which we have been forgiven is the surest way to keep awake our love and our gratitude to Jesus Christ. F. W. Boreham tells us of a letter which the old Puritan, Thomas Goodwin, wrote to his son. " When I was threatening to become cold in my ministry, and when I felt Sabbath morning coming and my heart not filled with amazement at the grace of God, or when I was making ready to dispense the Lord's Supper, do you know what I used to do? I used to take a turn up and down among the sins of my past life, and I always came down again with a broken and a contrite heart, ready to preach, as it was preached in the beginning, the forgiveness of sins." " I do not think," he said, " I ever went up the pulpit stair that I did not stop for a moment at the foot of it and take a turn up and down among the sins of my past years. I do not think that I ever planned a sermon that I did not take a turn round my study table and look back at the sins of my youth and of all my life down to the present; and many a Sabbath morning, when my soul had been cold and dry, for the lack of prayer during the week, a turn up and down in my past life before I went into the pulpit always broke my hard heart and made me close with the gospel for my own soul before I began to preach." When we think how we have hurt God and hurt those who love us and hurt our fellow men, and when we remember how God and men have forgiven us, that memory must awake the flame of gratitude within our hearts.

(iii) The memory of his sin was the constant urge to greater effort. It is quite true that a man can never earn the approval of God, and that he can never deserve the love of God; but it is also true that he can never stop trying to do something to show how much he appreciates the love and the mercy which have made him what he is. Whenever we love anyone we cannot help trying always to demonstrate our love. It comes naturally and instinctively to us to do so. When we remember how much God loves us and how little we deserve it, when we remember that it was for us that Jesus Christ hung and suffered there on Calvary, then it must compel us to effort which will tell God that we realize what He has done for us, and which will show Jesus Christ that His sacrifice was not in vain.

(iv) The memory of his sin was bound to be a constant encouragement to others. Paul uses a vivid phrase and picture. He says that what happened to him was a kind of outline-sketch of what was going to happen to those who would accept Christ in the days to come. The word he uses is *hupotupōsis*. It means an outline, a sketch-plan, a first draft, a preliminary model. It is as if Paul would say, " Look what Christ has done for me! If someone like me can be saved, there is hope for anyone yet." Suppose a man was very seriously ill and had to go through a very dangerous operation, it would be the greatest encouragement to him if he met and talked with someone who had undergone the same operation and who had emerged completely cured. Paul did not shrinkingly conceal his record; he blazoned it abroad, that others might know it and take courage and be filled with hope that the grace which had changed Paul could change them too.

Paul's sin was not something which he tried to forget. As Greatheart said to Christian's boys: " You must know that Forgetful Green is the most dangerous place in all these parts." Paul's sin was something which he refused to forget, for every time he remembered the greatness of his sin, he remembered the still greater greatness of Jesus Christ. It was not that he brooded unhealthily over his sin; it was that he remembered his sin to awaken rejoicing in the greatness of the grace of Jesus Christ.

THE SUMMONS WHICH CANNOT BE DENIED

I *Timothy* I: 18, 19

> I entrust this charge to you, Timothy lad, because it is the natural consequence of the messages which came to the prophets from God, and which marked you out as the very man for this work, so that, in obedience to these messages, you may wage a fine campaign, maintaining your faith and a good conscience all the time; and there are some who, in matters of the faith, have repelled the guidance of conscience, and have come to shipwreck. Amongst them are Hymenaeus and Alexander, whom I have handed over to Satan, that they may be disciplined out of their insults to God and His Church.

THE first section of this passage is highly compressed. What lies behind it is this. There must have been a meeting of the prophets of the Church. The prophets were men who were known to be within the confidence and the counsels of God. " Surely the Lord will do nothing but He revealeth His secret unto His servants the prophets " (*Amos* 3: 7). This meeting of the prophets thought about the situation which was threatening the Church and came to the conclusion that Timothy was the very man to deal with it. We can see the prophets acting in exactly the same way in *Acts* 13: 1-3. At that time the Church was faced with the great decision whether or not to take the message of the gospel out to the Gentiles; and it was to the prophets that there came the message of the Holy Spirit, saying: " Separate me Barnabas and Saul for the work whereunto I have called them " (*Acts* 13: 2). That was what had happened to Timothy. He had been marked out by the prophets as the man to deal with the situation in the Church. It may well have been that Timothy shrank from the greatness of the task which faced him, and in this passage Paul encourages him and kindles him with certain considerations.

(i) Paul says to him: " You are a man who has been chosen and you cannot refuse your task." It was something like that that happened to John Knox. He had been teaching in St. Andrews. His teaching was supposed to be private but many came to it, for he was obviously a man with a message. So the people urged him " that he would take the preaching place upon him. But he utterly refused, alleging that he would not run where God had not called him. . . . Whereupon they privily among themselves advising, having with them in council Sir David Lindsay of the Mount, they concluded that they would give a charge to the said John, and that publicly by the mouth of their preacher." John Knox was a man chosen, and yet a man who hesitated to take the tremendous responsibility upon himself. So Sunday came and Knox was in

Church and John Rough the preacher was preaching. " The said John Rough, preacher, directed his words to the said John Knox, saying: ' Brother, ye shall not be offended, albeit that I speak unto you that which I have in charge, even from all those that are here present, which is this: In the name of God, and of His Son Jesus Christ, and in the name of these that presently call you by my mouth, I charge you that you refuse not this holy vocation, but . . . that you take upon you the public office and charge of preaching, even as you look to avoid God's heavy displeasure, and desire that He shall multiply His graces with you.' And in the end he said to those that were present: ' Was not this your charge to me? And do ye not approve this vocation?' They answered: ' It was: and we approve it.' Whereat the said John, abashed, burst forth in most abundant tears, and withdrew himself to his chamber. His countenance and behaviour, from that day till the day that he was compelled to present himself to the public place of preaching, did sufficiently declare the grief and trouble of his heart; for no man saw any sign of mirth in him, neither yet had he pleasure to accompany any man, many days together." John Knox was chosen; John Knox did not want to answer the call; but John Knox had to, for the choice had come from God. Years afterwards the Regent Morton uttered his famous epitaph by John Knox's graveside: " In respect that he bore God's message, to whom he must make account for the same, he (albeit he was weak and an unworthy creature, and a fearful man) feared not the faces of men." The consciousness of being chosen gave him courage. So Paul says to Timothy: " You have been chosen; you cannot let down God and man." To every one of us there comes God's choosing; and when we are summoned to some work for Him, we dare not refuse it.

(ii) It may be that Paul was saying to Timothy: " Timothy, be true to your name." The name *Timothy*—its full form is *Timotheos*—is composed of two Greek words,

timē which means *honour*, and *theos* which means *God*.
The very name *Timothy* means *honour to God*. It is as if
Paul said to Timothy: " Timothy, live up to your name."
We are called by the name *Christian*, one of Christ's folk,
and to that name we must be true.

(iii) Finally, Paul says to Timothy: " You are a man
to whom a task has been entrusted." " I entrust this
charge to you," says Paul. The word which Paul uses for
to entrust is *paratithesthai*. That word is used of entrusting
something valuable and precious to someone's safe keeping.
It is used, for instance, of making a deposit in a bank, of
entrusting some person to another person's care. It always
implies that a trust has been reposed in someone, and that
for that trust that person will be called to account. So
Paul says to Timothy: " Timothy, into your hands I am
placing a sacred trust. See that you do not fail." God
has reposed His trust in us. Into our hands He has put
His honour and His Church. We too must see to it that
we do not fail.

DESPATCHED ON GOD'S CAMPAIGN

1 *Timothy* 1: 18, 19 (*continued*)

WHAT then is entrusted to Timothy? And for what purpose
is Timothy despatched? He is despatched to fight a *good
campaign*. The picture of life as a campaign is one which
has always fascinated men's thoughts. Maximus of Tyre
said: " God is the general; life is the campaign; man
is the soldier." Seneca said: " For me to live, my dear
Lucilius, is to be a soldier." When a man became a follower
of the goddess Isis, and when he was initiated into the
Mysteries connected with the goddess's name, the summons
to him was: " Enrol yourself in the sacred soldiery of
Isis."

There are three things to be noted here.
(i) It is not to a *battle* that we are summoned; it is to

a *campaign*. Life is one long campaign; life is a service from which there is no release. Life is not a short, sharp struggle after which a man can lay aside his arms and rest in peace; to the end of the day life is an unceasing campaign. To change the metaphor, life is not a sprint; it is a marathon race. It is there that the danger of life enters in. It is necessary to be for ever on guard and on the watch. " Eternal vigilance is the price of liberty." The temptations of life, the wrong things of life, never cease their attack and their search for a chink in the armour of the Christian. There are no periods of relaxation in the Christian life. It is one of the commonest dangers in life that we proceed in a series of spasms. We have a period of real effort and of real campaign, and then a period when we let things slide. We must remember that we are summoned to a campaign which goes on as long as life goes on.

(ii) It is to a *fine* campaign that Timothy is summoned. Here again we have the word *kalos* of which the Pastorals are so fond. This word *kalos* does not mean only something which is good and strong; it means something which is fine and attractive and winsome and lovely. The soldier of Christ is not a conscript who serves grimly, grudgingly and unwillingly; he is a volunteer who serves with a certain knightly chivalry. He is not the slave of duty; he is the servant of joy.

(iii) Timothy is bidden to take with him two weapons of equipment. (*a*) He must take *faith*. Even when things are at their darkest he must have faith in the essential rightness of his cause, and faith in the ultimate triumph of God. It was faith which kept John Knox when he was in despair. Once when he was a slave on the galleys, the ship came in sight of St. Andrews. He was so weak that he had to be lifted up bodily that he might see. They showed him the church steeple and asked him if he knew it. " Yes," he said, " I know it well: and I am fully persuaded, how weak that ever I now appear, that I shall not depart this life till that my tongue shall glorify His godly name in the same place." He describes his feelings in 1554 when he had to flee from the country to escape the vengeance of Mary Tudor, " when," as he said, " not only the ungodly, but even my faithful brethren, yea, and my own self, that is, all natural understanding, judged my cause to be irremediable." Then he goes on: " The frail flesh, oppressed with fear and pain, desireth deliverance, ever abhorring and drawing back from obedience giving. O Christian brethren, I write by experience. . . . I know the grudging and murmuring complaints of the flesh; I know the anger, wrath, and indignation which it conceiveth against God, calling all His promises in doubt, and being ready every hour utterly to fall from God. *Against which remains only faith.*" The Christian soldier needs in the darkest hour the faith that will not shrink. (*b*) He must take the defence of a *good conscience.* That is to say, the Christian soldier must at least try to live in accordance with his own teaching and his own doctrine. He must at least be able to say: " I have always tried to practise what I preach and to live by what I teach." The virtue is gone out of a man's message when his conscience condemns him as he speaks.

A STERN REBUKE

I *Timothy* I: 18, 19 (*continued*)

THE passage closes with a stern rebuke to two members of the Christian Church who have injured the Church, grieved Paul, and made shipwreck of their own lives. Hymenaeus is mentioned again in 2 *Timothy* 2: 17; and Alexander may well be the Alexander who is referred to in 2 *Timothy* 4: 14. Paul has three complaints against these men.

(i) They had rejected the guidance of conscience. They had allowed their own wishes and desires to speak with more power and persuasiveness than the voice of God. They had made their will, not God's will, the dictator of their lives.

(ii) Inevitably they had relapsed into evil practices. Once they had abandoned God, life had become soiled and debased and unworthy. When God went from life, beauty went from life along with Him.

(iii) They had taken to false teaching. Again it is almost inevitable. When a man takes the wrong way, his first instinct is to find justifications and excuses for himself. He takes the Christian teaching and twists and distorts it to suit himself. Out of the right he finds subtle and perverted arguments to justify the wrong. He finds arguments in the words of Christ to justify the ways of the devil. The moment a man disobeys the voice of conscience, his conduct becomes debased and his thinking becomes twisted.

So Paul goes on to say that he has " handed them over to Satan." What is the meaning of that terrible phrase? We cannot be sure what it means, but there are three real possibilities.

(i) He may be thinking of the Jewish practice of excommunication. According to Synagogue practice, if a man was an evil-doer he was first publicly rebuked. If that was ineffective, he was banished from the Synagogue for a period of thirty days. If he was still stubbornly unrepentant, he was put under the ban, which made him a person accursed, debarred from the society of men and the fellowship of God. In such a case a man might well be said to be handed over to Satan.

(ii) Paul may be saying that he has barred them from the Church and turned them loose in the world. In a heathen society it was inevitable that men should draw a hard and fast line between the Church and the world. The Church was God's territory; the world was Satan's territory; and to be debarred from the Church was to be handed over to that territory which was under the sway of Satan. The phrase may mean that these two troublers of the Church were abandoned to the world.

(iii) There is a third explanation which is the most likely of the three. Satan was held to be responsible for human suffering and human pain. There was a man in the Corinthian Church who had been guilty of the terrible sin of incest. Paul's advice is that that man should be delivered unto Satan " for the destruction of the flesh, that the spirit may be saved in the day of the Lord Jesus Christ " (I *Corinthians* 5: 5). The idea is that the Church should pray for some physical chastisement to fall on that man so that, by the pain of his body, he might be brought to the senses of his mind. In the case of Job it was Satan who brought the physical suffering upon Job (*Job* 2: 6, 7). In the New Testament itself we have the terrible end of Ananias and Sapphira (*Acts* 5: 5, 10), and the blindness which fell upon Elymas because of his opposition to the gospel (*Acts* 13: 11). It may well be that it was Paul's prayer that these two men should be subjected to some painful visitation, which would be to them a warning and a punishment.

That is all the more likely because it is Paul's hope, not that these men will be obliterated and destroyed, but that they will be disciplined out of the evil of their ways. To Paul, as it ought to be to us, punishment was never mere vindictive vengeance; it was always remedial discipline. It was never meant simply to hurt; it was always meant only to cure.

THE UNIVERSALITY OF THE GOSPEL

I *Timothy* 2: 1-7

So then the first thing I urge you to do is to offer your requests, your prayers, your petitions, your thanksgivings for all men. Pray for kings and for all who are in authority, that they may enjoy a life that is tranquil and undisturbed, and that they may act in all godliness and reverence. That is the fine way to live, the way which meets with the approval of

God, our Saviour, who wishes all men to be saved, and to come to a full knowledge of the truth. For there is one God, and one Mediator, between God and man, the man Jesus Christ, who gave Himself a ransom for all. It was thus He bore His witness to God in His own good times, a witness to which I have been appointed a herald and an envoy (I am speaking the truth: I do not lie), a teacher to the Gentiles, a teacher whose message is based on faith and truth.

BEFORE we begin to study this passage in detail we must note one thing which shines out from it in a way that no one can fail to see. There are few passages in the New Testament which so stress and underline the universality of the gospel. Prayer is to be made for *all* men; God is the Saviour who wishes *all* men to be saved; Jesus gave His life a ransom for *all*. As Walter Lock writes: " God's will to save is as wide as His will to create." This is a note which sounds in the New Testament again and again. Through Christ God was reconciling the *world* unto Himself (2 *Corinthians* 5: 18, 19). God so loved the *world* that He gave His Son (*John* 3: 16). It was Jesus' confidence that, if He was lifted up on His Cross, soon or late He would draw *all* men unto Him (*John* 12: 32). E. F. Brown writing on this passage calls it " the charter of missionary work." He says that it is the proof that all men are *capax dei*, capable of receiving God. Men may be lost, but they can be found. Men may be ignorant, but they can be enlightened. Men may be sinners, but they can be saved. George Wishart, the fore-runner of John Knox, writes in his translation of the First Swiss Confession: " The end and intent of the Scripture is to declare that God is benevolent and friendly-minded to mankind; and that He hath declared that kindness in and through Jesus Christ, His only Son; the which kindness is received by faith." That is why prayer must be made for all. God wants all men, and therefore God's Church must want all men.

(i) The gospel includes *high and low*. Both the Emperor

in his power and the slave in his helplessness were included in the sweep of the gospel. Both the philosopher in his wisdom and the simple man in his ignorance need the grace and the truth that the gospel can bring. Within the gospel there are no class distinctions. King and commoner, rich and poor, aristocrat and peasant, master and man are all included in its limitless embrace.

(ii) The gospel includes *good and bad*. A strange danger has come to the Church in modern times. It would seem that in a great many cases the principle is that a man has to be respectable before he is allowed into the Church, and that the Church looks askance at sinners who seek an entry to its doors. It is in fact very difficult for the sinner to enter the modern Church without being the target of suspicious and questioning and critical and even unfriendly looks, and without being the subject of whispered and openly expressed criticism and condemnation and curiosity. But the New Testament is clear that the Church exists, not only to edify the good, but to welcome and to save the sinner. C. T. Studd, that great missionary, used to repeat four lines of doggerel:

> " Some want to live within the sound
> Of Church or Chapel bell;
> I want to run a rescue shop
> Within a yard of hell."

One of the great saints of modern times, and indeed of all time, is Toyohiko Kagawa. It was to the Shinkawa slums that Kagawa went to find men and women for Christ. He lived there in the filthiest and the most depraved slums in the world. W. J. Smart describes the situation: " His neighbours were unregistered prostitutes, thieves who boasted of their power to outwit all the police in the city, and murderers who were not only proud of their murder record but always ready to add to their local prestige by committing another. All the people, whether sick, or feeble-minded or criminal, lived in conditions of abysmal misery, in streets slippery with filth, where rats crawled out of open sewers to die. The air was always filled with stench. An idiot girl who lived next door to Kagawa had vile pictures painted on her back to decoy lustful men to her den. Everywhere human bodies rotted with syphilis." Kagawa wanted people like that, and so does Jesus Christ, for He wants *all* men, good and bad alike.

(iii) The gospel embraces *Christian and non-Christian.* Prayer is to be made for *all* men. The Emperors and rulers and governors for whom this letter bids us to pray were not Christians; they were in fact hostile to the Church; and yet they were to be borne to the throne of grace by the prayers of the Church. For the true Christian there is no such thing as an enemy in all this world. None is outside his prayers, for none is outside the love of Christ, and none is outside the purpose of God, who wishes *all* men to be saved.

THE WAY OF PRAYER

I Timothy 2: 1-7 (continued)

IN this passage four different words for prayer are grouped together. It is true that they are not to be sharply distinguished; nevertheless when we examine each of them in turn they have something to tell us of the way of prayer.

(i) The first is the word *deēsis*, which we have translated *request*. *Deēsis* is not exclusively a religious word; it can be used of a request made either to a fellow man or to God. But the fundamental idea of *deēsis* is a sense of need. No one will make a request unless a sense of need has already wakened the desire to make that request. Prayer begins with a sense of need. It begins with the conviction that we cannot deal with life ourselves. It begins with the sense of our own inadequacy. It begins in the sense of human weakness. That sense of human weakness is the basis of all human approach to God.

" Let not conscience make you linger,
    Nor of fitness fondly dream;
    All the fitness He requireth
        Is to feel your need of Him."

Prayer begins with the realization of the helplessness of manhood.

(ii) The second is the word *proseuchē*, which we have translated *prayer*. The basic difference between *deēsis* and *proseuchē* is that *deēsis* may be addressed either to man or God, but *proseuchē* is never used of anything else but approach to God. There are certain needs which only God can satisfy. There are certain needs which can only be brought to Him. There is a strength which He alone can give; a forgiveness which He alone can grant; a certainty which He alone can bestow. It may well be that our weakness haunts us because we so often take our needs to the wrong place.

(iii) The third word is *enteuxis*, which we have translated *petition*. Of the three words this is the most interesting word. It is a word with a most interesting history. It is the noun from the verb *entugchanein*. Originally the verb *entugchanein* meant simply *to meet*, or *to fall in* with a person; then it went on to mean *to hold intimate conversation with a person*; then it acquired a special and a technical meaning; it meant *to enter into a king's presence and to submit a petition to him*. *Enteuxis* acquired the technical meaning of a petition offered to a governor or a king. That tells us much about prayer. It tells us that the way to God stands open to us; that there is given to us this priceless gift of intimate talk with God; that we have the right to bring our petitions to one who is a king. The Christian is the man who has the right to take his needs into the royal presence of God.

" Thou art coming to a King;
    Large petitions with thee bring;
    For His grace and power are such,
    None can ever ask too much."

It is impossible to ask too great a boon from the King.

(iv) The fourth word is the word *eucharistia*, which we have translated *thanksgiving*. Thanksgiving is an integral part of prayer. Prayer does not mean only asking God for things; prayer also means thanking God for things. For too many of us prayer is an exercise in complaint, when it should be an exercise in thanksgiving. Epictetus, who was not a Christian but a Stoic philosopher, used to say: " What can I, who am a little old lame man, do, except give praise to God? " We have the right to bring our needs and our desires and our requests to God; but we have also the duty of bringing our thanksgivings continually to Him.

PRAYER FOR THOSE IN AUTHORITY

vs. 2

2 Timothy 2: 1-7 *(continued)*

THIS passage definitely and distinctly commands prayer for kings and emperors and for all those who are set in authority. This was a cardinal principle of communal Christian prayer. Emperors might be persecutors. Those in authority might be determined to stamp out the Christians. But the Christian Church never, even in the times of bitterest persecution, ceased to pray for them.

It is extraordinary to trace how all throughout the days of the early Church, those days of bitter persecution, the Church still regarded it as an absolute duty to pray for the Emperor and his subordinate kings and governors. " Fear God," said Peter. " Honour the Emperor " (I *Peter* 2: 17), and we must remember that that Emperor was none other than Nero, that monster of cruelty. Tertullian insists that for the Emperor the Christian prayed for " long life, secure dominion, a safe home, a faithful senate, a righteous people, and a world at peace " (*Apology* 30). " We pray for our rulers," he wrote, " for the state of the world, for the peace of all things and for the postponement

of the end " (*Apology* 39). He writes: " The Christian
is the enemy of no man, least of all of the Emperor, for
we know that, since he has been appointed by God, it is
necessary that we should love him, and reverence him,
and honour him, and desire his safety, together with that
of the whole Roman Empire. Therefore we sacrifice for
the safety of the Emperor " (*Ad Scapulam* 2). Cyprian,
writing to Demetrianus, speaks of the Christian Church
as " sacrificing and placating God night and day for your
peace and safety" (*Ad Demetrianum* 20). In A.D. 311 the
Emperor Galerius actually asked for the prayers of the
Christians, and promised them mercy and indulgence
if they prayed for the state. Tatian writes: " Does the
Emperor order us to pay tribute? We willingly offer it.
Does the ruler order us to render service or servitude?
We acknowledge our servitude. But a man must be
honoured as befits a man, but only God is to be reverenced "
(*Apology* 4). Theophilus of Antioch writes: " The honour
that I will give the Emperor is all the greater, because
I will not worship him, but I will pray for him. I will worship
no one but the true and real God, for I know that the
Emperor was appointed by Him. . . . Those give real
honour to the Emperor who are well-disposed to him,
who obey him, and who pray for him " (*Apology* 1: 11).
Justin Martyr writes: " We worship God alone, but in all
other things we gladly serve you, acknowledging kings
and rulers of men, and praying that they may be found
to have pure reason with kingly power " (*Apology* 1: 14, 17).
The greatest of all the prayers for the Emperor is in Clement
of Rome's First Letter to the Church at Corinth which
was written about A.D. 90 when the savagery of Domitian
was still fresh in men's minds: " Thou, Lord and Master,
hast given our rulers and governors the power of sover-
eignty through Thine excellent and unspeakable might,
that we, knowing the glory and honour which Thou hast
given them, may submit ourselves unto them, in nothing
resisting Thy will. Grant unto them, therefore, O Lord,

health, peace, concord, stability, that they may administer
the government which Thou hast given them without
failure. For Thou, O heavenly Master, King of the Ages,
givest to the sons of men glory and honour and power
over all things that are upon the earth. Do Thou, Lord,
direct their counsel according to that which is good and well-
pleasing in Thy sight, that, administering the power
which Thou hast given them in peace and gentleness with
godliness, they may obtain Thy favour. O Thou, who alone
art able to do these things, and things far more exceeding
good than these for us, we praise Thee through the High
Priest and Guardian of our souls, Jesus Christ, through
whom be the glory and the majesty unto Thee both now
and for all generations, and for ever and ever. Amen "
(I *Clement* 61). The Church always regarded it as a bounden
duty to pray for those set in authority over the kingdoms
of the earth. The Church brought even her persecutors
before the throne of grace.

THE GIFTS OF GOD

I *Timothy* 2: I-7 (*continued*)

THE Church prayed for certain things for those in authority.

(i) The Church prayed for " a life that is tranquil and
undisturbed." That was the prayer for a time of peace,
free from war, free from rebellion, free from anything
which would disturb the peace of the realm. That is the
good citizen's prayer for his country.

(ii) But the Church prayed for much more than that.
It prayed for " a life that is lived in godliness and reverence."
Here we are confronted with two great words which are
keynotes of the Pastoral Epistles. They are words which
describe qualities which not only the ruler, but which
every Christian must covet.

First, there was *godliness*, which is *eusebeia*. This is one
of the great and almost untranslatable Greek words. It

describes reverence both towards God and man. It describes that attitude of mind which respects man and honours God and respects oneself. Eusebius defined it as " reverence towards the one and only God, and the kind of life that He would wish us to lead." To the Greek, Socrates was the great example of *eusebeia*, and Xenophon describes Socrates in the following terms: " So pious and devoutly religious that he would take no step apart from the will of heaven; so just and upright that he never did even a trifling injury to any living soul; so self-controlled, so temperate, that he never at any time chose the sweeter in place of the bitter; so sensible and wise and prudent that in distinguishing the better from the worse he never erred " (Xenophon, *Memorabilia*, 4, 8, 11). This word *eusebeia* comes very near to that great Latin word *pietas*. Warde Fowler describes the Roman *pietas*: " The quality known to the Romans as *pietas* rises, in spite of trial and panger, superior to the enticements of individual passion and selfish ease. Aeneas's *pietas* became a sense of duty to the will of the gods, as well as to his father, his son and his people; and this duty never leaves him." Clearly this *eusebeia* is a tremendous thing. It never forgets the reverence due to God; it never forgets the rights due to men; it never forgets the respect due to self. It lives for ever conscious of duty human and divine. It describes the character of the man who never fails God, man or himself.

Second, there was reverence, which is *semnotēs*. Here again we are in the realm of the untranslatable. The corresponding adjective *semnos* is constantly applied to the gods. R. C. Trench says that the man who is *semnos* " has on him a grace and a dignity, not lent by earth." He says that he is one who " without demanding it challenges and inspires reverence." Aristotle was the great ethical teacher of the Greeks. He had a way of describing every virtue as the mean between two extremes. On the one side there was an extreme of excess, and on the other side there was an extreme of defect, and in between there was the mean, the happy medium, in which virtue lay. So Aristotle describes *semnotēs*. He says that it is the mean between *areskeia*, which is *subservience*, and *authadeia*, which is *arrogance*. It may be said that for the man who is *semnos* all life is one long act of worship; all life is lived in the presence of God; he moves through the world, as it has been put, as if the world was the temple of the living God. He never forgets the holiness of God or the dignity of man. He is the man whose attitude to God and to men is right.

These are two great qualities which indeed are regal qualities but which every man must covet and for which every man must pray.

ONE GOD AND ONE SAVIOUR

I Timothy 2: 1-7 (*continued*)

PAUL concludes this passage with a statement of the greatest truths of the Christian faith.

(i) There is one God. We are not living in a world such as the Gnostics produced when they produced their theories of two gods, hostile to each other. We are not living in a world such as the heathen produced when they produced their horde of gods, often in competition and at war with one another. Missionaries tell us that one of the greatest reliefs which Christianity brings to the heathen is the conviction that there is only one God. Before that, they live in a world haunted by hundreds of gods; they can never know when they have omitted the honour which is the due of some god, and have so offended him. They live for ever terrified of the gods. It is an emancipation and a liberation when they discover that there is one God whose name is Father and whose nature is Love.

(ii) There is one Mediator. Even the Jews would have

said that there are many mediators between God and man.
A mediator is one who stands between two parties and
who acts as a go-between or who brings them together.
The Jews would have said that the angels were mediators.
The Testament of Dan (6: 2) has it: " Draw near unto
God, and unto the angel who intercedes for you, for he is a
mediator between God and man." The Greeks would
have said that there are all kinds of mediators. Plutarch
said that it was an insult to God to conceive that He was
in any way directly involved in the world; He was only
involved in the world through angels and demons and
demi-gods who were, so to speak, His liaison officers
between Himself and the world. Neither in Jewish nor
in Greek thought had a man *direct* access to God. But,
through Jesus Christ, the Christian has direct access to
God, with nothing to bar the way between. Further,
there is only *one* Mediator. E. F. Brown tells us that that
is, for instance, what the Hindus find it so hard to believe.
They find it hard to believe that God can have only one
method of salvation for all mankind. They say: " Your
religion is good for you, and ours for us." But unless
there is one God and one Mediator then there can be no
such thing as the brotherhood of man. If there are many
gods and many mediators it means that there are many
gods and many mediators competing for the loyalty and
the allegiance and the love of men. Religion then becomes
something which divides men instead of uniting men. It
is because there is one God and one Mediator that men
are brethren one of another.

So Paul goes on to call Jesus the one who gave His life a
ransom for all. That simply means that it cost God the
life and the death of His Son to bring men back to Himself.
There was a man who lost a son in the war. He had been
a man who lived a most careless and even a godless life;
but his son's death brought him to his senses, and brought
him face to face with God as he had never been before
in all his life. He became a changed man. One day he

was standing before the local war memorial, looking at his son's name upon it. And very gently he said: "I guess he had to go down to lift me up." That is what Jesus did; it cost the life and the death and the pain and the sacrifice of Jesus Christ to tell men of the love of God and to bring men home to God.

Then Paul says certain things of himself. He claims to himself four offices.

(i) He is a *herald* of the story of Jesus Christ. A herald is a man who proclaims the truth. A herald is a man who makes a statement and who says: "This is true." A herald is a man who brings a proclamation that is not his own, but which comes from the king.

(ii) He is a *witness* to the story of Christ. A witness is a man who says: "This is true, and I know it." A witness is a man who says, not only: "This is true," but also: "This works." A witness is a man who tells, not only the story of Christ, but also the story of what Christ has done for him.

(iii) He is an *envoy*. An envoy is one whose duty is to commend and to present his country in a foreign land. An envoy in the Christian sense is therefore one who commends the story of Christ to others. The envoy wishes to communicate that story to others, so that it will mean as much to others as it does to him.

(iv) He is a *teacher*. The *herald* is the person who proclaims the facts; the *witness* is the person who proclaims the power of the facts; the *envoy* is the person who commends the facts; the *teacher* is the person who leads men into the meaning of the facts. It is not enough to know that Christ lived and died; we must think out what that life and death meant. A man has a head as well as a heart; he has a brain as well as emotions; he has intellect as well as feelings. He must not only feel the wonder of the story of Christ; he must think out its meaning for himself and for the world.

BARRIERS TO PRAYER

I *Timothy* 2: 8-15

So, then, it is my wish that men should pray everywhere, lifting up holy hands, with no anger in their hearts and no doubts in their minds. Even so it is my wish that women should modestly and wisely adorn themselves in seemly dress. This adornment should not consist in braided hair, and ornaments of gold, and pearls, but—as befits women who profess to reverence God—they should adorn themselves with good works. Let a woman learn in silence and with all submission. I do not allow a woman to teach or to dictate to a man. Rather, it is my advice that she should be silent. For Adam was formed first, and then Eve; and Adam was not deceived, but the woman was deceived, and so became guilty of transgression. But women will be saved through childbearing, if they continue in faith and love, and if they wisely walk the road that leads to holiness.

THE early Church took over the Jewish attitude of prayer. The Jew prayed standing, with his hands outstretched with the palms upwards. Later Tertullian was to say that that attitude of prayer depicted the attitude of Jesus upon the Cross.

The Jews had always known about the barriers which kept a man's prayers from God. Isaiah heard God say to the people: "When ye spread forth your hands, I will hide mine eyes from you; yea, when ye make many prayers, I will not hear; your hands are full of blood" (*Isaiah* 1: 15). Here too certain things are demanded.

(i) He who prays must stretch forth and hold up holy hands. He must hold up to God hands which do not touch or handle the forbidden things. This does not mean for one moment that the sinner is debarred from God; but it does mean that there is no reality in the prayers of the man who prays and then goes out to soil his hands with forbidden things, as if he had never prayed. It is not thinking of the man who is helplessly in the grip of some sin or some passion or some habit and who is desperately

74

fighting against it, and who is bitterly conscious of his failure. It is thinking of the man whose prayers are a sheer formality, who prays and then goes out to live as if he had never prayed.

(ii) He who prays must have no anger in his heart. It has been said that "forgiveness is indivisible." Human and divine forgiveness go hand in hand. Again and again Jesus stresses the fact that we cannot hope to receive the forgiveness of God so long as we are in bitterness and enmity with our fellow men. "If thou bring thy gift to the altar, and then rememberest that thy brother hath aught against thee, leave there thy gift before the altar, and go thy way; first be reconciled to thy brother, and then come and offer thy gift" (*Matthew* 5: 23, 24). "If ye forgive not men their trespasses, neither will your Father forgive your trespasses" (*Matthew* 6: 15). Jesus tells the story of what happened to the unforgiving servant, how he himself found no forgiveness, and then he ends: "So likewise shall my heavenly Father do also unto you, if ye from your hearts forgive not every one his brother their trespasses" (*Matthew* 18: 35). To be forgiven, we must be forgiving. The *Didachē*, which is the earliest Christian book on public worship, and which dates from about A.D. 100, has it: "Let no one who has a quarrel with his neighbour come to us, until they are reconciled." The bitterness in a man's heart is a barrier which hinders his prayers from reaching God.

(iii) He who prays must have no doubts in his mind. This phrase can mean two things. The word which is used is *dialogismos*. *Dialogismos* can mean both an *argument*, and a *doubt*. If we took it in the sense of *argument*, it would simply repeat what has gone before. It would simply restate the fact that bitterness, and quarrels, and angry arguments, and venomous debates are a hindrance to prayer. It is better to take it in the sense of *doubt*. Before prayer is answered there must be belief that God will answer. If a man prays hopelessly and pessimistically,

75

if he prays with no real belief that prayer is any use, then his prayer falls wingless to the ground. Before a man can be cured, he must believe that he can be cured; before a man can lay hold on the grace of God, he must believe in the grace of God. We must take our prayers to God in the complete confidence that God is the God who hears and who answers prayer.

WOMEN IN THE CHURCH

2 *Timothy* 2: 8-15 (*continued*)

THE second part of this passage deals with the place of women in the Church. This is a passage which cannot be read out of its historical context. It springs entirely from the situation in which it was written. It is written against a double background.

(i) It is written against a Jewish background. Now in Jewish eyes, women *officially* had a very low position. It is true that no nation ever gave a bigger place to women in home and in family things than the Jews did; but officially the position of woman was very low. In Jewish law a woman was not a person; she was a thing. She was entirely at the disposal or her father or of her husband. A woman was forbidden to learn the law; to instruct a woman in the law was to cast pearls before swine. Women had no part in the Synagogue service; they were shut apart in a section of the Synagogue, or in a gallery, where they could not be seen, and were allowed no share in the service. A man came to the Synagogue to *learn*; but, at the most, a woman came to *hear*. In the Synagogue the lesson from Scripture was read by members of the congregation; but not by women, for that would have been to lessen " the honour of the congregation." It was absolutely forbidden for a woman to teach in a school; she might not even teach the youngest children. A woman was exempt from the stated demands of the Law. It was not obligatory on her to attend the sacred feasts and festivals. Women, slaves and children were classed together. In the Jewish morning prayer, a man thanked God that God had not made him " a Gentile, a slave or a woman." In the *Sayings of the Fathers* Rabbi Josē ben Johanan is quoted as saying: " ' Let thy house be opened wide, and let the poor be thy household, and talk not much with a woman. ' He said it in the case of his own wife, much more in the case of his companion's wife. Hence the wise have said: ' Everyone that talketh much with a woman causes evil to himself, and desists from the works of the Law, and his end is that he inherits Gehenna. ' " A strict Rabbi would never greet a woman on the street, not even his own wife or daughter or mother or sister. It was said of women: " Her work is to send her children to the Synagogue; to attend to domestic concerns; to leave her husband free to study in the schools; to keep house for him until he returns." We must remember that it was out of a Jewish background like that that the Church arose.

(ii) It is written against a Greek background. The Greek background made things doubly difficult. The place of women in Greek religion was low. The Temple of Aphrodite in Corinth had a thousand priestesses who were sacred prostitutes and who every evening plied their trade on the city streets. The Temple of Diana in Ephesus had its hundreds of priestesses called the *Melissae*, which means the *bees,* and whose function was the same. The respectable Greek woman led a very confined life. She lived in her own quarters into which no one but her husband came. She did not even appear at meals. She never at any time appeared on the street alone; she never went to any public assembly, still less did she ever speak or take any active part in such an assembly. The fact is that if in a Greek town Christian women had taken an active and a speaking and a teaching part in the work of the Christian Church, the Church would inevitably have gained the reputation of being the resort of loose and immoral women. The plain fact of the situation was that in any Greek society no other regulations than these could have been laid down.

Further, in Greek society, there were women whose whole life consisted in elaborate dressing and braiding of the hair. In Rome, Pliny tells us of a bride, Lollia Paulina, whose bridal dress cost the equivalent of £432,000. Even the Greeks and the Romans themselves were shocked at the love of dress and the love of display and the love of adornment which characterized some of their women. The great Greek religions were called the Mystery religions, and they had precisely the same regulations about dress. There is an inscription which reads as follows: " A consecrated woman shall not have gold ornaments, nor rouge, nor face-whitening, nor a head-band, nor braided hair, nor shoes, except those made of felt or of the skins of sacrificed animals." The Christian Church did not lay down these regulations as in any sense permanent regulations, but as things which were necessary in the situation in which the early Church found itself.

In any event there is much on the other side. It may be true that in the old story it was the woman who was created second, and it was the woman who fell to the seduction of the serpent who was the tempter; but it was Mary of Nazareth who bore and who trained the child Jesus; it was Mary of Magdala who was first to see the risen Lord; it was four women who of all the disciples stood by the Cross. Priscilla with her husband Aquila was a valued teacher in the early Church, a teacher who led Apollos to a knowledge of the truth (*Acts* 18: 26). Euodia and Syntyche, in spite of their quarrel, were women who laboured in the gospel (*Philippians* 4: 2, 3). Philip, the evangelist, had four daughters who were prophetesses (*Acts* 21: 9). The aged women were to teach (*Titus* 2: 3). Paul held Lois and Eunice in the highest honour (2 *Timothy* 1: 5), and there is many a woman's name held in honour in *Romans* 16. All the things in this chapter are mere

temporary regulations laid down to meet a given situation.
If we want Paul's real and permanent view on this matter,
we get it in *Galatians* 3: 28: "There is neither Jew nor
Greek, there is neither bond nor free, there is neither male
nor female: for ye are all one in Christ Jesus." In Christ
the differences of place and honour and prestige and function
within the Church were all wiped out.

And yet this passage ends with a real truth. Women, it
says, will be saved in child-bearing. There are two possible
meanings here. Just faintly possibly this may be a reference
to the fact that Mary, a woman, was the mother of Jesus.
It may be that it means that women will be saved—as
all others will—by this supreme act of child-bearing by
which the Son of God was born into the world. But it is
much more likely that the meaning of this passage is
much simpler; and that what it means is that women will
find life and salvation, not in attending meetings, and not
in addressing meetings, but in motherhood, which is their
crown. Whatever else is true, a woman is queen within
her home.

We must not read this passage as a barrier to all women's
work and service within the Church; we must read it in
the light of its Jewish background and in the light of the
situation in a Greek city. And we must look for Paul's
permanent views in the passage which tells us that the
differences are wiped out, and that men and women,
slaves and freemen, Jews and Gentiles, are all eligible to
serve Christ.

THE LEADERS OF THE CHURCH

I *Timothy* 3: 1-7

There is a saying which everyone must believe—if a
man aspires to the office of overseer in the Church,
it is a fine work on which his heart is set. An overseer
must be a man against whom no criticism can be
made; he must have been married only once; he
must be sober, prudent, well-behaved, hospitable

and possessed of an aptitude for teaching. He must not over-indulge in wine, nor must he be the kind of man who assaults others, but he must be gentle and peaceable, and free from the love of money. He must manage his own house well, keeping his children under control with complete dignity. (If a man does not know how to manage his own house, how can he take charge of the congregation of God?) He must not be a recent convert, in case he becomes inflated with a sense of his own importance, and so fall into the same condemnation as the devil did. He must have earned the respect of those outside the Church, that he may not fall into reproach and into the snare of the devil.

THIS is a very important passage from the point of view of Church government. It deals with the man whom the Authorised Version calls the *bishop,* and whom we have called in the translation the *overseer.*

In the New Testament there are two words which describe the principal office-bearers of the Church, the office-bearers who were to be found in every congregation, and on whose conduct and administration the welfare of these congregations depended.

(i) There was the man who was called the *elder* (*presbuteros*). The eldership is the most ancient of all offices within the Church. The Jews had their elders, and they traced the origin of them to the occasion when Moses, in the desert wanderings, appointed seventy men to help him in the task of controlling and caring for the people (*Numbers* 11: 16). Every Synagogue had its elders, and these elders were the real leaders of the Jewish community. They presided over the worship of the Synagogue; they administered rebuke and discipline where these were necessary; they settled the disputes and the arguments and the cases which other nations would have taken to the law-courts. Amongst the Jews the elders were the respected men who exercised a fatherly oversight over the spiritual and material affairs of every Jewish community. But there were more nations than the Jews who had an eldership. The presiding body of the Spartans was called the *gerousia*, which means *the board of the elder men.* The Parliament of Rome was called the *senate*, which comes from *senex*, which means *an old man.* In England the men who looked after the affairs of the community were called the *aldermen*, which means the *elder men.* In Egypt in New Testament times every Egyptian village had its village elders who looked after the affairs of the community. The elders had a long history, and they had a place in the life of almost every community.

(ii) But sometimes the New Testament uses another word; it uses the word *episkopos*, which the Authorised Version translates *bishop,* and which literally means *overseer*, or *superintendent.* This word too has a long and an honourable history. The Septuagint, the Greek version of the Hebrew scriptures, uses it to describe those who were the *task-masters*, who were over the public works and public building schemes (I *Chronicles* 34: 17). The Greeks used it to describe the men who were appointed to go out from the mother city to regulate the affairs of a newly founded colony in some distant place. They used it to describe what we would call *commissioners* who were appointed to regulate the affairs of a city. The Romans used it to describe the magistrates who were appointed to oversee the sale of food within the city of Rome. It is used of the special delegates appointed by a king to see that the rules and laws and regulations he had laid down were carried out. This word *episkopos* always implies two things. First, it implies *oversight* over some area or sphere of work; second, it implies *responsibility* to some higher power and authority. It is a word with an honourable and responsible history.

The great question at issue here is: What was the relationship in the early Church between the elder, the *presbuteros*, and the overseer, the *episkopos*, the man whom the Authorised Version calls the *bishop*, and whom we have called the *overseer*?

Modern scholarship is practically unanimous in holding that in the early Church the *presbuteros* and the *episkopos*, the elder and the bishop or overseer, were one and the same person. The grounds for that identification are as follows: (*a*) Elders were everywhere appointed. After the first missionary journey, Paul and Barnabas appointed elders in all the Churches they had founded (*Acts* 14: 23). Titus is instructed to appoint and ordain elders in all the cities of Crete (*Titus* 1: 5). (*b*) The qualifications of a *presbuteros* and of an *episkopos* are to all intents and purposes identical (I *Timothy* 3: 2-7; *Titus* 1: 6-9). (*c*) At the beginning of *Philippians*, Paul's greetings are to the *bishops and the deacons* (*Philippians* 1: 1). It is quite impossible that Paul would have sent no greetings at all to the *elders*, who, as we have already seen, were in every Church; and therefore the *bishops* and the *elders*, must be one and the same body of people. (*d*) When Paul was on his last journey to Jerusalem he sent for the *elders* of Ephesus to meet him at Miletus (*Acts* 20: 17), and in the course of his talk to them he says that God has made them *overseers*, *episkopoi*, bishops to feed the Church of God (*Acts* 20: 28). That is to say, Paul addresses precisely the same body of men, first as *elders*, and second, as bishops or overseers. (*e*) When Peter is writing to his people he talks to them as an *elder* to *elders* (I *Peter* 5: 1), and then he goes on to say that their function is *oversight* of the flock of God (I *Peter* 5: 2), and the word he uses for *oversight*, is the verb *episkopein* from which the word *episkopos*, bishop, comes. All the evidence from New Testament times goes to prove that the *presbuteros* and the *episkopos*, the elder and the bishop or overseer, were one and the same person.

Two questions arise. First, if they were the same, why then are there two names for them? The answer is that *presbuteros*, elder, described these leaders of the Church as they personally were. They were the elder men, the older and the respected members of the community. The word *episkopos*, bishop, overseer, on the other hand,

describes *their function and their task,* which was to oversee
and to superintend the life and the work of the Church.
The one word describes the man; the other word describes
the function of the man.

The second question is: If the elder and the bishop were
originally the same, how did the bishop become what he
did become? The answer is simple. Inevitably the body
of the elders would acquire a leader. Someone to lead and
to preside would be essential and would inevitably emerge.
The more organized the Church became, the more such a
figure would be necessary and would be bound to arise.
And the elder who stood out as leader came to be called
the *episkopos,* the *superintendent* of the Church. But it is
to be noted that he was simply a leader amongst equals.
He was in fact the elder whom circumstances and personal
qualities had combined to make a leader for the work of
the Church.

It will be seen then that to translate *episkopos* by the
word *bishop* in New Testament times now gives the word
a wrong and a misleading meaning. It is better to translate
it *overseer* or *superintendent.*

THE APPOINTMENT AND THE DUTIES OF THE
LEADERS OF THE CHURCH

I *Timothy* 3: 1-7 (*continued*)

THIS passage is further interesting in that it tells us something of the appointment and the duties and the conditions
of service of the leaders of the Church.

(i) They were officially and formally set apart for their
office. Titus was to ordain elders in every Church (*Titus*
1: 5). The office-bearer of the Church is not made an
office-bearer in secret; he is ordained and set apart to
office in the eyes of men. Men know his position, and to
men he stands for the Church; the honour of the Church is
publicly delivered into his hands.

(ii) They had to undergo a period of testing. They had first to be proved (I *Timothy* 3: 10). No one builds a bridge or a piece of machinery with metal which has not been subjected to trial and to test. The Church might do well to be more strict than she is in the testing of those who are chosen out for leadership.

(iii) They were paid for the work which they had to do. The labourer is worthy of his hire (I *Timothy* 5: 18). The Christian leader does not work for pay, but on the other hand he has to live, and the duty of the Church which chose him for the work was also to supply him with the means to live.

(iv) They were liable to censure (I *Timothy* 5: 19-22). In the early Church the office-bearer had a double function. True, he was the leader and the director of the Church; but also he was the servant and officer of the Church. He had to answer for his stewardship. No Christian office-bearer must ever adopt an attitude in which he considers himself answerable to no one. He is answerable to God, and he is answerable to the people over whom God gave him the task of presiding.

(v) They had the duty of *presiding over* the Christian assembly and of *teaching* the Christian congregation (I *Timothy* 5: 17). The Christian office-bearer has the double duty of *administration* and *instruction*. It may well be that one of the tragedies of the modern Church is that the administrative function of the office-bearer has usurped the teaching function almost entirely. It is, for instance, a saddening thing to see how few elders of the Church are actively engaged in the teaching work of Sunday Schools.

(vi) It is an interesting piece of advice that the office-bearer *should not be a recent convert.* Two reasons are given for that. The first of them is quite clear. It is " in case he becomes inflated with a sense of his own importance." The second reason is not so clear. It is, as the Authorised Version has it, " lest he fall into the condemnation of the

84

devil." There are three possible explanations of that strange phrase. (a) It was pride which caused the fall of the devil. It was through his pride that Lucifer rebelled against God, and was expelled from heaven. And this may simply be a second warning against the danger of pride. (b) It may mean that, if the too quickly advanced convert becomes guilty of pride, he gives the devil a chance to level his charges against him. A conceited Church office-bearer gives the devil a chance to say to critics of the Church: " Look! There's your Christian! There's your Church member! That's what an office-bearer is like! " The office-bearer who is guilty of pride gives the devil a chance to whisper his accusation against the Church in the ear of those for whom any stick is good enough wherewith to beat the Church. (c) The word *diabolos* has two meanings. It means *devil*, and that is the way in which the Authorised Version has taken it here. But it also means *slanderer*. It is in fact the word that is used for *slanderer* in verse II, in the phrase where the women are forbidden to be slanderers. So then this phrase may mean that the recent convert, who has been appointed to office, and who has acquired, as we say, a swelled head, gives a chance to the slanderers to direct their slanders against the Church. His unworthy conduct is ammunition for those who are ill-disposed to and critical of the Church. No matter how we take it, the great point is that the proud and conceited Church official is a bad debt to the Church.

But as the early Church saw it, the responsibility of the office-bearer of the Church did not begin and end in the Church. He had two other spheres of responsibility, and if he failed in them, he was bound also to fail in the Church.

(i) His first sphere of duty was his own home. If a man did not know how to rule his own household, how could he engage upon the task of ruling the congregation of the Church? (I *Timothy* 3: 5). A man who had not succeeded in making a Christian home could hardly be expected to succeed in making a Christian Church. A man who had not instructed his own household and family could hardly be the right man to instruct the family of the Church. Church work is no virtue and no credit to a man, if in the performance of it, he neglects his own home and family. Like charity, Christian work begins at home.

(ii) He has a second sphere of responsibility in the world. He must have " a good report from them who are without " (I *Timothy* 3: 7). He must be a man who has gained the respect of his fellow men in the ordinary day-to-day tasks and business of life and living. Nothing has hurt the Church more than the sight of people who are active and high in the Church and whose business and social life belies the faith which they profess and the precepts which they teach. The Christian office-bearer must first of all be a good man.

THE CHARACTER OF THE CHRISTIAN LEADER

I *Timothy* 3: 1-7 (*continued*)

WE have just seen that the Christian leader must be a man who has won the respect of all. In this passage there is a great series of words and phrases describing this Christian character; and it will be worth while to look at each of them in turn. Before we do that it will be interesting to set beside them two famous descriptions of the necessary character written by the great heathen thinkers. Diogenes Laertius (7: 116-126) hands down to us the Stoic description of the good man. He must be married; he must be without pride; he must be temperate; and he must combine prudence of mind with excellence of outward behaviour. A writer called Onosander has a description of the character of the ideal commander. He must be prudent, self-controlled, sober, frugal, enduring in toil, intelligent, without love of money, neither young nor old, if possible the father of a family, able to speak competently, and of good reputation. It is interesting to see how, when it comes to a description of real manhood, the pagan and the Christian descriptions coincide.

The Christian leader must be *a man against whom no criticism can be made (anepilēptos)*. The word *anepilēptos* is used of a position which is not open to attack, of a life which is not open to censure, of an art or technique which is so perfect that no fault can be found with it, of an agreement which is unassailable and inviolable. The Christian leader must be a man who is not only free from such faults as can be assailed by definite charges; he must be a man of such fine character that he is even beyond criticism. The Rheims version of the New Testament translates this Greek word by the very unusual English word *irreprehensible*, unable to be found fault with. The Greeks themselves defined the word as meaning " affording nothing of which an adversary can take hold." Here is the ideal of perfection. We will not be able fully to attain to it; but the fact remains that the Christian leader must seek to offer to the world a life of such purity and nobility that he leaves no loophole even for criticism of himself.

The Christian leader must have been married only once. The Greek of this literally means that the Christian leader must be " the husband of one wife." There are some people who would take this to mean that the Christian leader must be a married man, and it is possible that the phrase could mean that; and it is certainly true that a married man can be a recipient of confidences and a bringer of help in a way that a single man cannot be, and that he can bring a special understanding of and sympathy to many a situation in life. There are some few who would take this to mean that the Christian leader cannot in any case marry a second time, even after his wife's death. To support that they would quote Paul's teaching in I *Corinthians* 7. But in its context here we can be quite certain that this means that the Christian leader must be a loyal husband, preserving marriage in all its purity. In

87

later days the *Apostolic Canons* laid it down: " He who is involved in two marriages, after his baptism, or he who has taken a concubine, cannot be an *episkopos*, a bishop."

We may well ask: Why should it be necessary to lay down what looks like too obvious a regulation? We must understand the state of the world against which this was written. It has been said, and said with much truth, that the only totally new virtue which Christianity brought into this world was the virtue of chastity. In many ways it is true to say that the ancient world was in a state of moral chaos. That was true even of the Jewish world. Astonishing as it may seem, there were certain Jews who still believed in and practised polygamy. In the *Dialogue with Trypho*, in which Justin Martyr discusses Christianity with a Jew, it is said that " it is possible for a Jew even now to have four or five wives " (*Dialogue with Trypho*, 134). Josephus can write: " By ancestral custom a man can live with more than one wife " (*Antiquities of the Jews*, 17: 1, 2). Apart altogether from these unusual cases divorce was tragically easy in the Jewish world. The Jews had the highest ideals of marriage. They said that a man must surrender his life rather than commit murder, idolatry or adultery. They had the belief that marriages are made in heaven. In the story of the marriage of Isaac and Rebecca it is said: " The thing proceedeth from the Lord " (*Genesis* 24: 50). This was taken to mean that the marriage was arranged by God. So it is said in *Proverbs* 19: 14: " A prudent wife is from the Lord." In the story of Tobit, the angel says to Tobit: " Fear not for she was prepared for thee from the beginning " (*Tobit* 6: 17). So the Rabbis said: " God sits in heaven arranging marriages." " Forty days before the child is formed a heavenly voice proclaims its mate."

But for all that the Jewish law allowed divorce. Marriage was indeed the ideal but divorce was permitted. Marriage was " inviolable but not indissoluble." The Jews held that once the marriage ideal had been shattered by cruelty

or infidelity or incompatibility, it was far better to allow
a divorce and to permit the two to make a fresh start
all over again. That may well be so, but the great tragedy
of the Jewish law of divorce was that the wife had no
rights whatsoever. Josephus says: " With us it is lawful
for a husband to dissolve a marriage, but a wife, if she
departs from her husband, cannot marry another, unless
her former husband put her away " (*Antiquities of the Jews*,
15: 8, 7). In a case of divorce by consent, in the time of
the New Testament, all that was required was two witnesses,
and no court case at all. A husband could send his wife
away for any cause; at the most a wife could petition
the court to urge her husband to write her a bill of divorce-
ment, but the court could not compel him even to do that.

In face of that situation among the Jews, things came
to such a pass that " women refused to contract marriages,
and men grew grey and celibate." A brake was put upon
this process by legislation introduced by Simon ben Shetah.
A Jewish wife always brought her husband a dowry which
was called *Kethubah*. Simon enacted that a man had
unrestricted use of the *Kethubah*, so long as he remained
married to his wife, but on divorce he was absolutely
liable to repay it, even if he had " to sell his hair " to do so.
This checked divorce; but the Jewish system was always
vitiated by the fact that the wife had no rights at all.

In the heathen world the state of things was infinitely
worse. There too, according to Roman law, the wife had
no rights. Cato said: " If you were to take your wife in
adultery, you could kill her with impunity, without any
court judgment; but if you were involved in adultery,
she would not dare to lift a finger against you, for it is
unlawful." Things grew so bad, and marriage grew so
irksome, that in 131 B.C. a well known Roman called
Metellus Macedonicus made a statement which Augustus
was afterwards to quote: " If we could do without wives,
we would be rid of that nuisance. But since nature has
decreed that we can neither live comfortably with them.

nor live at all without them, we must look rather to our
permanent interests than to passing pleasure."

Even the Roman poets saw the dreadfulness of the
situation. "Ages rich in sin," wrote Horace, "were the
first to taint marriage and family life. From this source
the evil has overflowed." "Sooner will the seas be dried
up," said Propertius, "and the stars be reft from heaven,
than our women reformed." Ovid wrote his famous, or
infamous, book *The Art of Love*, and never from beginning
to end mentions married love. He wrote cynically: "These
women alone are pure who are unsolicited, and a man who
is angry at his wife's love affair is nothing but a rustic
boor." Seneca declares: "Anyone whose affairs have
not become notorious, and who does not pay a married
woman a yearly fee, is despised by women as a mere lover
of girls; in fact husbands are got as a mere decoy for
lovers." "Only the ugly," he said, "are loyal." "A
woman who is content to have only two followers is a
paragon of virtue." Tacitus commends the supposedly
barbarian German tribes for "not laughing at evil, and
not making seduction the spirit of the age." When a
marriage took place, the home to which the couple were
going was decorated with green bay leaves. Juvenal says
that there were those who entered on divorce before the
bays of welcome had faded. In 19 B.C. a man named
Quintus Lucretius Vespillo erected a tablet to his wife,
which said: "Seldom do marriages last until death
undivorced; but ours continued happily for forty-one
years." The happy marriage was the astonishing exception.

Ovid and Pliny had three wives; Caesar and Antony
had four; Sulla and Pompey had five; Herod had nine;
Cicero's daughter Tullia had three husbands. The Emperor
Nero was the third husband of Poppaea and the fifth
husband of Statilla Messalina.

It was not for nothing that the Pastorals laid it down
that the Christian leader must be the husband of one wife.
In a world where even the highest places were deluged

in immorality, the Christian Church must demonstrate the Christian chastity, the inviolability of the marriage bond, and the sanctity of the Christian home.

THE CHARACTER OF THE CHRISTIAN LEADER

I *Timothy* 3: 1-7 (*continued*)

THE Christian leader must be *sober* (*nēphalios*), and a little further on we read that he must not *over-indulge in wine*, he must not be *paroinos*. In the ancient world wine was continually used. In conditions in which the water supply was very inadequate and sometimes dangerous, wine was the most natural drink of all. It is wine which cheers the heart of God and man (*Judges* 9: 13). In the restoration of Israel she will plant her vineyards and drink her wine (*Amos* 9: 14). Strong drink is given to those who are ready to perish, and wine to those whose hearts are heavy (*Proverbs* 31: 6). That is not to say that the ancient world was not fully alive to the dangers which come from drink. *Proverbs* speaks of the disaster which comes to the man who looks on the wine when it is red (*Proverbs* 23: 29-35). Wine is a mocker and strong drink is raging (*Proverbs* 20: 1). There are terrible stories of what happened to people through over-indulgence in wine. There is the case of Noah (*Genesis* 9: 18-27); of Lot (*Genesis* 19: 30-38); of Ammon (2 *Samuel* 13: 28, 29). But although the ancient world used wine as the commonest of all drinks it used it most abstemiously. When wine was drunk, it was drunk in the proportion of two parts of wine to three parts of water. A man who was drunken would be disgraced in ordinary heathen society, let alone in the Church. The interesting thing is the double meaning that both words in this section possess. *Nēphalios* means *sober*, but it also means *watchful* and *vigilant*. *Paroinos* means *addicted to wine*, but it also means *quarrelsome* and *violent*. The point that the instruction of the Pastorals is here making is that the

91

Christian must allow himself no pleasure and no indulgence which would lessen his Christian vigilance or soil his Christian conduct.

There follow two great Greek words which describe two great qualities which must characterize the Christian leader. The Christian leader must be *prudent* (*sōphrōn*) and *well-behaved* (*kosmios*).

We have translated *sōphrōn* by the English word *prudent*, but it is really one of these untranslatable words. It is variously translated *of sound mind, discreet, prudent, self-controlled, chaste, having complete control over sensual desires*. The Greeks derived it from two words which mean *to keep one's mind safe and sound*. The corresponding noun is *sōphrosunē*, and the Greeks wrote and thought much about it. It is the opposite of intemperance and lack of self-control. Plato defined it as " the mastery of pleasure and desire." Aristotle defined is as " that power by which the pleasures of the body are used as law commands." Philo defined it as " a certain limiting and ordering of the desires, which eliminates those which are external and excessive, and which adorns those which are necessary with timeliness and moderation." Pythagoras said that it was " the foundation on which the soul rests." Iamblichus said that " it is the safeguard of the most excellent habits in life." Euripides said that it was " the fairest gift of God." Jeremy Taylor called it " reason's girdle and passion's bridle." Trench describes *sōphrosunē* as " the condition of entire command over the passions and desires, so that they receive no further allowance than that which law and right reason admit and approve." Gilbert Murray, the great classical scholar, wrote of this word *sōphrōn*: "There is a way of thinking which destroys and a way which saves. The man or woman who is *sōphrōn* walks among the beauties and perils of the world, feeling love, joy, anger, and the rest; and through all he has that in his mind which saves. Whom does it save? Not him only, but, as we should say, the whole situation. It saves the imminent evil from coming to be." E. F. Brown quotes in illustration of *sōphrosunē* a prayer of Thomas Aquinas which asks for " a quieting of all our impulses, fleshly and spiritual."

The man who is *sōphrōn* is the man who has every part of his nature under perfect control, which is to say that the man who is *sōphrōn* is the man in whose heart Christ reigns supreme.

The companion word is the word *kosmios*, which we have translated *well-behaved*. If a man is *kosmios* in his outer conduct it is because he is *sōphrōn* in his inner life. This word *kosmios* means *orderly, honest, decorous*. In Greek it has two very special usages. It is very common in tributes and in inscriptions to the dead. And it is very common to describe the man who is a good citizen. Plato defines the man who is *kosmios* as " the citizen who is quiet in the land, who duly fulfils in his place and order the duties which are incumbent upon him as such." This word has more in it than simply good behaviour. It describes the man whose life is beautiful and in whose character all things are harmoniously blended and integrated. He is the man in whom strength and beauty join hands.

The leader of the Church must be a man who is *sōphrōn*, a man whose every instinct, passion and desire are under perfect control; he must be a man who is *kosmios*, a man whose inner control has issued in outward beauty; the leader must be a man in whose heart the power of Christ reigns, and on whose life the beauty of Christ shines.

THE CHARACTER OF THE CHRISTIAN LEADER

1 *Timothy* 3: 1-7 (*continued*)

THE Christian leader must be *hospitable* (*philoxenos*). This is a quality on which the New Testament lays much stress. Paul bids the Roman Church to be " given to hospitality" (*Romans* 12: 13). "Use hospitality to one another," says Peter, "without grudging" (I *Peter* 4: 9). In the *Shepherd of Hermas*, one of the very early Christian writings, it is laid down: "The *episkopos* must be hospitable, a man who gladly and at all times welcomes into his house the servants of God." The Christian leader must be a man with an open heart and an open house.

The ancient world was very careful of the rights of the guest and the stranger. The stranger was under the protection of Zeus Xenios, Zeus, the Protector of Strangers. In the ancient world, inns were notoriously bad. In one of Aristophanes' plays Heracles asks his companion where they will lodge for the night; and the answer is: "Where the fleas are fewest." Plato speaks of the inn-keeper being like a pirate who holds his guests to ransom. Inns tended to be dirty and expensive and, above all, immoral. The ancient world itself had a system of what were called *Guest Friendships*. Over generations families had arrangements with each other to give each other accommodation and hospitality. Often the members of the families came in the end to be unknown to each other by sight. They identified themselves by means of what were called *tallies*. The stranger seeking accommodation would produce one half of some object; the other partner would possess the other half of the tally; and if the two halves fitted each other then the friend knew that he had found his guest, and the guest knew that the stranger was indeed the ancestral friend of his household.

In the Christian Church there were wandering teachers and preachers; they needed hospitality. There were many slaves who had no homes of their own; it was a great privilege to them to have the right of entry to a Christian home. The whole Church was a little island of Christianity in a pagan world; and it was of the greatest blessing that Christians should have Christian doors which were ever open to them, and Christian homes in which they could meet people like-minded to themselves. We still live in a world where there are many who are far from home, many who are strangers in a strange place, many who live in conditions where it is hard to be a Christian. The door of the Christian home, and the welcome of the Christian heart, should be open to all such.

The Christian leader must be possessed of an *aptitude for teaching* (*didaktikos*). It has been said that the duty of the Christian leader is " to preach to the unconverted and to teach the converted." There are two things to be said about this. It is one of the disasters of modern times that the teaching ministry of the Church has not been exercised as it should be. There is any amount of topical preaching; there is any amount of exhortation; but there is little use in exhorting a man to be a Christian when he does not know what being a Christian means. Instruction is a primary duty of the Christian preacher and leader. But the second thing is this. The finest and the most effective teaching is not done by *speaking*, but by *being*. Our ultimate duty is not to talk to men about Christ, but to show men Christ. Even the man with no gift of words can teach by living in such a way that in him men see the reflection of the Master. A saint has been defined as someone " in whom Christ lives again."

The Christian leader *must not be a man who assaults others*. The Greek word is *plēktēs*, a *striker*. That this instruction was not unnecessary is seen in one of the very early regulations of the *Apostolic Canons*: " A bishop, priest or deacon who smites the faithful when they err, or the unbelievers when they commit injury, and desires by such means as this to terrify them, we command to be deposed; for nowhere hath the Lord taught us this. When He was reviled, He reviled not again, but the contrary. When He was smitten, He smote not again; when He suffered, He threatened not." It will not be likely that any Christian or Christian leader will nowadays strike another Christian, but the fact remains that blustering, bullying, irritable, bad-tempered speech or action is forbidden to the Christian.

The Christian leader must be *gentle*. The word is *epieikēs*, and here we have another of these completely untranslatable words. The noun is *epieikeia*, and Aristotle describes it as " that which corrects justice." He said it was that which " is just and better than justice." He said that it was that quality which corrects the law when the law errs because of its generality. What he means is this. Sometimes it may actually be unjust to apply the strict letter of the law. There can arise cases in life when to apply the strict letter of the law can actually be injustice. Trench said that *epieikeia* means " retreating from the letter of right better to preserve the spirit of right." He said that it was " the spirit which recognizes the impossibility of cleaving to all formal law . . . that recognizes the danger that ever waits upon the assertion of legal rights, lest they should be pushed into moral wrongs . . . the spirit which rectifies and redresses the injustice of justice." Aristotle describes in full the action of *epieikeia*: " To pardon human failings; to look to the law-giver, not to the law; to the intention, not to the action; to the whole, not to the part; to the character of the actor in the long run and not in the present moment; to remember good rather than evil, and the good that one has received rather than the good that one has done; to bear being injured; to wish to settle a matter by words rather than deeds." If there is a matter under dispute, it can be settled by consulting a book of practice and procedure, or it can be settled by consulting Jesus Christ. If there is a matter of debate, it can be settled in law, or it can be settled in love. It can be brought to the test of legal enactments, or it can be brought to the footstool of the throne of the grace of God. The whole atmosphere of many a Church would be radically changed if there was more *epieikeia* within it.

The Christian leader must be *peaceable* (*amachos*). The

Greek word means *disinclined to fight*. There are people who, as we might put it, are "trigger-happy" in their relationships with other people. But the real Christian leader wants nothing so much as he wants peace with his fellow men.

The Christian leader must be *free from the love of money*. He will never do anything simply for profit's sake. He will know that there are values which are beyond all money price.

THE MEN OF CHRISTIAN SERVICE

I *Timothy* 3: 8-10, 12, 13

> In the same way, the deacons must be men of dignity, men who are straight, men who are not given to over-indulgence in wine, men who are not prepared to stoop to disgraceful ways of making money; they must hold the secret of the faith which has been revealed to them with a clear conscience. The deacons too must first of all be put upon probation, and, if they emerge blameless from the test, let them become deacons. . . . Deacons must be married only once; they must manage their own children and their own homes well. For those who make a fine job of the office of deacon win for themselves a fine degree of honour, and they gain much boldness in their faith in Christ Jesus.

IN the early Church the function of the deacons lay much more in the sphere of practical service. The Christian Church inherited a magnificent organization of charitable help from the Jews. No nation has ever had such a sense of responsibility for the poorer brother and sister as the Jews had and still have. The Synagogue had a regular organization for dealing with and helping such people. The Jews rather discouraged the giving of individual help to individual people. They preferred that help should be given through the community and especially through the Synagogue. Each Friday in every community two official collectors went round the markets and called on each house, collecting donations for the poor and needy in money and in goods. This material so collected was distributed to those in need by a committee of at least two, or of more than two if more were necessary for the work. The poor of the community were given enough food for fourteen meals, that is for two meals a day for the week. But no one could receive any donation from this fund if he already possessed a week's food in the house. This fund for the poor was called the *Kuppah,* or the *basket.* In addition to this there was a daily collection of food from house to house for those who were actually in emergency need for the day. This fund was called the *Tamhui,* or the *tray.* The Christian Church inherited this charitable organization, and no doubt it was the duty and the task of the deacons to carry it out in practice.

Many of the qualifications of the deacon are the same as the qualification for the *episkopos* or overseer or elder. They are to be men of dignified character; they are to be abstemious; they are not to soil their hands with disreputable ways of making money; they have to undergo a test and a time of probation; they must practise what they preach, so that they can hold the revelation of the Christian faith with a clear conscience.

One new qualification is to be added; they were to be *straight.* The Greek is that they must not be *dilogos*; *dilogos* means *speaking with two voices,* saying one thing to one and another to another. In *The Pilgrim's Progress* John Bunyan puts into By-ends mouth a description of the people who live in the town of Fair-speech. There is my Lord Turn-about, my Lord Time-Server, my Lord Fair-speech, after whose ancestors the town was named, Mr. Smooth-man, Mr. Facing-both-ways, Mr. Any-thing; and the parson of the parish, Mr. Two-tongues. A deacon, in his going from house to house, and in his dealing with those who needed and who requested charity, had to be a straight man. Again and again he would be tempted to evade issues by a little timely hypocrisy and smooth speaking. But the man who would do the work of the Christian Church must be straight.

It is clear that the man who performs the office of deacon well can look for promotion to the high office of elder. And if he performs it well, he will gain such a confidence in the faith that he can look any man in the face with boldness.

WOMEN WHO SERVE THE CHURCH

I *Timothy* 3: II

> In the same way, the women must be dignified; they must not be given to slanderous gossip; they must be sober; they must be in all things reliable.

As far as the Greek goes, this could refer to the wives of the deacons, or to women who are engaged in a similar service. It seems far more likely that it refers to women who are also engaged upon this work of charity. There must have been acts of kindness and of help and of charity which only a woman could properly do for another woman. Certainly in the early Church there were deaconesses. They had the duty of instructing female converts and in particular of presiding and attending at their baptism, for baptism was by total immersion.

It was very necessary that such women workers should be warned against slanderous gossip and should be bidden to be absolutely reliable. When a young doctor graduates and before he begins to practise, to this day he takes the Hippocratic oath, and part of that oath is a pledge and promise never to repeat anything that he has heard in the house of a patient, or anything that he has heard about a patient, even if he has heard it on the street. In the work of helping the poor, things might easily be heard, and things might easily be repeated and infinite damage might be done. It is not any insult to women that the Pastorals specially forbid gossip to them. In the nature of life a woman runs more risk of gossip than a man. A man's work takes him out into the world; he has his business and his activities and all his wider interests; a woman of necessity lives in a narrower sphere, and for that very reason has fewer things to talk about; and she is always in danger of talking about these personal relationships from which slanderous gossip arises. Whether man or woman, a tale-bearing, confidence-repeating Christian is a monstrous and a dangerous thing.

In Greek civilization it was essential that the women workers of the Church should preserve their dignity. The respectable Greek woman lived in the greatest seclusion; she never went out alone; she never even shared the meals with her men folk; she lived a completely secluded life. Pericles had said that the duty of an Athenian mother was to live so retired a life that her name should never be mentioned among men for praise or blame. Xenophon tells how a country gentleman who was a friend of his told about the young wife whom he had just married and whom he dearly loved. " What was she likely to know when I married her? Why, she was not yet fifteen when I introduced her to my house, and she had been brought up always under the strictest supervision; as far as could be managed, she had not been allowed to see anything, hear anything or ask any questions." That is the way in which respectable Greek girls were brought up. Xenophon gives a vivid picture of one of these girl-wives gradually " growing accustomed to her husband and becoming sufficiently tame to hold conversation with him."

Christianity emancipated women. It liberated them from what was really a kind of slavery. But there were dangers. She who was liberated might misuse her new-found freedom; the respectable world might be shocked by such an emancipation; and so the Church had wisely to lay down its regulations. It was by wisely using freedom, and not by misusing it, that women came to hold the proud position in the Church which they hold to-day.

THE PRIVILEGE AND THE RESPONSIBILITY OF LIFE WITHIN THE CHURCH

I *Timothy* 3: 14, 15

> I am writing these things to you, hoping, as I write, to come to you soon. But I am writing, so that, if I am delayed, you may know how to behave yourselves in the household of God, which is the assembly of the living God, and the pillar and buttress of the truth.

HERE in one phrase is the whole reason why the Pastoral Epistles were written; they were written to tell men how to behave within the Church. The word for *to behave* is *anastrephesthai*; it describes what we would call a man's *walk and conversation.* It describes his whole life and character; but it specially describes him in his relationships with other people. As it has been said, the word in itself lays it down that a Christian Church member's personal character must be excellent and that his personal relationships with other people should be a true fellowship. Within the Church a man should be in fellowship with God, and in fellowship with his fellow men. A Church is a body of people who are friends with God and friends with each other. Then Paul goes on to use four great words which describe four great functions of the Church.

(i) The Church is the *household* (*oikos*) of God. First and foremost the Church must be a family. In a despatch written after one of his great naval victories, Nelson ascribed his victory to the fact that he " had the happiness to command a band of brothers." Unless a Church is a band of brothers it is not a true Church at all. Love of God can only exist where brotherly love exists.

(ii) The Church is the assembly (*ekklēsia*) of the living God. The word *ekklēsia* literally means a company of people who have been called out. It does not mean that they have been *selected* or *picked out*. In Athens the *ekklēsia* was the governing body of the city; and the governing body consisted of *all* the citizens met in assembly. But, very naturally, at no time did all the citizens attend. The summons went out to come to the Assembly of the City, but only some of the citizens answered to it and came. God's summons, God's invitation, God's call has gone out to every man; but only some men have accepted it; and those who have accepted it are the *ekklēsia*, the assembly, the Church of the living God. It is not that God has been selective; it is not that God has chosen some and rejected others; it is that not all men have accepted it. The invitation and the call come to all; but to an invitation there must be an answer, and to a call there must be a response.

not predestination

(iii) The Church is the *pillar* of the truth. In Ephesus, to which these letters were written, the word *pillar* would have a special significance. The greatest glory of Ephesus was the Temple of Diana or Artemis. "Great is Diana of the Ephesians" (*Acts* 19: 28). That temple was one of the seven wonders of the world. One of the features of that temple was its pillars. There were in it one hundred and twenty-seven pillars, every one of them the gift of a king. All of them were made of marble, and some of them were studded with jewels and overlaid with gold. The people of Ephesus knew well how beautiful a thing a pillar could be. It may well be that the idea of the word *pillar* here is not so much *support*—that is contained in the word *buttress*—as *display*. Often the statue of a famous man is set on the top of a pillar that it may stand out above all ordinary things and so be clearly seen, even from a distance. The idea here is that the Church's duty is to hold up the truth in such a way that all men can see it.

It is the Church's duty to display and to demonstrate the truth.

(iv) The Church is the *buttress* (*hedraiōma*) of the truth. The buttress is the support of the building. It keeps the building standing four-square and intact. In a world which does not wish to face the truth, the Church holds up the truth for all to see. In a world which would often gladly eliminate unwelcome and unpleasant truth, the Church supports the truth against all who would seek to destroy it.

Last verse Chapter 3

A HYMN OF THE CHURCH

I *Timothy* 3: 16

As everyone must confess, great is the secret which God has revealed to us in our religion:

Beautiful

He who was manifested in the flesh:
He who was vindicated by the Spirit:
He who was seen by angels:
He who has been preached among the nations:
He in whom men have believed all over the world:
He who was taken up into glory.

THE great interest of this passage is that here we have a fragment of one of the hymns of the early Church. It is a kind of setting of men's belief in Christ to poetry and to music. It is a hymn in which men sang their creed. We cannot look in poetry and in a hymn for the precision of statement for which we would look in a creed; but we must try to see what each line in this hymn is saying to us.

(i) *He who was manifested in the flesh.* Right at the beginning this hymn stresses the real manhood and the real humanity of Jesus. It says: "Look at Jesus, and you will see life as God would have lived it, if God had been a man." It says: "Look at Jesus, and here you will see the mind and the heart and the action of God, in a form that men can understand."

(ii) *He who was vindicated by the Spirit.* This is a difficult line. There are three things which it can mean. (*a*) It could mean that all through His earthly days Jesus was kept sinless by the power of the Spirit. It is the Spirit who gives a man guidance, who tells him at every moment in life what to do and what to say. Our error is that we so often refuse the guidance of the Spirit. It was Jesus' perfect submission to the Spirit of God which kept Him without sin. (*b*) It could mean that Jesus' claims were vindicated by the power and the action of the Spirit who dwelt in Him. When Jesus was accused by the scribes and Pharisees of effecting cures by the power of the devil, His answer was: " If I cast out devils *by the Spirit of God,* then the kingdom of God is come unto you " (*Matthew* 12: 28). The power that was in Jesus was the power of the Spirit, and the mighty acts He performed in that power were the vindication of the tremendous claims which He made. (*c*) It may be that this is a reference to the Resurrection. Men took Jesus and crucified Him as a criminal upon a cross; but through the power of the Spirit He rose again; the verdict of men was demonstrated to be false, and He was vindicated because by the power of the Spirit He rose again and conquered death. No matter how we take this line, the meaning is that the Spirit is the power who proved Jesus to be what He claimed to be.

(iii) *He who was seen by angels.* Again there are three possible meanings for this line. (*a*) It might be a reference to Jesus' life before He came to this earth. In the heavenly places the Son of God was seen by angels and was worshipped by them, before He came to earth. (*b*) It may be a reference to His life on earth. Even on earth the hosts of heaven were looking on at this tremendous contest with evil. Amidst the unseen cloud of witnesses the angels were looking down. (*c*) It was the belief of all men in the time of Jesus and of the earthly Church, that the air was full of demonic and angelic powers. Many of these powers were hostile to God and to man, and bent on the destruction of Jesus. Now Paul at least once argued that they were bent on the destruction of Jesus through ignorance, and that Jesus brought to them and to men the wisdom which had been hidden since the world began (I *Corinthians* 2: 7, 8). If this phrase is to be connected with that belief, it means that Jesus brought the truth even to the angelic and demonic powers who had never known it. However we take it, this phrase means that the work of Jesus is so tremendous that it includes both heaven and earth.

(iv) *He who has been preached among the nations.* Here we have the great truth that Jesus was the exclusive possession of no race and of no country. He was not the Messiah who had come to raise the Jews to earthly greatness; He was the Saviour of all nations, of the whole wide world.

(v) *He in whom men have believed all over the world.* Here is an almost miraculous truth stated with utter simplicity. After Jesus had died and had risen again and had ascended to His glory, the number of His followers was one hundred and twenty (*Acts* I: 15). All that His followers had to offer was the story of a Galilaean carpenter, crucified on a hilltop in Palestine, as a criminal. And yet before seventy years had passed that story had gone out to the ends of the earth, and men of every nation accepted this crucified Jesus as Saviour and Lord. Here in this simple phrase there is the whole wonder of the divine expansion of the Church, an expansion which on any human grounds was incredible.

(vi) *He who was taken up into glory.* This is a reference to the Ascension. The story of Jesus begins in heaven and ends in heaven. He lived as a servant; He was branded as a criminal; He was crucified on a cross; He rose with the nailprints still upon Him; but the end is glory.

THE SERVICE OF GOD OR THE SERVICE OF SATAN

1 Timothy 4: 1-5

The Spirit clearly says that in the later times some will desert from the faith, through paying attention to spirits who can do nothing but lead them astray, and to teachings which come from the demons, teachings of false men whose characteristic is insincerity, teachings of men whose conscience has been branded with the mark of Satan, teachings of those who forbid marriage, and who order men to abstain from foods which God created in order that men might gratefully take their share of them in the company of those who believe and who really know the truth; for everything that God has made is good, and nothing is to be rejected, but it is to be gratefully received; for it is hallowed by the word of God and by prayer.

THE Christian Church had inherited from the Jews the fixed belief that in this world things would be a great deal worse before they were better. The Jews always thought of time in terms of two ages. There was *this present age*, which was altogether bad and altogether in the grip of the evil powers; there was *the age to come*, which was to be the perfect age of God and of goodness. But the one age would not pass into the other without a last convulsive struggle. In between the two ages there would come *The Day of the Lord*. On that day the world would be shaken to its foundations; there would be a last supreme battle with evil, a last universal judgment, and then the new day would dawn. The New Testament writers took over that picture. Being Jews, they had been brought up in it. One of the expected things of the last age was heresies and false teachers. "Many false prophets shall rise, and they shall deceive many" (*Matthew* 24: 11). "False Christs and false prophets shall rise, and shall shew signs and wonders, to seduce, if it were possible, even the elect" (*Mark* 13: 22). In these last days Paul looks for the emergence of "the man of sin, the son of perdition," who would set himself up against God (2 *Thessalonians* 2: 4).

Into the Church at Ephesus such false teachers had come. The way in which that false teaching is regarded in this passage is something to make us think, and to make us think very seriously. At that time, as we have seen so often, men believed in evil spirits and evil demons, who haunted the air and who were out to ruin men. It was from these evil spirits and demons that this false teaching came. But though it came *from* the demons, it came *through* men. It came through men whose characteristic was a smooth hypocrisy; it came through men whose consciences had been branded by Satan. The idea behind the brand is this; it sometimes happened that a slave was branded with a mark which identified him as belonging to a certain owner, as cattle are branded nowadays. These false teachers bear upon their consciences the very brand of Satan; they are marked out as his slaves, as his property, as belonging to him.

Now here is the threatening and the terrible thing. We know that God and God's Spirit are everywhere looking for men to use. God is always searching for men who will be His instruments, His weapons, His tools in the world. But here we come face to face with the terrible fact that the forces of evil are also looking for men to use. Just as God seeks men for His purposes, the forces of evil seek men for their purposes. Here is the terrible responsibility of manhood. Man can accept the service of God, or the service of the devil. Man can become an instrument of the Supreme Good or the Supreme Evil. Men are faced with the eternal choice—to whom are we to give our lives, to God or to God's enemy? Are we to decide to be used by God, or are we to decide to be used by the devil?

ENSLAVERS OF MEN AND INSULTERS OF GOD

I *Timothy* 4: 1-5 (*continued*)

THE heretics of Ephesus were propagating a heresy with very definite consequences for life. As we have already seen, these heretics were Gnostics; and the essence of Gnosticism was that spirit is altogether good and that matter is altogether evil. One of the consequences of that heresy was that there were men who preached that the body was evil, that everything to do with the body, every physical instinct and function is evil, that the world is evil, that everything in the world is evil, that even the fairest things in the world must be abandoned and despised. In Ephesus this issued in two definite errors. These heretics insisted that men must, as far as possible, abstain from food, for food is material and food is evil; food ministers to the body and the body is evil; further, they insisted that a man must abstain from marriage, for the body is evil and the instincts of the body are evil and must be entirely suppressed.

This was an ever-recurring heresy in the Church; in every generation men arose who tried to be stricter than God. When the *Apostolic Canons* came to be written, it came to be necessary to set it down in black and white: " If any overseer, priest or deacon, or anyone on the priestly list, abstains from marriage and flesh and wine, not on the ground of asceticism (that is, for the sake of discipline), but through abhorrence of them as evil in themselves, forgetting that all things are very good, and that God made man male and female, but blaspheming and slandering the workmanship of God, either let him amend, or be deposed and cast out of the Church. Likewise a layman also " (*Apostolic Canons* 51). Irenaeus, writing towards the end of the second century, tells how certain followers of Saturninus " declare that marriage and generation are from Satan. Many likewise abstain from animal food, and draw away multitudes by a feigned

108

temperance of this kind " (Irenaeus, *Against Heresies*, I, 24, 2). This kind of thing came to a head in the monks and hermits of the fourth century. They went away and lived in the Egyptian desert, entirely cut off from men. They spent their lives mortifying the flesh. One never ate cooked food and was famous for his "fleshlessness." Another stood all night by a jutting crag so that it was impossible for him to sleep. Another was famous because he allowed his body to become so dirty and neglected that vermin dropped from him as he walked. Another deliberately ate salt in midsummer, and then abstained from drinking water. " A clean body," they said, " necessarily means an unclean soul."

The answer to these men was that by doing things like that they were insulting God, for God is the creator of the world; and repeatedly God's creation is said to be good. " And God saw everything that He had made and behold it was very good " (*Genesis* I: 31). " Every moving thing that liveth shall be meat for you " (*Genesis* 9: 3). " God created man in His own image . . . male and female created He them. And God blessed them, and God said unto them, Be fruitful and multiply and replenish the earth " (*Genesis* I: 27, 28). So far from being evil, everything that God has made is good.

But all God's gifts have to be used in a certain way.

(i) They have to be used *in the memory that they are gifts of God*. There are things which come to us so regularly and so unfailingly that we begin to forget that they are gifts, and we begin to take them as rights. We are to remember that all that we have is a gift from God, that we cannot draw another breath without God, that there is not a living and growing thing which could have life apart from God.

(ii) They have to be used *in sharing*. All selfish use is forbidden. No man can monopolize God's gifts; every man must share God's gifts.

(iii) They are to be used *with gratitude*. Always there is to be grace before meat. The Jew always said his grace. He had a grace for different things. When he ate fruits he said: "Blessed art Thou, King of the Universe, who createst the fruit of the tree." When he drank wine he said: "Blessed art Thou, King of the Universe, who createst the fruit of the vine." When he ate vegetables he said: "Blessed art Thou, King of the Universe, who createst the fruit of the earth." When he ate bread he said: "Blessed art Thou, King of the Universe, who bringest forth bread from the ground." The very fact that we thank God for a thing makes that thing sacred. Nothing remains unclean when it has been first offered to God. Not even the demons can touch it when it has been touched by the Spirit of God.

It is Christian teaching that the true Christian does not serve God by enslaving himself with rules and regulations and insulting God's creation; he serves God by gratefully accepting God's good gifts and remembering that he lives in a world where God made all things well, and by never forgetting to share God's gifts with others and to offer God the thanks of his heart for them.

ADVICE TO AN ENVOY OF CHRIST

I Timothy 4: 6-9

If you lay these things before the brothers, you will be a fine servant of Jesus Christ, if you feed your life on the words of faith, and of the fine teaching of which you have been a student and a follower. Refuse to have anything to do with irreligious stories like the tales old women tell to children. Train yourself towards the goal of true godliness. The training of the body has only a limited value; but training in godliness has a universal value for mankind, because it has the promise of life in this present age, and life in the age to come. This is a saying which deserves to be accepted by all. The reason why we toil and struggle so hard is that we have set our hopes on the living God, who is the Saviour of all men, and especially of those who believe.

HERE is a passage close-packed with practical advice, not only for Timothy, but for any teacher or any servant of the Church who is charged with the duty of work and leadership in the Church.

(i) It tells us *how to instruct others.* The word that is used for *laying these things* before the brothers is a most suggestive word (*hupotithesthai*). It does not mean *to issue orders*; it means rather to counsel, to advise, to point out, to suggest. It is a gentle, a humble, and a modest word. It means that the teacher and the leader must never dogmatically and pugnaciously and belligerently lay down the law. It means that he must not issue his instructions with the dogmatism of a dictator or the arrogance of a tyrant. It means that he must act rather as if he was reminding men of what they already knew, or suggesting to them, not that they should learn from him, but that they should discover from their own hearts, what is right. The guidance which is given in gentleness will always be more effective than the bullying instructions which are laid down with force. It is always true that men can be led when they will refuse to be driven.

(ii) It tells us *how to face* the task of teaching. Timothy is told that he must feed his life on the words of faith. No man can give out without taking in. He who would teach must himself be continually learning. It is the reverse of the truth that when a man becomes a teacher he ceases to be a learner. A man must ever feed his own mind before he can feed the minds of others; he must daily know Jesus Christ better before he can bring Christ to others. To bring others to the faith a man must himself feed upon the faith.

(iii) It tells us *what to avoid.* Timothy is to avoid profitless tales like the tales which old women tell to children. It is always necessary to remain at the centre of the faith. It is easy to get lost in side-issues and in by-ways. It is easy to get entangled in things which are at best fripperies

III

and embroideries. It is on the great central truths and realities that a man must ever feed his mind and nourish his faith.

(iv) It tells us *what to seek.* Timothy is told that as an athlete trains his body, so the Christian must train his soul in godliness. It is not that bodily and physical fitness is despised. It is the conviction of the Christian faith that the body is the temple of the Holy Spirit. But there are certain things in Paul's mind here. First, in the ancient world, especially in Greece, the gymnasia were dangerous places. Every town had its gymnasium; for the Greek youth between the ages of sixteen and eighteen, gymnastics were the main part of education. But the ancient world was riddled with homosexuality, and the gymnasia were notorious as the hotbeds of that particular sin. Second, what Paul is doing here is that he is pleading for a sense of proportion. Bodily and physical training is good, and even essential; but its use is limited. It only develops part of a man; and it only produces results which last for so short a time, for the body passes away. Training in godliness, in goodness, develops the whole man in body, mind and spirit, and its results affect not only time, but eternity as well. The Christian is not the athlete of the gymnasium, he is the athlete of God. The greatest of the Greeks well recognized this. Isocrates wrote: " No ascetic ought to train his body as a king ought to train his soul." " Train yourself by submitting willingly to toils, so that when they come on you unwillingly you will be able to endure them."

(v) Finally, this passage shows us *the basis of the whole matter.* No one has ever claimed that the Christian life is an easy way; *but its goal is God.* It is because a man hopes in God, it is because he sees God at his journey's end, it is because life is lived in the presence of God and ends in His still nearer presence, that the Christian is willing to endure as he does. The greatness of the goal makes the toil of the struggle worth while.

THE ONLY WAY TO SILENCE CRITICISM

1 Timothy 4: 10-16

Make it your business to hand on and to teach these commandments. Do not give anyone a chance to despise you because you are young; but in your words and in your conduct, in love, in loyalty and in purity, show yourself an example of what believing people should be. Until I come, devote your attention to the public reading of the scriptures, to exhortation and to teaching. Do not neglect the special gift which was given to you, when the voices of the prophets picked you out for the charge which has been given to you, when the body of the elders laid their hands upon you. Think about these things; find your whole life in them, that your progress may be evident to all. Take heed to yourself and to your teaching; stick to them; for if you do, you will save yourself and those who hear you.

ONE of the difficulties which Timothy would have to overcome was the fact that he was young. We are not to think of him as a mere stripling. After all, it was fifteen years since he had first become Paul's helper. The word that is used for *youth* (*neotēs*) can in Greek describe anyone of military age, that is up to the age of forty. But the Church has always liked its office-bearers to be men of maturity. *The Apostolic Canons* later laid it down that a man was not to become a bishop until he was over fifty, for by then " he will be past youthful disorders." But Timothy was young in comparison with Paul, and there would be many who would watch him with a critical eye, ever ready to find fault and to criticize. When the elder William Pitt, the great Earl of Chatham, was making a speech in the House of Commons at the age of thirty-three, he said: " The atrocious crime of being a young man . . . I will neither attempt to palliate or deny." The Church has always regarded youth with a certain suspicion, and under that suspicion Timothy would inevitably fall.

The advice that was given to Timothy is the hardest possible advice to follow, and yet it was the only possible

For the Youth

Hardest advice

advice. The advice was that Timothy must silence criticism by conduct. Plato, the great Greek philosopher, was once falsely accused of dishonourable conduct. " Well," he said, " we must live in such a way that all men will see that the charge is false." Arguments and verbal defences cannot silence criticism; conduct can. What then were to be the marks of Timothy's conduct?

(i) First, there was to be love. Agapē, the Greek word for the greatest of the Christian virtues, is a largely untranslatable word. The real meaning is unconquerable benevolence. If a man has agapē, no matter what other people do to him or say of him, no matter how other people treat him, he will seek nothing but their good. He will never be bitter, never resentful, never vengeful; he will never allow himself to hate; he will never refuse to forgive. No matter what his fellow men are like in themselves, and no matter what they do to him, he will seek only their good. Now clearly this is the kind of love which takes the whole of a man's personality to achieve. Ordinarily love is something which we cannot help. Love of our nearest and dearest is an instinctive thing which is part of a man's being. The love of a man for a maid is an experience unsought and unachieved. It comes unbidden. Ordinarily love is a thing of the heart; but clearly this Christian love is more than a thing of the heart; it is a thing of the will. It is not something which a man cannot help; it is an achievement and a conquest. Christian love is that conquest of self whereby we are enabled to develop an unconquerable caring for other people. So then the first authenticating mark of the Christian leader is that he cares for others, no matter what others do to him. That is something of which any Christian leader who is quick to take offence and prone to bear grudges should constantly think.

(ii) Second, there is loyalty. Loyalty is an unconquerable fidelity to Christ, no matter what that fidelity may cost. It is not difficult to be a good soldier when things are going well. But the really valuable soldier is the soldier who can fight well when his body is weary and his stomach is empty, when the situation seems hopeless and when he is in the midst of a campaign the movements of which he cannot understand. The second authenticating mark of the Christian leader is a loyalty to Christ which defies circumstances, which is true whatever light may shine or shadow fall.

(iii) Third, there is *purity*. Purity is an unconquerable allegiance to the standards of Jesus Christ. When Pliny was reporting back to Trajan about the Christians in Bithynia, where he was governor, he wrote: " They are accustomed to bind themselves by an oath to commit neither theft, nor robbery, not adultery; never to break their word; never to deny a pledge that has been made when summoned to answer for it." The Christian pledge was to a life of purity. The Christian ought to have a standard of honour and honesty, a standard of self-control and chastity, a standard of discipline and consideration, that are far above the standards of the world. The simple fact is that the world will never have any use for Christianity, until the Christian Church can prove that it produces the best men and women in the world. The third authenticating mark of the Christian leader is a life lived on the standards of Jesus Christ, and not on the standards of the world.

THE DUTIES OF THE CHRISTIAN LEADER WITHIN THE CHURCH

1 *Timothy* 4: 10-16 (*continued*)

CERTAIN duties are laid upon Timothy, the young leader designate of the Church. He is to devote himself to the public reading of scripture, to exhortation and to teaching. In that instruction we have the pattern of the Christian Church service.

vs 13

The very first description of a Christian service which
we possess is in the works of Justin Martyr. About the
year A.D. 170 Justin Martyr wrote a defence of Christianity
to the Roman government, and in it (Justin Martyr,
First Apology, 1: 67) he describes a service of the early
Church: " On the day called the day of the Sun a gathering
takes place of all who live in the towns or in the country
in one place. The Memoirs of the Apostles or the writings
of the prophets are read as long as time permits. Then
the reader stops, and the leader by word of mouth impresses
and urges to the imitation of these good things. Then we
all stand together and send forth prayers." So then in
the pattern of any Christian service there should be three
things.

(i) There should be *the reading and the exposition of
scripture*. Men ultimately do not gather together to hear
the opinions of a preacher; they gather together to hear
the word of God. The Christian service is Bible-centred.

(ii) There should be *teaching*. The Bible is a difficult
book, and therefore it has to be explained. Christian
doctrine is not easy to understand, but a man must be
able to give a reason for the hope that is in him. There
is little use in exhorting a man to be a Christian, if he
does not know what being a Christian is. The Christian
preacher is the man who has given many years of his life
to gain the necessary equipment to explain the faith to
others. He has been set free from the ordinary duties
and tasks of life in order to think, to study and to pray
that he may better expound the word of God. There can
be no lasting Christian faith in any Church without a
teaching ministry.

(iii) There should be *exhortation*. The Christian message
must always end in Christian action. After any preaching
of the word there must be something to be done. Someone
has said that every sermon should end with the challenge:
" What about it, chum? " It is not enough to present the
Christian message as something to be studied and known

and understood; it has to be presented as something to be done. Christianity is truth, but it is truth in action.

(iv) There is prayer. The whole gathering meets in the presence of God; it thinks in the Spirit of God; it goes out in the strength of God. Neither the preaching nor the listening during the service, nor the consequent action in the world is possible without the help of the Spirit of God.

It would do us no harm sometimes to test our modern services by the pattern of the first services of the Christian Church.

THE PERSONAL DUTY OF THE CHRISTIAN LEADER

I *Timothy* 4: 10-16 (*continued*)

HERE in this passage there is set out in the most vivid way the personal duty of the Christian leader.

(i) He must remember that he is *a man set apart for a special task by the Church.* The Christian leader does not make sense apart from the Church. His commission came from the Church; his work is within the fellowship of the Church; his duty is to build others into the Church. That is precisely the reason why the really important work of the Christian Church is never done by any itinerant evangelist, but is always done by the settled ministry of the Church. Without the Church the Christian leader is a meaningless figure.

(ii) He must remember *the duty to think about these things.* The great danger of the Christian leader is intellectual sloth and the shut mind. The danger is that he forgets to study and allows his thoughts to run in well-worn grooves. The danger is that he never gets outside the orbit of a limited number of favourite ideas. The danger is that new truths, new methods, the attempt to restate the faith in contemporary terms comes merely to irritate and to annoy him. The Christian leader must be a Christian thinker or he fails in his task; and to be a Christian thinker is to be an adventurous thinker so long as life lasts.

(iii) He must remember *the duty of concentration*. He must find his whole life in the things he teaches. The danger of the Christian leader is that he may dissipate his energies on many things which are not central to the Christian faith. He is presented with the invitation to many duties; he is confronted with the claims of many spheres of service; but his only duty is concentration on the task for which he was set apart. There was a prophet who confronted Ahab with a kind of parable. He said that in a battle a man brought him a prisoner to guard, telling him that if the prisoner escaped his own life would be forfeit. But he allowed his attention to wander, and " as thy servant was busy here and there he was gone " (I *Kings* 20: 35-43). It is easy for the Christian leader to be busy here and there, and to let the central things go. Concentration is a prime duty of the Christian leader.

(iv) He must remember *the duty of progress*. His progress must be evident to all men. It is all too true of most of us that the same things conquer us year in and year out; that we are the victim of the same faults of temperament and of character; that we fail for the same reasons; that as year succeeds year, we are no further on. The Christian leader pleads with others to become more like Christ. How can he do so with honesty unless he himself from day to day becomes more like the Master whose he is and whom he seeks to serve? When Kagawa decided to become a Christian, his first prayer was: " God, make me like Christ." The Christian leader's prayer must first be that he may grow more like to Christ, for only thus will he be able to lead others to Christ.

THE DUTY TO REPRIMAND

I *Timothy* 5: 1, 2

If you have occasion to reprimand an older man, do not do so sharply, but appeal to him as you would

to a father. Treat the younger men like brothers;
the older women as mothers; the younger women as
sisters, in complete purity.

IT is always a difficult thing to reprimand anyone with
graciousness; and to Timothy there would sometimes fall
a duty that was doubly difficult—the duty of reprimanding
a man who was older than himself. Chrysostom writes:
" Rebuke is in its own nature offensive particularly when
it is addressed to an old man; and when it proceeds from
a young man too, there is a threefold show of forwardness.
By the manner and mildness of it, therefore, he would
soften it. For it is possible to reprove without offence,
if one will only make a point of this; it requires great
discretion, but it may be done."

Rebuke and reprimand are always a problem. We may
so dislike the task of speaking a warning word to someone
that we may shirk it altogether. Many a person would
have been saved from sorrow and shipwreck, if someone
had only spoken a warning and a rebuking word in time.
There can be no more poignant tragedy in life than to hear
someone say to us: " I would never have come to this,
if you had only spoken in time." It is always wrong to
shirk the word that should be spoken.

We may rebuke and reprimand a person in such a way
that there is clearly nothing but anger in our voice and
nothing but bitterness in our minds and hearts. A rebuke
given solely in anger, a rebuke given in such a way that
it seems to come from dislike and loathing and contempt
and disgust may produce fear; it may cause hurt and
pain; but it will almost inevitably produce resentment;
and its ultimate effect may well be simply to confirm the
mistaken person in the error of his ways. The rebuke of
anger and the reprimand of contemptuous dislike are
seldom effective, and are far more likely to do more harm
than good.

It was said of Florence Allshorn, the great missionary
teacher, that, when she was Principal of a women's college,

she always rebuked her students, when need arose, as
it were with her arm around them. The rebuke which
clearly comes from love is the only effective rebuke. If
we ever have cause to reprimand anyone, we must do so
in such a way as to make it clear that we do this, not
because we find a cruel and a hurting pleasure in it, not
because we wish to do it, but because we are under the
compulsion of love, and because we seek to help and not
to hurt.

THE RELATIONSHIPS OF LIFE

1 *Timothy* 5: 1, 2 (*continued*)

THESE two verses lay down the spirit which the different
age relationships of life should display.

(i) To older people we must show *affection and respect*.
An older man is to be treated like a father, and an older
woman like a mother. The ancient world knew well the
deference and the respect which were due to age. Cicero
writes: " It is, then, the duty of a young man to show
deference to his elders, and to attach himself to the best
and most approved of them, so as to receive the benefit
of their counsel and influence. For the inexperience of
youth requires the practical wisdom of age to strengthen
and direct it. And this time of life is above all to be pro-
tected against sensuality and trained to toil and endurance
of both mind and body, so as to be strong for active duty
in military and civil service. And even when they wish to
relax their minds and give themselves up to enjoyment,
they should beware of excesses and bear in mind the
rules of modesty. And this will be easier, if the young are
not unwilling to have their elders join them, even in their
pleasures " (Cicero, *De Officiis*, 1: 34). Aristotle writes:
" To all older persons too one should give honour appropriate to their age, by rising to receive them and finding
seats for them and so on " (Aristotle, *Nicomachean Ethics*,
9: 2). It is one of the tragedies of life that youth is so

often apt to find age a nuisance. To age there must always be given the respect and the affection which are due to those who have lived long and fared far upon the pathway of life and of experience. There is a famous French phrase which says with a sigh: " If youth but had the knowledge, if age but had the power." But when there is mutual respect and affection, then the wisdom and the experience of age can co-operate with the strength and the adventurousness and the enthusiasm of youth, to the great profit of both.

(ii) To our contemporaries we must show *brotherliness*. The younger men are to be treated like brothers. Aristotle has it: " To comrades and brothers one should allow freedom of speech and common use of all things " (Aristotle, *Nicomachean Ethics*, 9: 2). With our contemporaries there should be tolerance and sharing. Those who are Christian can never be strangers to each other; they must be brothers in the Lord.

(iii) To those of the opposite sex our relationships must always be marked with *purity*. The Arabs have a phrase for a man of chivalry. They call him " a brother of girls." There is a famous phrase which speaks of " Platonic friendship." Love must be kept for one; it is a fearful thing when physical things dominate the relationship between the sexes, and when a man cannot see a woman without thinking in terms of the body. There must be a fellowship of mind and heart between Christ's people which is cleansed of lust and rendered secure by the highest kind of mutual Christian love.

CHURCH AND FAMILY DUTY

I *Timothy* 5: 3-8

> Honour widows who are genuinely in a widow's destitute position. But if any widow has children or grandchildren, let such children learn to begin by discharging the duties of religion in their own homes;

and let them learn to give a return for all that their parents have done for them; for this is the kind of conduct that meets with God's approval. Now she who is genuinely in the position of a widow, and who is left all alone, has set her hope on God, and night and day she devotes herself to petitions and prayers. But she who lives with voluptuous wantonness is dead even though she is still alive. Pass on these instructions that they may be irreproachable. If anyone fails to provide for his own people, and especially for the members of his own family, he has denied the faith and is worse than an unbeliever.

THE Christian Church inherited a fine tradition of charity to those in need. No people has ever cared more for its needy and its aged than the Jewish people did and does. Here advice is given for the care of widows. There may well have been two classes of women here. There were certainly widows who had become widows in the normal way by the death of their husbands. But it has been suggested that it may be that another class of women are also involved. It was not uncommon in the pagan world, in certain places, for a man to have more than one wife, for polygamy was not yet dead. Now when a man became a Christian, he could not go on being a polygamist, and he therefore had to choose which wife he was going to live with. That inevitably meant that some of his wives had to be sent away. These women who were sent away were clearly in a very unhappy and a very unfortunate position. The same thing can happen in the mission field to-day. And it may be that such women as these were also reckoned as widows, and were given the support of the Church.

Jewish law laid it down that at the time of his marriage a man ought to make provision for his wife, in the event of his death, and should she become a widow. The very first office-bearers whom the Christian Church appointed, had this duty of caring fairly and justly for the widows (Acts 6: 1). Ignatius lays it down: " Let not widows be neglected. After the Lord be thou their guardian." The

Apostolic Constitutions enjoin the bishop: " O bishop, be mindful of the needy, both reaching out thy helping hand and making provision for them as the steward of God, distributing the offerings seasonably to every one of them, to the widows, the orphans, the friendless, and those tried with affliction." The same book has an interesting and kindly instruction: " If anyone receives any service to carry to a widow or poor woman . . . let him give it the same day." As the proverb has it: " He gives twice who gives quickly," and the Church was concerned that those in poverty might not have to wait and want while some servant of the Church delayed.

But it is to be noted that the Church did not propose to assume the responsibility for older people whose children were still alive and well able to support them. The ancient world was very definite that it was the duty of children to support aged parents, and, as E. K. Simpson has well said: " A religious profession which falls below the standard of duty recognised by the world is a wretched fraud." The Church would never have agreed that the Church's charity should become an excuse for children to evade their responsibility. It was Greek law from the time of Solon that sons and daughters were, not only morally, but also legally bound to support their parents. Anyone who refused that duty lost his civil rights. Aeschines, the Athenian orator, says in one of his speeches: " And whom did our law-giver (Solon) condemn to silence in the Assembly of the people? And where does he make this clear? ' Let there be,' he says, ' a scrutiny of public speakers, in case there be any speaker in the Assembly of the people who is a striker of his father or mother, or who neglects to maintain them or to give them a home '." Demosthenes says: " I regard the man who neglects his parents as unbelieving in and hateful to the gods, as well as to men." Philo, writing of the commandment to honour parents, says: " When old storks become unable to fly, they remain in their nests and are fed by their children, who go to endless exertions

to provide their food because of their piety." To Philo
it was clear that even the animal creation acknowledged
its obligations to aged parents, and how much more must
men? Aristotle in the *Nicomachean Ethics* lays it down:
" It would be thought in the matter of food we should
help our parents before all others, since we owe our nourish-
ment to them, and it is more honourable to help in this
respect the authors of our being, even before ourselves."
As Aristotle saw it, a man must himself starve before he
would see his parents starve. Plato in *The Laws* has the
same conviction of the debt that is owed to parents:
" Next comes the honour of loving parents, to whom, as
is meet, we have to pay the first and greatest and oldest
of debts, considering that all which a man has belongs to
those who gave him birth and brought him up, and that
he must do all that he can to minister to them; first, in
his property; secondly, in his person; and thirdly, in
his soul; paying the debts due to them for their care and
travail which they bestowed upon him of old in the days
of his infancy, and which he is now able to pay back to
them, when they are old and in the extremity of their
need."

It is the same with the Greek poets. When Iphigenia
is speaking to her father Agamemnon, in Euripides'
Iphigenia at Aulis, she says (the translation is that of A. S.
Way):

" 'Twas I first called thee father, thou me child.
'Twas I first throned my body on thy knees,
And gave thee sweet caresses and received.
And this thy word was: ' Ah, my little maid,
Blest shall I see thee in a husband's halls
Living and blooming worthily of me? '
And as I twined my fingers in thy beard,
Whereto I now cling, thus I answered thee:
' And what of thee? Shall I greet thy grey hairs,
Father, with loving welcome in mine halls,
Repaying all thy fostering toil for me? ' "

The joy of the child was to look forward to the day when she could repay all that her father had done for her.

When Euripides tells how Orestes discovered that an unkind fate had made him unwittingly slay his own father, he makes Orestes say:

> " He fostered me a babe, and many a kiss
> Lavished upon me. . . .
> O wretched heart and soul of mine!
> I have rendered foul return! What veil of gloom
> Can I take for my face? Before me spread
> What cloud, to shun the old man's searching eye? "

To Euripides the most haunting sin on earth was failure in duty to a parent.

The New Testament ethical writers were certain that support of parents was an essential part of Christian duty. It is a thing to be remembered. We live in a time when even the most sacred duties are pushed on to the state, and when we expect, in so many cases, public charity to do what private piety ought to do. As the Pastorals see it, help given to a parent is two things. First, it is an honouring of the recipient. It is the only way in which a child can demonstrate the honour and esteem which are within his heart. Second, it is an admission of the claims of love. It is love honouring its debt to love. It is repaying love received in time of need with love given in time of need; and only with love can love be repaid.

There remains one thing left to say, and to leave it unsaid would be unjust and unfair. This very passage goes on to lay down certain of the qualities of the people whom the Church is called upon to support. What is true of the Church is true within the family. If a person is to be supported, that person must be supportable. If a parent is taken into a home and then by thoughtless, inconsiderate, unkind, unwise conduct causes nothing but trouble, then another situation arises. There is a double duty here; it is the duty of the child to support the parent, but it is the duty of the parent to be such that that support is possible within the structure of the home.

AN HONOURED AND A USEFUL OLD AGE

1 *Timothy* 5: 9-10

> Let a woman be enrolled as a widow only if she is
> more than sixty years of age; if she has been the
> wife of one husband; if she has earned an attested
> reputation for good works; if she has nourished
> children; if she has been hospitable to strangers;
> if she has helped those in trouble; if she has washed
> the feet of the saints; if she has devoted herself to
> every good work.

FROM this passage it is clear that the Church had an
official register of widows. And it seems that the word
widow is being used in a double sense. Women who were
aged and whose husbands had died and whose lives were
lovely and useful were the responsibility of the Church;
but it is also true that, perhaps as early as this, and certainly
later in the early Church, there was an official order of
widows, an order of elderly women who were set apart
for special duties in the life and work of the Church.

In the later regulations of the *Apostolic Constitutions*,
which tell us what the life and organization of the Church
were like in the third century, it is laid down: " Three
widows shall be appointed, two to persevere in prayer for
those who are in temptation, and for the reception of
revelations, when such are necessary, but one to assist
women who are visited with sickness; she must be ready
for service, discreet, telling the elders what is necessary,
not avaricious, not given to too much love of wine, so that she
may be sober and able to perform the night services, and
other loving duties." On widows there was laid the duties
of constant prayer, and constant loving help for those in
trouble.

Such widows were not ordained as the elders and the
bishops were; they were set apart by prayer for the work
which they had to do. They were not to be set apart for
that task until they were over sixty years of age. That
was an age which the ancient world also considered to be

specially suited for concentration on the spiritual life. Plato, in his picture and plan for the ideal state, held that sixty was the right age for men and women to become priests and priestesses. The religious people of the East regard sixty as the right age to retire from the ordinary activities of the world in order to engage on a life of contemplation.

The Pastoral Epistles are always intensely practical books; and here in this passage we find seven qualifications which the Church's widows must satisfy.

They must have been the wife of one husband. In an age when the marriage bond was lightly regarded and almost universally dishonoured, they must be examples of purity and fidelity.

They must have earned an attested reputation for good works. The office-bearer of the Church, male or female, has within his or her keeping, not only his or her personal reputation and good name, but also the good name of the Church. Nothing discredits a Church like unworthy office-bearers; and nothing is so good an advertisement for a Church as an office-bearer who has taken his or her Christianity into the work and activity of daily life and living.

They must have nourished children. This may well mean more than one thing. It may mean that widows must have given proof of their Christian piety by bringing up their own families in the Christian way. But it can mean more than that. In an age when the marriage bond was very lax, and when men and women changed their partners with bewildering rapidity, children were regarded as a misfortune. The last thing that people wanted was a child. This was the great age of child exposure. When a child was born, he was brought and laid before his father's feet. If the father stooped and lifted the child, that meant that the father acknowledged the child and was prepared to accept responsibility for his upbringing. If the father turned and walked away, then the child was quite literally thrown out, like an unwanted piece of rubbish. It often happened that such unwanted children were collected by conscienceless and unscrupulous people and, if they were girls, were brought up to stock the public brothels, and if they were boys were trained up to be slaves or gladiators for the public games. In such circumstances it would be a Christian duty to rescue such children from death and worse than death, and to bring them up in a Christian home. So then this may mean that widows must be women who had been prepared to give a home to orphaned and to abandoned children.

They must have been hospitable to strangers. Inns in the ancient world were notoriously dirty, notoriously expensive, and notoriously immoral. So then those who opened their homes to the Christian traveller, or the Christian stranger in a strange place, or to young people whose work and study took them far from home, were doing a most valuable service to the Christian community. The open door of the Christian home is always a precious thing.

They must have washed the feet of the saints. That need not necessarily be taken literally, although the literal sense is included. To wash a person's feet was the task of a slave; it was the most menial of duties. This means that Christian widows must have been willing to accept the humblest tasks in the service of Christ and of His people. The Church needs its leaders who will live in prominence; but no less the Church needs those who are prepared to do the tasks which receive no prominence and little thanks.

They must have helped those in trouble and in prison. In days of persecution it was no small thing to visit and to help Christians who were suffering for their faith. To do so was to identify oneself with them and to accept the risk of coming to a like punishment and imprisonment. The Christian must stand by those in trouble for their faith, even if, in so doing, he brings trouble on himself.

They must have devoted themselves to all good works. Every man concentrates his life on something; the Christian concentrates his life on obeying Christ and helping men.

When we study these qualifications for those who were to be enrolled as widows, we see that they are indeed the qualifications for the life of every Christian who loves Christ and who loves his fellow men.

THE PRIVILEGE AND THE DANGERS OF SERVICE

I *Timothy* 5: 9-10 (*continued*)

As we have already said, if not as early as the time of the Pastoral Epistles, certainly in later days, the widows became an accepted order in the Christian Church. Their place and their work in the Christian Church are dealt with in the first eight chapters of the third book of *The Apostolic Constitutions*, and it is worth while looking at these chapters to see the use that such an order could be and the perils and dangers into which such an order almost inevitably ran.

(i) It is laid down that women who would serve the Church must be women of discretion. Particularly they must be discreet in speech and talk: " Let every widow be meek, quiet, gentle, sincere, free from anger, not talkative, not clamorous, not hasty of speech, not given to evil-speaking, not captious, not double-tongued, not a busybody. If she see or hear anything that is not right, let her be as one that does not see, and as one that does not hear." Such Church officials must be very careful when they talk about the faith, and when they discuss it with outsiders: " For unbelievers when they hear the doctrine concerning Christ, not explained as it ought to be, but defectively, especially that concerning His Incarnation or His Passion, will rather reject it with scorn, and laugh at it as false, than praise God for it." There is nothing more dangerous than an official of the Church

who talks about private things which ought to be kept
secret. A Church office-bearer or minister should no more
repeat a confidence than a priest would repeat a secret
of the confessional. A Church office-bearer must be equipped
to communicate the gospel in a way that will make men
think more and not less of Christian truth.

(ii) It is laid down that women who serve the Church
must not be gadabouts: " Let the widow therefore own
herself to be the ' altar of God,' and let her sit in her own
house, and not enter into the houses of the unfaithful, under
any pretence to receive anything; for the altar of God never
runs about, but is fixed in one place. Let therefore the
virgin and the widow be such as do not run about, or gad
to the houses of those who are alien from the faith. For
such as these are gadders and impudent." The curious
and restless gossip is ill-equipped to serve the Church.

(iii) It is laid down that widows who accept the charity
of the Church are not to be greedy. "There are some
widows who esteem gain their business; and since they
ask without shame, and receive without being satisfied,
render other people more backward in giving. . . . Such
a woman is thinking in her mind of where she can go to
get, or that a certain woman who is her friend has forgotten
her, and she has something to say to her. . . . She murmurs
at the deaconess who distributed the charity, saying,
' Do you not see that I am in more distress and need of
your charity? Why therefore have you preferred her
before me? ' " It is an ugly thing to seek to live off the
Church rather than for the Church.

(iv) It is laid down that such women must do all they
can to help themselves: " Let her take wool and assist
others rather than herself want from them." The charity
of the Church does not exist to make people lazy and
dependent.

(v) Such women are not to be envious and jealous:
" We hear that some widows are jealous, envious calumni-
ators, and envious of the quiet of others. . . . It becomes

them when one of their fellow-widows is clothed by anyone, or receives money, or meat, or drink, or shoes, at the refreshment of their sister, to thank God."

There we have at one and the same time a picture of the faults of which the Church is all too full, and of the virtues which should be the marks of the true Christian life.

THE PERILS OF IDLENESS

1 *Timothy* 5: 11-16

> Refuse to enrol the younger women as widows, for when they grow impatient with the restrictions of Christian widowhood, they wish to marry, and so deserve condemnation, because they have broken the pledge of their first faith; and, at the same time, they learn to be idle and to run from house to house. Yes, they can become more than idle; they can become gossips and busybodies, saying things which should not be repeated. It is my wish that the younger widows should marry, and bear children, and run a house and home, and give our opponents no chance of abuse. For, even as things are, some of them have turned aside from the way to follow Satan. If any believing person has widowed relations, let such a person help them, and let not the Church be burdened with the responsibility, so that it may care for those who are genuinely in the position of widows.

A PASSAGE like this reflects the situation in society in which the early Church found itself.

It is not that younger widows are condemned for marrying again. What is condemned is this. Sorrow and death might enter into the home of a younger couple. The husband dies; and then the widow in the first bitterness of sorrow, and on the religious impulse of the moment, might decide to remain a widow all her life, and to dedicate her life to Christ and the Church. Now a woman doing that was regarded as having taken Christ as her bridegroom, and as being herself the bride of Christ. So then, if she broke her vows, and wished to marry again, she was regarded as having broken her marriage vow to Christ. She would have been better never to have taken the vow. No one inside or outside the Church would have thought any the less of her, if she had not taken it. But having taken it, her duty is to be true to it, and to keep her life consecrated to Christ.

What complicated this matter very much was the social background of the times. In the ancient world it was next to impossible for a single or a widowed woman to earn her living honestly. There was hardly anything that she could do; there was practically no trade or profession open to her. The result was inevitable; she was almost driven to prostitution in order to live. All this passage has got to be read against a background where it was almost completely impossible for a single woman to be independent through honest work. She either had to marry, or had to dedicate her life completely to the service of the Church; there was no halfway house between the two.

In any event the perils of idleness remain the same in any age and generation. There was the danger of becoming *restless*; there was the danger, that, because a woman had not enough to do, she might become one of those creatures who drift from house to house in an empty social round. It was almost inevitable that such a woman would become a *gossip*; because she had nothing important to talk about, she would tend to talk scandal, to repeat tales from house to house, each time with a little more embroidery and a little more malice and sting in the telling. The best way to avoid worthless, gossiping talk is to pack life with activity and to store the mind with knowledge so that there is always something which is worth talking about. Such a woman ran a risk of becoming a *busybody*. Since she had nothing of her own to take up her attention, she would be very apt to be over-interested and over-interfering in the affairs of others. It was true then, as it is true now, that " Satan finds some mischief still for idle hands to do.''

The full life is always the safe life, and the empty life is always the life in peril.

So the advice is that these younger women should marry, and should engage upon the greatest task of all, the task of rearing a family and making a home. Here again we have another example of one of the main thoughts of the Pastoral Epistles. The Pastoral Epistles are always concerned with how the Christian appears to the outside world. Does the individual Christian give the outside world an opportunity to criticize the Church, or, does he or she give the outside world a reason to admire the Church? The world is quick to use any scandal to discredit the Church. It is always true that " the greatest handicap the Church has is the unsatisfactory lives of professing Christians," and it is always true that the greatest argument for Christianity is a genuinely Christian life. And there is no argument in all the world for Christianity like the beauty and the joy and the fellowship of a truly Christian home.

RULES FOR PRACTICAL ADMINISTRATION

1 *Timothy* 5: 17-22

> Let elders who discharge their duties well be judged worthy of double honour, especially those who toil in preaching and in teaching; for Scripture says: " You must not muzzle the ox when he is treading the corn," and, " The workman deserves his pay."
>
> Do not accept an accusation against an elder unless on the evidence of two or three witnesses.
>
> Rebuke those who persist in sin in the presence of all, so that the others may develop a healthy fear of sinning.
>
> I adjure you before God and Christ Jesus and the chosen angels that you keep these regulations impartially, and that you do nothing because of your own prejudices or predilection.
>
> Do not be too quick to lay your hands on any man, and do not share the sins of others. Keep yourself pure.

THIS passage consists of a series of the most practical regulations for the life and administration of the Church.

(i) Elders are to be properly honoured, and properly paid. When threshing was done in the East, the sheaves of corn were laid on the threshing-floor; then oxen in pairs were driven repeatedly across them; or the oxen were tethered to a post in the middle, like a pivot, and made to march round and round on the grain; or sometimes a threshing sledge was harnessed to them and the sledge was drawn to and fro across the corn; but in all cases the oxen were left unmuzzled; they were free to eat as much of the grain as they wished, as a reward for the work which they were doing. The actual law that the ox must not be muzzled is in *Deuteronomy* 25: 4. The saying that the workman deserves his pay is actually a saying of Jesus (*Luke* 10: 7). It is most likely a proverbial saying which He quoted. Any man who works deserves his support, and the harder he works, the more he has earned and the more he deserves. Christianity has never had anything to do with the soft and sentimental ethic which clamours for equal shares for all. A man's reward must always be proportioned to a man's toil. But it is to be noted what kind of elders are to be specially honoured and specially rewarded. It is those who toil in *preaching* and *teaching* who are to be so honoured. The elder who stopped at giving advice and counsel, whose service consisted in words and discussion and argument, who regarded the duties of the eldership as finished when he had sat round a table and talked is not in question here. The man whom the Church really honoured was the man who worked to edify and to build up the Church by his preaching of the truth to the people, and his educating of the young and of the new converts in the Christian way.

(ii) It was Jewish law that no man should be condemned on the evidence of a single witness: " One witness shall not rise up against a man for any iniquity, or for any sin, in any sin that he sinneth. At the mouth of two witnesses, or at the mouth of three witnesses, shall the matter be established " (*Deuteronomy* 19: 15). The *Mishnah*, the codified Rabbinic law, in describing the process of trial says: " The second witness was likewise brought in and examined. If the testimony of the two was found to agree, the case for the defence was opened." That is to say, if a charge was supported by the evidence of only one witness, it was held that there was no case to answer. In later times the Church regulations laid it down that the two witnesses must be Christians, for it would have been easy for a malicious heathen to fabricate a false charge against a Christian elder in order to discredit him, and through him to discredit the Church. In the early days of the Church, the Church authorities did not hesitate to apply discipline, and Theodore of Mopseuestia, one of the early fathers, points out how necessary this regulation was, because the elders were always liable to be disliked and were specially open to malicious attack " due to the retaliation by some who had been rebuked by them for sin." A man who had been disciplined might well seek to get his own back by maliciously charging an elder with some irregularity or some sin. This permanent fact remains, that this would be a happier world, and the Church would be a happier Church, if people would realize that it is nothing less than a sin to spread and to repeat stories about people of whose truth they are not, and cannot be, sure. Irresponsible, slanderous and malicious talk does infinite damage and causes infinite heartbreak, and such talk will not go unpunished by God.

RULES FOR PRACTICAL ADMINISTRATION

1 *Timothy* 5: 17-22 (*continued*)

(iii) Those who persist in sin are to be publicly rebuked. That public rebuke had a double value. It sobered the sinner into a consideration of his ways, and wakened him into a sense of shame; and it made others have a care that they did not involve themselves in a like humiliation. The threat of publicity is no bad thing, if it keeps a man in the right way, even from fear. A wise leader will know when there is a time to keep things quiet, and a time for public rebuke. But whatever happens, the Church must never give the world the impression that it is condoning sin.

(iv) Timothy is urged to administer his office without favouritism and without prejudice. B. S. Easton writes: "The well-being of every community depends on impartial discipline." There is nothing which does more harm than when some people are treated as if they could do no wrong, and when others are treated as if they could do no right. Justice is a universal virtue, and in it the Church must surely never fall below the impartial standards which even the world rightly demands.

(v) Timothy is warned not to be too hasty "in laying hands on any man." That may mean one of two things. (a) It may mean that he is not to be too quick in laying hands on any man to ordain him to office in the Church. Before a man gains promotion in business, or in teaching, or in the army or the navy or the air force, he must give proof that he has earned it and that he deserves it. No man should ever start at the top. A man must give proof that he deserves a position of responsibility and leadership. This is doubly important in the Church; for a man who is raised to high office, and who then fails in it or brings discredit on it, brings dishonour, not only on himself, but also on the Church. In a critical world the Church cannot be too careful in regard to the kind of men whom she chooses as her leaders. (b) In the early Church it was the custom to lay hands on a penitent sinner who had given proof of his repentance and who had returned to the fold of the Church. It is laid down: "As each sinner repents, and shows the fruits of repentance, lay hands on him, while all pray for him." Eusebius, the Church historian, tells us that it was the ancient custom that repentant sinners should be received back with the laying on of hands and with prayer. If that be the meaning here, it will be a warning to Timothy not to be too quick to receive back the man who had brought disgrace on the Church; to wait until he has shown that his penitence is genuine, and that he is truly determined to mould his life to fit his penitent professions. That is not for a moment to say that such a man is to be held at arms' length, and treated with suspicion and distrust. Such a man has to be treated with all sympathy and with all help and guidance in his period of probation. The Christian fellowship at such a time must do everything to help such a man to redeem himself and to begin again. But it is to say that membership of the Church is never to be treated lightly, and that a man must show his penitence for the past and his determination for the future, not before he is received into the *fellowship* of the Church, but before he is received into the *membership* of the Church. The fellowship of the Church exists to help such people to redeem themselves, but the membership of the Church is for those who have truly and honestly pledged their lives to Christ.

ADVICE FOR TIMOTHY

1 *Timothy* 5: 23

> Stop drinking only water, and use a little wine for the sake of your stomach, to help your frequent illnesses.

HERE is a sentence which shows the real intimacy of these letters. Amidst the affairs of the Church, and the problems of administration, Paul finds time to slip in a little bit of loving advice to Timothy about his health.

There had always been a strain of asceticism in Jewish religion. When a man took the Nazirite vow (*Numbers* 6: 1-21) he was pledged never to touch or taste any of the product of the vine: " He shall separate himself from wine and strong drink, and shall drink no vinegar of wine, or vinegar of strong drink, neither shall he drink any liquor of the grapes, nor eat moist grapes, or dried. All the days of his separation shall he eat nothing that is made of the vine tree, from the kernels even to the husk " (*Numbers* 6: 3, 4). The Rechabites also were pledged to abstain from wine. The *Book of Jeremiah* tells how Jeremiah went and set before the Rechabites wine and cups: " But they said, We will drink no wine; for Jonadab, the son of Rechab our father, commanded us saying, Ye shall drink no wine, neither ye nor your sons for ever; neither shall he build house, nor sow seed, nor plant vineyard, nor have any " (*Jeremiah* 35: 5-7). Now Timothy was on one side a Jew— his mother was a Jewess (*Acts* 16: 1)—and it may well be that Timothy had from his mother inherited this strict and ascetic way of living. On his father's side Timothy was a Greek. Now, we have already seen that at the back of the Pastorals there is the heresy of gnosticism which saw all matter, all bodily things, and all earthly things as evil. We saw that that belief could issue in an asceticism which starved and ill-treated the body. And it may well be that Timothy was even unconsciously influenced by this Greek asceticism as well.

Here we have a great truth which the Christian and the worker for Christ forgets at his peril, the truth that we dare not neglect the body. No man ought ever to be too busy to look after his own health. And often a man will find that his spiritual dullness and flatness and aridity comes from the simple fact that his body is tired and neglected. No machine will run well unless it is duly cared for; and neither will the body. We wish to do Christ's work as well as we can; we will not and cannot do it well unless we are physically fit to do it. There is no virtue —rather the reverse—in neglect of and contempt for the body. *Mens sana in corpore sano*, a healthy mind in a healthy body, was the old Roman ideal, and it is the Christian ideal too.

This is a text which has much troubled those who are advocates of total abstinence. It must be remembered that this text does not give any man a licence to indulge in drink to excess; it simply approves the use of wine where wine may be medicinally helpful. If it does lay down any principle at all, E. F. Brown has well stated that principle: " It shows that while total abstinence may be recommended as a wise counsel, it is never to be enforced as a religious obligation." Paul is simply saying that there is no virtue in an asceticism which does the body more harm than good.

THE IMPOSSIBILITY OF ULTIMATE CONCEALMENT

I *Timothy* 5: 24, 25

> Some men's sin are plain for all to see, and lead the way to judgment; the sins of others will duly catch up on them. Even so there are good deeds which are plain for all to see, and there are things of a very different quality which cannot be hidden.

THIS is a saying which bids us to leave things to God and to be content. There are obvious sinners, whose sins are clearly leading to their own disaster and to their own punishment; and there are secret sinners who behind a front of unimpeachable rectitude live a life that is in essence evil and ugly. What man cannot see, God does see. " Man sees the deed, but God sees the intention." " God," as someone said, " does not pay every Friday night." There is no escape from the ultimate confrontation with the God who sees and knows everything.

There are some whose good deeds are plain for all to see, and who have already won the praise and thanks and honour and congratulations of men. There are some whose good deeds have never been noticed. They have never been appreciated, never thanked, never praised, never valued as they ought to have been. They have always been taken for granted. They need not feel either disappointed or embittered. God knows the good deed also, and God will repay, for God is never in any man's debt.

Here we are told that we must neither grow angry at the apparent escape of others, nor embittered at the apparent thanklessness of men, but that we must be content to leave all things to the ultimate judgment of God.

HOW TO BE A SLAVE AND A CHRISTIAN

Timothy 6: 1, 2

> Let all those who are slaves under the yoke hold their own masters to be worthy of all respect, in order that no one may have an opportunity to speak evil of the name of God and the Christian teaching. If they have masters who are believers, let them not try to take advantage of them because they are brothers, but rather let them render even better service, because those who lay claim to that service are believers and beloved.

BENEATH the surface of this passage there are certain supremely important Christian principles for everyday life and work.

The Christian slave was in a peculiarly difficult position. If he was the slave of a heathen master, he might very easily make it clear that he regarded his master as bound for perdition and himself as the heir of salvation. His Christianity might well give him a feeling of intolerant superiority which would create an impossible situation. On the other hand, if his master was a Christian, the slave would be tempted to take advantage of the new relationship and to trade upon it. He might use the new relationship as an excuse for producing inefficient work and then expecting to escape all punishment. He might think that the fact that both he and his master were Christians entitled him to all kinds of special consideration and special allowances. He might use the fact of his own and his master's Christianity to be a lazy and an inefficient servant

who was exempt from discipline and punishment. There
was an obvious problem here. We must note two general
things.

(i) In those early days the Church did not emerge as the
opponent and the would-be destroyer of slavery by violent
and sudden means. And the Church was wise. There
were something like 60,000,000 slaves in the Roman
Empire. Simply because of their numbers the slaves were
always regarded as potential enemies. If ever there was
a slave revolt it was put down with merciless force, because
the Roman Empire could not afford to allow the slaves
to rise. If a slave ran away, if he was caught he was either
executed or branded on the forehead with the letter F,
which stood for *fugitivus*, which means *runaway*. There
was indeed a Roman law which stated that if a master
was murdered all his slaves could be examined under
torture, and could indeed be put to death in a body.
E. K. Simpson wisely writes: " Christianity's spiritual
campaign would have been fatally compromised by stirring
the smouldering embers of class-hatred into a devouring
flame, or opening an asylum for runaway slaves in its
bosom." For the Church to have encouraged slaves to
revolt and rebel and rise against their masters would
have been fatal. It would simply have caused civil war,
mass murder, and the complete discredit of the Church.
What then happened? What happened was that as the
centuries went on Christianity so permeated civilization
that in the end the slaves were freed voluntarily and not
by force. Here is a tremendous lesson. It is the proof
that neither men nor the world nor society can be reformed
by force and by legislation. The reform must come through
the slow penetration of the Spirit of Christ into the human
situation. Things have to happen in God's time, not in
ours. In the end the slow way is the sure way, and the
way of violence always defeats itself.

(ii) There is here the further truth, as it has been put,
that " spiritual equality does not efface civil distinctions."

One of the continual dangers of Christianity is that a man may unconsciously regard his Christianity as an excuse for and a defence of slackness and inefficiency. Because he is a Christian and his master is a Christian, he may expect to be treated with special leniency and special consideration. But the fact that both master and man are Christian does not in any way release the employee from doing a good day's work and from earning his wage. It does not entitle him to any special familiarity. The Christian is under the same obligation to submit to discipline, to earn his pay and to do a good day's work as any other man.

(iii) What then is the duty of the Christian slave as the Pastorals see it ? The duty of the Christian slave is to be a good slave. If he is not, if he is slack and careless, if he is disobedient and insolent, he merely supplies the world with ammunition to criticize the Church. The Christian workman must commend his Christianity by being a better workman than other people. In particular, his work will be done in a new spirit. He will not now think of himself as being unwillingly compelled to work; he will think of himself as rendering service to his master, to God and to his fellow men. His aim will be, not to see how little can be forced out of him, but how much he can willingly do. Nothing would more commend Christianity than good Christian workmen. As George Herbert had it:

> " A servant with this clause
>   Makes drudgery divine:
> Who sweeps a room, as for Thy laws
>   Makes that and the action fine."

FALSE TEACHERS AND FALSE TEACHING

I *Timothy* 6: 3-5

If any man offers a different kind of teaching, and does not apply himself to sound words (it is the words of our Lord Jesus Christ I mean) and to godly teaching, he has become inflated with pride. He is a man of no understanding; rather he has a diseased addiction to subtle speculations and battles of words, which can only be a source of envy, strife, the exchange of insults, evil suspicions, continual altercations of men whose minds are corrupt and who are destitute of the truth, men whose belief is that religion is a means of making gain.

THE circumstances of life in the ancient world presented the false teacher with an opportunity which he was not slow to take. On the Christian side, the Church was full of wandering prophets, whose very way of life gave them a certain prestige. The Christian service was much more informal than it is now. Anyone who felt he had a message was free to give it; and the door was wide open to men who were out to propagate a false and mistaken and misleading message. On the heathen side, the ancient world knew all about the wandering so-called philosopher who was out for gain. There were men who were called *sophists*, which means *wise men*. These men made it their business, so to speak, to sell philosophy. They had two lines. They claimed for a fee to be able to teach men to speak well and to argue cleverly; they were the men who with their smooth tongues and their adroit minds were skilled in " making the worse appear the better reason." They had turned philosophy into a way of becoming rich and well-to-do. Their other line was to give demonstrations of public speaking. The Greek had always been fascinated by the spoken word; he loved an orator; and these wandering sophists went from town to town, giving their oratorical demonstrations. They went in for advertising on an intensive scale; they even went the length of delivering by hand personal invitations to their displays. The most famous of them drew people literally by the thousand to their lectures; they were in their day the equivalent of the modern film star. Philostratus tells us that Adrian, one of the most famous of them, had such a popular power that, when his messenger appeared with the news that he was to speak, even the senate and the circus emptied, and the whole population flocked to the Athenaeum to hear him. Obviously such displays would bring in a great deal of money. They had three great faults.

Their speeches were quite unreal. They would offer to speak on any subject, however remote and recondite and unlikely, that any member of the audience might propose. They would undertake to argue any question. This is the kind of question they would argue; it is an actual example: A man goes into the citadel of a town to kill a tyrant who has been grinding down the people; not finding the tyrant himself, he kills the tyrant's son; the tyrant comes in and sees his dead son with the sword in his body, and in his grief kills himself; the man then claims the reward for killing the tyrant and bringing back liberty to his people; should he receive it? Truly they were sick with an addiction to abstruse and futile speculations, and truly they were experts in wordy warfare.

Their one thirst was for applause. Competition between them was a bitter and a cut-throat affair. Plutarch tells of a travelling sophist called Niger who came to a town in Galatia where a prominent orator resided. A competition was immediately arranged. Niger had to compete or lose his reputation. He was suffering from a fishbone in his throat and had difficulty in speaking; but for the sake of prestige he had to go on. Inflammation set in soon after, and in the end he died. Dio Chrysostom paints a picture of a public place in Corinth with all the different kinds of competitors in full blast: " You might hear many poor wretches of sophists shouting and abusing each other, and their disciples, as they call them, squabbling, and many writers of books reading their stupid compositions, and many poets singing their poems, and many jugglers exhibiting their marvels, and many soothsayers giving the meaning of prodigies, and a thousand rhetoricians twisting lawsuits, and no small number of traders driving their several trades." There you have just that interchange of insults, that envy and strife and bitterness, that constant wordy altercation of men with decadent minds that the writer of the Pastorals deplores. " A sophist," wrote Philostratus, " is put out in an extempore speech by a serious-looking audience and tardy praise and no clapping." " They are all agape," said Dio Chrysostom, " for the murmur of the crowd. . . . Like men walking in the dark they move always in the direction of the clapping and the shouting." Lucian writes: " If your friends see you breaking down, let them pay the price of the suppers you give them by stretching out their arms and giving you a chance of thinking of something to say in the intervals between the rounds of applause." The ancient world well knew just the kind of false teacher who was invading the Church.

Their thirst was for praise, and their criterion was numbers. Epictetus has some vivid pictures of the sophist talking to his disciples after his performance. " ' Well, what did you think of me to-day?' ' Upon my life, sir, I thought you were admirable.' ' What did you think of my best passage?' ' Which was that?' ' Where I described Pan and the Nymphs.' ' Oh, it was excessively well done.' " " ' A much larger audience to-day, I think,' says the sophist. ' Yes, much larger,' responds the disciple. ' Five hundred, I should guess.' ' O, nonsense! It could not have been less than a thousand.' ' Why, that is more than Dio ever had. I wonder why it was? They appreciated what I said, too.' ' Beauty, sir, can move a stone.' " These performing sophists were " the pets of society." They became senators, governors, ambassadors. When they died monuments were erected to them, with inscriptions such as, " The Queen of Cities to the King of Eloquence."

The Greeks were intoxicated with the spoken word. Among the Greeks, if a man could speak, his fortune was made. It was against a background like that that the Church was growing up; and it is little wonder that this type of teacher invaded the Church. The Church gave him a new area in which to exercise his meretricious gifts and to gain a tinsel prestige, and a not unprofitable following. In Greek society it was inevitable that such men should invade the Church.

THE CHARACTERISTICS OF THE FALSE TEACHER

1 *Timothy* 6: 3-5 (*continued*)

HERE in this passage there are set out the characteristics of the false teacher; and they are characteristics which were not peculiar to the sophists of the time of the early Church; they are permanent marks of a certain kind of teacher.

(i) His first characteristic is conceit. His first aim is self-display. His desire is not to display Christ, but to display himself. There are still preachers and teachers who are more concerned to gain a following for themselves than for Jesus Christ. They are more concerned to press their own views upon people than they are to bring to men the word of God. When people meet together for worship they are not concerned to listen to what any man thinks; they are eager to hear what God says. The great preacher and teacher is not a purveyor of his own ideas; he is an echo of God. In a lecture on his own old teacher A. B. Bruce, W. M. Macgregor said: " One of our own Highland ministers tells how he had been puzzled by seeing Bruce again and again during lectures take up a scrap of paper, look at it and then proceed. One day he caught at the chance of seeing what this paper contained, and discovered on it an indication of the words: ' O, send out Thy light and Thy truth,' and thus he realized with awe that into his classroom the professor brought the majesty and the hopefulness of worship." The great teacher does not offer men his own farthing candle of illumination; he offers them the light and the truth of God.

(ii) His concern is with abstruse and recondite speculations. There is a kind of Christianity which is more
concerned with argument than life. To be a member of a
discussion circle or a Bible study group and spend very
enjoyable hours in the discussion of doctrines does not necessarily make a Christian. J. S. Whale in his book *Christian
Doctrine* has certain scathing things to say about this
pleasant intellectualism: " We have as Valentine said of
Thurio, ' an exchequer of words, but no other treasure.'
Instead of putting off our shoes from our feet because
the place whereon we stand is holy ground, we are taking
nice photographs of the Burning Bush from suitable
angles: we are chatting about theories of the Atonement
with our feet on the mantelpiece, instead of kneeling
down before the wounds of Christ." As Luther had it:
" He who merely studies the commandments of God
(*mandata Dei*) is not greatly moved. But he who listens
to God commanding (*Deum mandantem*), how can he
fail to be terrified by majesty so great? " As Melanchthon
had it: " To know Christ is not to speculate about the
mode of His Incarnation, but to know His saving benefits."
Gregory of Nyssa drew a revealing picture of Constantinople
in his day: " Constantinople is full of mechanics and
slaves, who are all of them profound theologians, preaching
in the shops and the streets. If you want a man to change
a piece of silver, he informs you wherein the Son differs
from the Father; if you ask the price of a loaf, you are
told by way of reply that the Son is inferior to the Father;
and if you enquire whether the bath is ready, the answer is
that the Son is made out of nothing." Subtle argumentation,
and glib theological statements do not make a Christian.
Such study and argument and speculation may well be
nothing other than a mode of escape from the challenge
of Christian living.

(iii) The false teacher is a disturber of the peace. He
is instinctively competitive; he is suspicious of all who
differ from him; when he cannot win in an argument he

is reduced to hurling insults at his opponent's theological position, and even at his character; in any argument the accent of his voice is bitterness and not love; and a discussion always drifts or plunges into an altercation. The false teacher has never learned the duty and the secret of speaking the truth in love. The source of this bitterness is the exaltation of self. The tendency of the false teacher is to regard any difference from or any criticism of his views as a personal insult. Wherever any teacher produces an attitude of bitterness, his falseness is demonstrated apart altogether from his views.

(iv) The false teacher commercializes religion. He is out for profit. He looks on his teaching and preaching, not as a vocation, but as a career. He is in the business, not to serve others, but to advance himself. One thing is certain—there is no place for careerists in the ministry of any Church. The Pastorals are quite clear and quite frank that the labourer is worthy of his hire; but the motive of his whole work must be public service and not private gain. His passion is, not to get, but to spend and to be spent in the service of Christ and of his fellowmen.

THE CROWN OF CONTENT

I *Timothy* 6: 6-8

> And in truth godliness with contentment is great gain. We brought nothing into the world, and it is quite clear that we cannot take anything out of it either; but if we have food and shelter, we shall be content with them.

THE word which is here used for *contentment* is the word *autarkeia*. *Autarkeia* was one of the great watchwords of the Stoic philosophers. By it they meant an entire and complete *self-sufficiency*. They meant a frame of mind which was completely independent of all outward and external things, and which carried the secret of happiness within itself. Content never comes from the possession of external things. As George Herbert wrote:

> " For he that needs five thousand pounds to live
> Is full as poor as he that needs but five."

Contentment comes from an inward attitude to life. In the Third part of *Henry the Sixth*, Shakespeare draws a picture of the king wandering in the country places unknown. He meets two gamekeepers and tells them that he is a king. One of them asks him:

" But, if thou be a king, where is thy crown? " And the king gives a great answer:

> " My crown is in my heart, not on my head;
> Not deck'd with diamonds and Indian stones,
> Nor to be seen; my crown is call'd content—
> A crown it is that seldom kings enjoy."

Long ago the old Greek philosophers had gripped the right end of the matter. Epicurus said of himself: " To whom little is not enough nothing is enough. Give me a barley cake and a glass of water and I am ready to rival Zeus for happiness." And when someone asked him for the secret of happiness and of content, his answer was: " Add not to a man's possessions but take away from his desires."

The great men have always been content with very little. One of the sayings of the Jewish Rabbis was: " Who is rich? He that is contented with his lot." Walter Lock quotes the kind of training on which a Jewish Rabbi engaged and the kind of life he lived: " This is the path of the Law. A morsel with salt shalt thou eat, thou shalt drink also water by measure, and shalt sleep upon the ground and live a life of trouble while thou toilest in the Law. If thou doest this, happy shalt thou be, and it shall be well with thee; happy shalt thou be in this world and it shall be well with thee in the world to come." The Rabbi had to learn to be content with that which is enough. E. F. Brown quotes a passage from the great preacher Lacordaire: " The rock of our present day is that no one knows how to live upon little. The great men of antiquity were generally poor. . . . It always seems to me that the retrenchment of useless expenditure, the laying aside of what one may call the relatively necessary, is the high road to Christian disentanglement of heart, just as it was to that of ancient vigour. The mind that has learned to appreciate the moral beauty of life, both as regards God and men, can scarcely be greatly moved by any outward reverse of fortune; and what our age wants most is the sight of a man, who might possess everything, being yet willingly contented with little. For my own part, humanly speaking, I wish for nothing. A great soul in a small house is the idea which has touched me more than any other."

It is not that Christianity pleads for poverty. There is no special virtue in being poor, and no happiness in having a constant struggle to make ends meet. But Christianity does plead for two things.

It pleads for the realization that it is never in the power of things to bring happiness. E. K. Simpson says: " Many a millionaire, after choking his soul with gold-dust, has died from melancholia." Happiness always comes from personal relationships. All the things in the world will not make a man happy if he knows neither friendship nor love. All the things in the world will never take away loneliness. The Christian knows that the secret of happiness lies, not in things, but in people.

It pleads for the concentration upon the things which are permanent, the things that a man can take with him when in the end he dies. We brought nothing into the world, and it is clear that we cannot take anything out of it either. The wise men of every age and faith have known this. " You cannot," said Seneca, " take anything more out of the world than you brought into it." The poet of the Greek anthology had it: " Naked I set foot on the earth; naked I shall go below the earth." As the Spanish proverb grimly puts it: " There are no pockets in a shroud." E. K. Simpson comments: " Whatever a man amasses by the way is in the nature of luggage, no part of his truest personality, but something he leaves behind at the toll-bar of death." Two things alone a man can take to God. He can take, and must take, himself; and therefore the great task of life is to built up a self and a character and heart and a soul that a man can take without shame to God. He can take, and must take, the relationship with God into which he has already entered in the days of his life. We have already seen that the secret of happiness lies in personal relationships, and the greatest of all personal relationships is the relationship to God. And the supreme thing that a man can take with him is the utter trusting conviction that he goes to One who is the friend and lover of his soul.

Content comes when we escape the servitude to things, when we find our wealth in the love and the friendship and the fellowship of men, and when we realize that our most precious possession is our friendship with God, made possible through Jesus Christ.

THE PERIL OF THE LOVE OF MONEY

1 *Timothy* 6: 9, 10

> Those who wish to be rich fall into temptation and a snare, and into many senseless and harmful desires for the forbidden things, desires which swamp men in a sea of ruin and total loss in time and in eternity. For the love of money is a root from which all evils spring; and some, in their reaching out after it, have been sadly led astray, and have transfixed themselves with many pains.

HERE is one of the most often quoted and misquoted sayings in the Bible. Scripture does not say that *money* is the root of all evil; it says that *the love of money* is the root of all evil. This is a truth of which the great classical thinkers were quite as conscious as the Christian teachers. " Love of money," said Democritus, " is the metropolis of all evils." Seneca speaks of, " the desire for that which does not belong to us, from which every evil of the mind springs." " The love of money," said Phocylides, " is the mother of all evils." Philo spoke of, " love of money which is the starting-place of the greatest transgressions of the Law." Athenaeus quotes a saying: " The belly's pleasure is the beginning and root of all evil." Money in itself is neither good nor bad; it is simply dangerous in that the love of it may become bad. With money a man can do much good; and with money he can do much evil. With money a man can selfishly serve his own desires; and with money he can generously answer to the cry of his neighbour's need. With money a man can buy his way to the forbidden things and facilitate the path of wrong-doing; and with money he can make it easier for someone else to live as God meant him to live. Money is not an evil, but it is a great responsibility. Money brings power, and power is always a double-edged thing, for it is powerful to good and powerful to evil. What then are the special dangers involved in the love of money?

(i) The desire for money tends to be a thirst which is insatiable. There was a Roman proverbial saying that wealth is like sea-water; so far from quenching a man's thirst, the more a man drinks of sea-water, the more he wants to drink. The strange thing about wealth is that there never seems to come a time when a man can say: " Enough! " He is always driven by the desire for a little more.

(ii) The desire for wealth is founded on an illusion. Basically the desire for wealth is founded on two things. It is founded, first, on the desire for security; and, second, when a man thinks that he has attained to a minimum of security, the desire for further wealth is founded on the desire for comfort and for luxury. But wealth cannot buy security. It cannot buy the greatest things. It cannot buy health; it cannot buy real love. It cannot preserve from sorrow and from death. The security which is founded on material things is foredoomed to failure and to collapse. Such a security is founded on the sand.

(iii) The desire for money tends to make a man selfish. It fosters the spirit of competition. If a man is driven by the desire for wealth it is nothing to him that someone has to remain poor in order that he may amass more, or that someone has to lose in order that he may gain. The desire for wealth fixes a man's thoughts upon himself, and others become merely means or obstacles in the path to his own enrichment. It is quite true that that *need* not happen; but it is also quite true that in point of fact it *does* happen.

(iv) The strange thing is that the desire for wealth is based on the desire for security, but it ends in nothing but worry and anxiety. The more a man has to keep, the more he has to lose. And, if he has great possessions, the tendency is for him to be haunted by the risk of losing them. There is an old fable about a peasant who rendered a great service to a king. The king rewarded him by giving him a great gift of money. For a time the man was thrilled, but the day came when he went to the king and besought him to take the gift back, for into his life there had entered the hitherto unknown worry that he might lose what he had. John Bunyan was right:

> " He that is down needs fear no fall,
>   He that is low, no pride;
> He that is humble ever shall
>   Have God to be his guide.
>
> I am content with what I have,
>   Little be it or much;
> And, Lord, contentment still I crave,
>   Because Thou savest such.
>
> Fulness to such a burden is
>   That go on pilgrimage;
> Here little, and hereafter bliss,
>   Is best from age to age."

The man who has least has least to lose; the man who has most may well be haunted with the fear of losing what he has.

(v) The love of money may easily lead a man into wrong ways of getting money, and therefore may lead him in the end into the pain and regret and remorse. That is true even physically. He may so drive his body in his passion to get, that he ruins his health, and makes his age a weariness instead of a rest. He may discover too late what damage his desire has done to others, and be saddled with remorse for things that cannot be undone and consequences which cannot be reversed.

To seek to be independent, to be able to pay one's debts, to provide a house and a home and an opportunity for one's family, prudently to provide for the future, is a Christian duty; but to evaluate everything in terms of money, to make the love of money the driving-force of life, cannot ever be anything else than the most perilous of sins.

CHALLENGE TO TIMOTHY

I *Timothy* 6: 11-16

But you, O man of God, flee from these things. Pursue righteousness, godliness, faith, love, endurance, gentleness. Fight the good fight of faith; lay hold on eternal life, to which you are called, now that you have witnessed a noble profession of your faith in the presence of many witnesses. I charge you in the sight of God. who makes all things alive, and in the sight of Christ Jesus, who, in the days of Pontius Pilate, witnessed His noble confession, that you keep the commandment, that you should be without spot and without blame, until the day when our Lord Jesus Christ appears, that appearance which in His own good times the blessed and only Potentate, the King of kings, and the Lord of lords will show, He who alone possesses immortality, He who dwells in the light that no man can approach, He whom no man has seen or ever can see, to whom be honour and everlasting power. Amen.

So the letter comes to an end with a tremendous challenge to Timothy, a challenge all the greater and all the more solemn because of the deliberate sonorous nobility of the words in which it is clothed.

Right at the very outset Timothy is challenged and put upon his mettle. He is addressed as *man of God*. That is one of the great Old Testament titles. It is a title which is given to Moses. *Deuteronomy* 33: 1 speaks of " Moses, the man of God." The title of *Psalm* 90 is, " A Prayer of Moses the man of God." It is a title of the prophets and the messengers of God. God's messenger to Eli is a man of God (I *Samuel* 2: 27). Samuel is described as a man of God (I *Samuel* 9: 6). Shemaiah, God's messenger to Rehoboam, was a man of God (I *Kings* 12: 22). John Bunyan in the *Pilgrim's Progress* calls Great-Grace " God's Champion." Here is the title of honour. When the charge is given to Timothy, he is not reminded of his own weakness and his own helplessness and his own inadequacy and his own sin; that might well have reduced him to pessimistic despair; he is rather challenged by the honour which is his, the honour of being God's man. It is the Christian way, not to depress a man by branding him as a lost and helpless sinner, but rather to uplift him by summoning him to be what he has got it in him to be. The Christian way is not to fling a man's humiliating past in his face, but to set before him the majestic splendour of his potential future. The very fact that Timothy was addressed as " Man of God " would make him square his shoulders and throw his head back as one who has received his commission from the King.

The virtues and the noble qualities which are set before Timothy are not just heaped haphazardly together. There is an order in them. First, there comes *righteousness*. *Righteousness*, *dikaiosunē*, is defined as " giving both to men and to God their due." Righteousness is the most comprehensive and inclusive of the virtues. The righteous man is the man who does his duty to God and to his fellow men. Second, there comes a group of three virtues which look towards God. *Godliness, eusebeia*, is the reverence of the man who throughout all his life never ceases to be aware that all life is lived in the presence of God. *Faith, pistis*, here means *fidelity*, and is the virtue of the man who, through all the chances and the changes of life, down even to the gates of death, is loyal to God. *Love, agapē*, is the virtue of the man who, even if he tried, cannot forget what God has done for him, and cannot forget the love of the heart of God to men. Third, there comes the virtue which looks to the conduct of life. It is *hupomonē*, which the Authorised Version translates *patience*. But *hupomonē* never means the spirit which sits with folded hands and simply bears things, letting the experiences of life flow like a tide over it. *Hupomonē* is victorious endurance, masculine constancy under trial. " It is unswerving constancy to faith and piety in spite of adversity and suffering." *Hupomonē* is the virtue which does not so much accept the experiences of life as it conquers these experiences. *Hupomonē* is the virtue which in spite of all things overcomes the world. Fourthly, there comes the virtue which looks to men. The Greek word is *paupatheia*, which the Authorised Version translates *gentleness*. It is one of these untranslatable words. It describes the spirit which never blazes into anger for its own wrongs, but which can be purely and devastatingly angry for the wrongs of others. It describes the spirit which knows how to forgive and yet knows how to wage the battle of righteousness. It describes the spirit which walks at once in humility and yet in pride of its high calling from God. It describes the virtue by which a man at one and the same time remembers the shame of being a sinner and the glory of being a son of God. It describes the virtue by which at all times a man is enabled rightly to treat his fellow men, and rightly to regard himself.

MEMORIES WHICH INSPIRE

I *Timothy* 6: 11-16 (*continued*)

As Timothy is challenged to the work and the task of the future, he is inspired with the memories of the past.

(i) He is to remember his baptism and the vows he took at it. We must remember that in the circumstances of the early Church baptism was naturally and inevitably adult baptism, for men were coming straight from heathenism to Christ. Baptism was confession of faith and witness to all men that a man had taken Jesus Christ as Saviour, Master and Lord. The earliest of all Christian confessions was the simple creed: " Jesus Christ is Lord " (*Romans* 10: 9; *Philippians* 2: 11). But it has been suggested that behind these words to Timothy there lies a confession of faith which said: " I believe in God the Almighty, Creator of heaven and earth, and in Christ Jesus who suffered under Pontius Pilate who will return to judge; I believe in the Resurrection from the dead and in the life immortal." It may well have been a creed like that to which Timothy gave his allegiance. So, then, first of all, Timothy is reminded that he is a man who has given his pledge. The Christian is first and foremost a man who has pledged himself to Jesus Christ.

(ii) He is to remember that he has made the same confession of his faith as Jesus did. When Jesus stood before Pilate, Pilate said: " Art Thou the King of the Jews? " and Jesus answered: " Thou sayest it " (*Luke* 23: 3). Jesus had witnessed that He was a King; and Timothy always had witnessed to the lordship of Christ. When the Christian confesses his faith, he does what his Master has already done; when the Christian suffers for his faith, he undergoes what his Master has already undergone. When we are engaged on some great enterprise, we can say: " Brothers, we are treading where the saints have trod," but when we confess our faith before men, we can say even more; we can say: " I stand with Christ ";

and surely such a memory must lift up our hearts and inspire our lives.

(iii) He is to remember that Christ comes again. He is to remember that life and work must necessarily be made fit for Christ to see. The Christian is not working to satisfy men; he is working to satisfy Christ. The Christian must take every task he does and offer it, not to men, but to Christ. The question which the Christian must always ask himself is not: " Is this good enough to pass the judgment of men? " but: " Is this good enough to win the approval of Jesus Christ? "

(iv) And above all he is to remember God. And what a memory that is! He is to remember the One who is King of every king, and Lord of every Lord; the one who possesses the gift of life eternal to give to men; the One whose holiness and majesty are such that no man can ever dare to look upon them. The Christian must ever remember God, and then he must say: " If God be for us, who can be against us? "

ADVICE TO THE RICH

I *Timothy* 6: 17-19

> Charge those who are rich in this world's goods not to be proud, and not set their hopes on the uncertainty of riches, but on God who gives them all things richly to enjoy. Charge them to do good; to find their wealth in noble deeds; to be ready to share all that they have; to be men who never forget that they are members of a fellowship; to lay up for themselves the treasure of a fine foundation for the world to come, that they may lay hold on real life.

SOMETIMES we think of the early Church as being composed entirely of poor people and of slaves. Here we see that even as early as this the Church had its wealthy members. They are not condemned for being wealthy; they are not told to give all their wealth away. What they are told is what not to do, and what to do with their riches.

Their riches must not make them proud. Because they have more money than other people they must not think themselves better than other people. There is nothing in this world which gives any man any right to look down on any other man, least of all the possession of wealth. They must not set their hopes on wealth. In the chances and the changes of life a man may be wealthy to-day and a pauper to-morrow; and it is folly to set one's hopes on that which can so easily be lost.

They are told that they must use their wealth to do good; that they must ever be ready to share; and that they must remember that a Christian is essentially a man who is a member of a fellowship. And they are told that such wise use of wealth will build for them a good foundation in the world to come. As someone put it: " What I kept, I lost; what I gave I have."

There is a famous Jewish Rabbinic story. There was a man called Monobaz who had inherited great wealth, but he was a good, a kindly and a generous man. In the time of famine he gave away all his wealth to help the poor. His brothers came to him and said: " Your fathers laid up treasure, and added to the treasure that they had inherited from their fathers, and are you going to waste it all? " He answered: " My fathers laid up treasure below: I have laid it up above. My fathers laid up treasure of Mammon: I have laid up treasure of souls. My fathers laid up treasure for this world: I have laid up treasure for the world to come."

Every time we could have given and did not give, lessens the wealth that is laid up for us in the world to come; every time we gave of what we had increases the riches that are laid up for us when this life comes to an end.

The whole teaching of the Christian ethic is, not that wealth is a sin, but that wealth is a very great responsibility. If a man's wealth ministers to nothing but his own pride and enriches no one but himself, then his wealth becomes his ruination, because it has impoverished his soul. But if a man uses his wealth to bring help and comfort to others, in becoming poorer, he becomes richer. In time and in eternity " it is more blessed to give than to receive."

A FAITH TO HAND ON

1 *Timothy* 6: 20, 21

> O Timothy, guard the trust that has been entrusted to you. Avoid irreligious empty talking; and the paradoxes of that knowledge which has no right to be called knowledge, which some have professed, and by so doing have missed the target of the faith.
> Grace be with you.

IT may well be that the name *Timothy* is here used in the fulness of its meaning. The name Timothy comes from two words, *timan*, *to honour*, and *theos*, *God*. The name *Timothy* means *he who honours God*. It may well be that this concluding passage begins by reminding Timothy of his name, and by urging him to be true to it.

This passage talks of the *trust* that has been entrusted to him. The Greek word for *trust* is *parathēkē*, which literally means a *deposit*. It was the word for money deposited with a banker or with a friend. When such money was in time demanded back it was a sacred duty to hand it back entire and whole and unharmed. Sometimes in Greek, children are called a sacred *parathēkē*, a sacred trust. If the gods gave a man a child, it was that man's duty to present that child, trained, disciplined and equipped to the gods. The Christian faith is like that. The Christian faith is something which we received from our forefathers, and something which we must pass on to our children. E. F. Brown quotes a famous passage from St. Vincent of Lerins: " What is meant by the *deposit*? (*parathēkē*). That which is committed to thee, not that which is invented by thee; that which thou hast received, not that which thou hast devised; a thing not of wit, but of learning; not of private assumption, but of public tradition; a thing brought to thee, not brought forth of thee; wherein thou must not be an author, but a keeper; not a leader, but a follower. Keep the deposit. Preserve the talent of the Catholic faith safe and undiminished; let that which is committed to thee remain with thee, and that deliver. Thou hast received gold, render gold." A man does well to remember that his duty is not only to himself, but also to his children and his children's children. If in our day the Church were to become weakened and enfeebled; if in our day the Christian ethic were to be more and more submerged in the world; if in our day the Christian faith were to be twisted and distorted, it would not only be we who were the losers; those of generations still to come would be robbed of something infinitely precious. We are not only the possessors, we are also the trustees of the faith. That which we have received, we must also hand on.

Finally the Pastorals condemn those who, as the Authorised Version has it, have given themselves to " the oppositions of science falsely so-called." First, we must note that here the word *science* is used in its original sense; it simply means *knowledge* (*gnōsis*), and has nothing to do with scientific knowledge as nowadays we use the word. What is being condemned is a false intellectualism, and a false stressing of human knowledge. But what is meant by *oppositions*? The Greek word is *antitheseis*. Very much later than this there was a heretic called Marcion who produced a book called *The Antitheseis* in which he quoted Old Testament texts and set beside them New Testament texts which contradicted them. This might very well mean: " Don't waste your time seeking out contradictions in Scripture. Use the Scriptures to live by and not to argue about." But there are two meanings more probable than that.

(i) The word *antithesis* could mean a *controversy*; and this might mean: " Avoid controversies; don't get yourself mixed up in useless and bitter arguments and differences."

161

This would be a very relevant bit of advice to a Greek congregation in Ephesus. The Greek had a passion for going to law. He found one of his main amusements in the law courts. The Greek would even go to law with his own brother, just for the pleasure of going to law. The Greek was a born litigant. This may well mean, " Don't make the Church a battle-ground of theological arguments and debates. Christianity is not something to argue about, but something to live by."

(ii) The word *antithesis* can mean a *rival thesis*. This is the most likely meaning, because it suits Jew and Gentile alike. The scholastics in the later days used to argue about questions like: " How many angels can stand on the point of a needle? " The Jewish Rabbis would argue about hair-splitting points of the law for hours and days and even years. They would balance one argument, one theory, one interpretation against another. The Greeks were the same, only in a still more serious way. There was a school of Greek philosophers, and a very influential school it was, called the Academics. The Academics held that in the case of everything in the realm of human thought, you could by logical argument arrive at precisely opposite conclusions. They therefore went on to hold that there is no such thing in this world as absolute binding truth; that all there is is two hypotheses of equal weight and strength. They then went on to argue that since that is so the wise man will never make up his mind about anything, but will hold himself for ever in a state of suspended judgment. The effect of that was of course to paralyse all action and to reduce men for ever to complete uncertainty about the truth. So Timothy is told: " Don't waste your time in subtle arguments; don't waste your time in ' dialectical fencing.' Don't be too clever to be wise. Listen rather to the unequivocal voice of the commandments of God than to the subtle disputations of over-clever minds."

So the letter draws to a close with a warning which our own

generation needs. Clever argument can never be made
a substitute for Christian action. The duty of the Christian
is not to sit in a study in isolation and to weigh arguments;
it is to live the Christian life in the dust and heat of the
world. In the end it is not intellectual cleverness, but
conduct and character which count.

And so there comes the closing blessing—" Grace be
with you." The letter ends with the beauty of the grace
of God.

AN APOSTLE'S GLORY AND AN APOSTLE'S
PRIVILEGE

2 Timothy I: I-7

This is a letter from Paul, who was made an apostle of
Christ Jesus by the will of God, and whose apostleship
was designed to make known to all men God's promise
of real life in Christ Jesus, to Timothy his own beloved
child. Grace, mercy and peace be to you from God,
the Father, and from Christ Jesus, our Lord.
I thank God, whom I serve with a clear conscience,
as my forefathers did before me, for all that you
are to me, just as in my prayers I never cease to
remember you, for, remembering your tears when we
parted, I never cease to yearn to see you, that I
may be filled with joy. And I thank God that I have
received a fresh reminder of that sincere faith which
is in you, a faith of the same kind as first dwelt in
your grandmother Lois and in your mother Eunice,
and which, I am convinced, dwells in you too. That
is why I send you this reminder to keep at white
heat the gift that is in you and which came to you
through the laying of my hands upon you; for God
did not give us the spirit of craven fear, but of power
and love and self-discipline.

WHEN Paul speaks of his own apostleship there are always
certain unmistakable notes in his voice. To Paul his
apostleship was always certain things. (*a*) His apostleship
was an *honour*. He was chosen to it by the will of God.
Every Christian must regard himself as a God-chosen

man. (b) His apostleship was a *responsibility*. God chose him because God wanted to do something with him. God wished to make him the agent and the instrument by which the tidings of new life went out to men. No Christian is ever chosen to be a Christian entirely for his own sake; he is chosen for what he can do for others. A Christian is a man who is lost in wonder, love and praise at what God has done for him, and who is aflame with eagerness to tell others what God can do for them. (c) His apostleship was a *privilege*. It is most significant to see what it was that Paul conceived it to be his duty to bring to others. It was the *promise* of God that Paul was convinced that he must broadcast throughout the world, not the *threat* of God. To Paul, Christianity was not the threat of damnation; it was the good news of salvation. It is worth remembering that the greatest evangelist and missionary the world has ever seen was out, not to terrify men by shaking them over the flames of hell, but to move them to astonished submission at the sight of the love of God. The dynamic of Paul's gospel was love, not fear.

As always when he speaks to Timothy, there is a warmth of loving affection in Paul's voice. " My beloved child," he calls him. Timothy was Paul's child in the faith. Timothy's parents had given Timothy physical life; but it was Paul who gave him eternal life. There is a joy in physical parenthood; but there is joy also in spiritual parenthood. And there is many a teacher and many a saintly person to whom God never gave the gift of a physical child who has the joy and the privilege of being a father or a mother in the faith. There is no joy in all the world like the joy of bringing one soul to Christ.

THE INSPIRING OF TIMOTHY

2 Timothy 1: 1-7 (*continued*)

PAUL'S object in writing is to inspire and to strengthen Timothy for his task in Ephesus. Timothy was young, and Timothy had a hard task in battling against the heresies and the infections that were bound to threaten and to invade the Church. So, then, in order to keep his courage high and his effort strenuous, Paul reminds Timothy of certain things.

(i) He reminds Timothy of his own belief and confidence in him. There is no greater inspiration than to feel that someone believes in us. An appeal to honour is always more effective than a threat of punishment. The fear to let those who love us down is a cleansing fear.

(ii) He reminds Timothy of his family tradition. Timothy was walking in a fine heritage, and if Timothy failed, not only would he smirch his own name, but he would lessen the honour of his family name as well. A fine parentage is one of the greatest gifts that a man can have. Let him thank God for it, and let him never bring dishonour to it.

(iii) He reminds Timothy of his setting apart to office and of the gift which was conferred upon him. Once a man enters upon the service of any society or association with a tradition and a history, anything that he does affects not only himself; and anything that he has to do has to be done not only in his own strength. There is given to him the strength of a tradition to draw upon and the honour of a tradition to preserve. That is specially true of the Church. He who serves the Church has the honour of the Church in his hands; he who serves the Church is upheld and strengthened by the consciousness of the communion of all the saints.

(iv) He reminds Timothy of the qualities which should characterize the Christian teacher. These qualities, as Paul at that moment saw them, are four. (a) There was *courage*. It is not craven fear, it is courage, that the Christian service should bring to a man. It always takes courage to be a Christian, and that courage comes from the continual consciousness of the presence of Christ. (b) There was *power*. In the true Christian there is the power to cope with things, the power to shoulder the back-breaking task, the power to stand erect in face of the shattering situation, the power to retain faith in face of the soul-searing sorrow, and the wounding disappointment. The Christian is characteristically the man who can pass the breaking-point and not break. (c) There is *love*. In Timothy's case this is love for the brethren, love for the congregation of the people of Christ over whom he is set. It is precisely that love which gives the Christian pastor his other qualities. The Christian pastor must love his people so much that he will never find any toil too great to undertake for them. He must love his people so much that no threatening situation will ever daunt him. No man need ever enter the ministry of the Church of Christ unless there is love for Christ's people within his heart. (d) There is *self-discipline*. The word is *sōphronismos*. Here is one of these great Greek untranslatable words. Someone has defined it as " the sanity of saintliness." Falconer defines it as " control of oneself in face of panic or of passion." It is Christ alone who can give us that self-mastery, that self-discipline, that self-control which will keep us alike from being swept away and from running away. No man can ever rule others unless he has first mastered himself. *Sōphronismos* is that divinely given self-mastery which makes a man a great ruler of others because he is first of all the servant of Christ and the master of himself.

A GOSPEL WORTH SUFFERING FOR

2 *Timothy* 1: 8-11

So, then, do not be ashamed to bear your witness to our Lord; and do not be ashamed of me His prisoner; but accept with me the suffering which the gospel brings, and do so in the power of God, who saved us, and who called us with a call to consecration, a call which had nothing to do with our own achievements, but which was dependent solely on His purpose, and on the grace which was given to us in Christ Jesus: and all this was planned before the world began, but now it stands full-displayed through the appearance of our Saviour Christ Jesus, who abolished death and brought life and incorruption to light by means of the good news which He brought, good news in the service of which I have been appointed a herald, and an apostle and a teacher.

IT is inevitable that loyalty to the gospel will bring trouble. For Timothy, loyalty to the gospel and loyalty to Paul meant loyalty to a man who was regarded as a criminal, because as Paul wrote he was in prison in Rome. But here Paul sets out the gospel in all its glory, as a gospel worth suffering for. Here sometimes by implication and sometimes by direct statement Paul brings out element after element in the glory of the gospel. There are few passages in the New Testament which have in them and behind them such a sense of the sheer grandeur of the gospel of Jesus Christ.

(i) It is the gospel of *power*. Any suffering which the gospel involves is to be borne in the power of God. To the ancient world the gospel was the power to live. That very age in which Paul was writing was the great age of suicide. The highest of the ancient thinkers were the Stoics; the Stoics had the highest principles; but the Stoics had their own way out when life became intolerable. They had a saying: " God gave men life, but God gave men the still greater gift of being able to take their own lives away." The gospel was, and is, power, power to conquer self, power to master circumstances, power to go on living when life is unlivable, power to be a Christian when being a Christian looks impossible.

(ii) It is the gospel of *salvation*. God is the God who saves us. The gospel is rescue. It is rescue from sin. It is that which liberates a man from the things which have him in their power; power to break with the habits which are unbreakable; power to conquer the sins which have become woven into the very fibre of life. The gospel is essentially that rescuing power which can make bad men good.

(iii) The gospel is the call to *consecration*. The gospel is not simply rescue from the consequences and the penalty of past sin. The gospel is a summons to walk the way of holiness. The sheer changing power of the gospel is a fact which is beyond all argument. In *The Bible in World Evangelism* A. M. Chirgwin quotes two amazing instances of this miraculous changing power of Christ. There was a New York gangster and ex-convict who had recently been in prison for robbery with violence. He was on his way to join his old gang with a view to taking part in another robbery when he picked a man's pocket in Fifth Avenue. He went into Central Park to see what he had succeeded in stealing, and he discovered to his disgust that he had picked a man's pocket of a New Testament. Since he had time to spare before he was due to meet his fellow gangsters, he began idly to turn over the pages and to read. Soon he was deep in the book, and he read to such effect that a few hours later he went to his old comrades and told them bluntly what he had been doing, and broke with them for ever. For that ex-convict and gangster the gospel was the call to holiness. There was a young Arab in Aleppo who had a bitter quarrel with a former friend. He told a Christian evangelist: " I had made up my mind to kill him. I hated him so much that I plotted revenge, even to the point of murder. Then," he went on, " one day I ran into you and you induced me to buy a copy of St. Matthew. I only bought it to please you. I never intended to read it. But as I was going to bed that night the book fell out of my pocket, and I picked it up and started to read. When I reached the place where it says: ' Ye have heard that it hath been said of old time, Thou shalt not kill. . . . But I say unto you that whosoever is angry with his brother without a cause shall be in danger of the judgment,' I remembered the hatred I was nourishing against my enemy. As I

read on my uneasiness grew until I reached the words,
' Come unto me all ye who labour and are heavy laden,
and I will give you rest. Take my yoke upon you, and
learn of me; for I am meek and lowly in heart; and ye
shall find rest unto your souls.' Then I was compelled
to cry: ' God be merciful to me a sinner.' Joy and peace
filled my heart and my hatred disappeared. Since then I
have been a new man, and my chief delight is to read God's
word." It was the gospel which set the ex-convict in
New York and the would-be murderer in Aleppo on the
road to holiness. It is there that so much of our Church
Christianity falls down. It does not change people; and
therefore it is not Christianity. The man who has known
the saving power of the gospel is a changed man, in his
business, in his pleasure, in his home, in his temperament,
in his character. There should be an essential difference
between the Christian and the non-Christian, because the
Christian has obeyed the summons to begin to walk the
road to holiness.

A GOSPEL WORTH SUFFERING FOR

2 Timothy 1: 8-11 (continued)

(iv) THE gospel is the gospel of *grace*. It is not dependent
on our achievements but on God's purpose. It is not
something which we have achieved, but something which
we accept. God did not call us because we are holy; God
called us to make us holy. If we had to win, to achieve,
to deserve the gospel and the love of God, our situation
would be helpless and hopeless. The gospel is the free
gift of God. God does not love us because we deserve
His love; God loves us out of the sheer generosity of
His heart.

(v) The gospel is the gospel of *God's eternal purpose*.
It was planned and designed before the world and time
began. We must never think that once God was stern law

and that since the life and death of Jesus, God has been forgiving love. From the beginning of time God's love has been seeking and searching for men, and God's grace and forgiveness have been offered to men. Love is the very essence of the eternal nature and being of God.

(vi) The gospel is the gospel of *life and immortality*. It is Paul's conviction that Christ Jesus brought life and incorruption to light. The ancient world feared death; or, if they did not fear death, they regarded it as one eternal night through which men must for ever sleep; death was extinction; at the best the ancient world regarded death as absorption in the being of God. But it was the message of Jesus that death was the way to life, and that so far from separating men from God, death brought men into God's nearer presence.

(vii) The gospel is the gospel of *service*. It was this gospel which made Paul a herald, an apostle and a teacher of the faith. It was not a gospel which left Paul in a comfortable feeling that now his own soul was saved and he did not need to worry any more. It was a gospel which laid on him the inescapable task of wearing himself out in the service of God and of his fellow men. This gospel laid three necessities on Paul. (*a*) It made him a herald. The word is *kērux*. *Kērux* in Greek is a word with a wide meaning. It has three main lines of meaning, and each of them has something to suggest about our Christian duty. The *kērux* was the herald who brought the announcement from the king. The *kērux* was the emissary when two armies were opposed to each other, and who brought the terms of or the request for truce and peace. The *kērux* was the man whom an auctioneer or a merchantman employed to shout his wares, and to invite people to come and buy. So the Christian must be the man who brings the message to his fellow men; he must be the man who brings men into truce and peace with God; he must be the man who calls on his fellow men to accept the rich offer which God is making to them. (*b*) It made him an *apostle*. An apostle, *apostolos*, is literally *one who is sent out*. The word can mean an *envoy*, or an *ambassador*. The *apostolos* did not speak for himself; he spoke for him who sent him. The *apostolos* did not come in his own authority; he came in the authority of him who sent him. The Christian is the envoy, the ambassador of Christ, come to speak for Christ, and to represent Christ to men. (c) It made him a *teacher*. There is a very real sense in which the teaching task of the Christian and of the Church is the most important task of all. It is certain that the task of the teacher is very much harder than the task of the evangelist. It is the task of the evangelist to appeal to men, to confront men with the message of the love of God. In a moment of vivid emotion, in a moment when his defences have been battered down, a man may respond to that summons. But a long road still remains. He must learn the meaning of it; he must learn the discipline of the Christian life. The seed has been planted; but the long slow process of growth has still to come. The foundations have been laid, but the edifice of the Christian life has still to be raised. The flame of evangelism has to be followed by the steady glow of Christian teaching. It may well be that people drift away from the Church, after their first decision, for the simple, yet fundamental, reason that they have not been taught into the truth and meaning of the Christian faith. Herald, ambassador, teacher—here is the threefold function of the Christian who would serve his Lord and his Church.

(viii) The gospel is the gospel of *Christ Jesus*. Without Him we would never have known it. It was full displayed through the *appearance* of our Lord Christ Jesus. The word that Paul uses for *appearance* is a word with a great history. It is the word *epiphaneia*. It was a word which the Jews repeatedly used of the great saving manifestations of God, for customs, in the terrible days of the Maccabaean struggles, when the enemies of Israel were deliberately seeking to obliterate God.

In the days of Onias the High Priest there came a certain Heliodorus to plunder the Temple treasury at Jerusalem. Neither prayers nor entreaties would stop him carrying out this sacrilege. And, so the story runs, even as Heliodorus was about to set hands on the treasury, " the Lord of Spirits and the Prince of Power caused a great *epiphaneia*. . . . For there appeared unto them an horse with a terrible rider upon him . . . and he ran fiercely and smote at Heliodorus with his forefeet. . . . And Heliodorus fell suddenly to the ground and was compassed with great darkness " (2 *Maccabees* 3: 24-30). What exactly happened we may never know; but in Israel's hour of need there came this tremendous *epiphaneia* of God. When Judas Maccabaeus and his little army were confronted with the might of Nicanor, they prayed: " O Lord, who didst send Thine angel in the time of Hezekiah king of Judaea, and didst slay in the host of Sennacherib an hundred fourscore and five thousand (cp. 2 *Kings* 19: 35, 36), wherefore now also, O Lord of Heaven, send a good angel before us for a fear and a dread unto them; and through the might of Thine arm let those be stricken with terror, that come against Thy holy people to blaspheme." And then the story goes on: " Then Nicanor and they that were with him came forward with trumpets and with songs. But Judas and his company encountered the enemy with invocation and prayer. So that, fighting with their hands and praying unto God with their hearts, they slew no less than thirty and five thousand men; for through the *epiphaneia* of God they were greatly cheered " (2 *Maccabees* 15: 22-27). Once again we do not know what happened, but once again God made a great and saving appearance for His people. So to the Jew this word *epiphaneia* denoted a rescuing and saving intervention of God.

To the Greek this was an equally great word. The accession of the Emperor to his throne was called his *epiphaneia.* It was his manifestation. Every Emperor came to the throne with high hopes; his coming was hailed as the dawn of a new and precious day, and of great blessings to come.

The gospel was full displayed with the *epiphaneia* of Jesus; and the very word shows that Jesus was God's great, rescuing intervention and manifestation into the world; and that the coming of Jesus was the beginning of the ascending by Jesus into the throne which in the end would be the throne of the Kingdom of God.

TRUST HUMAN AND DIVINE

2 Timothy 1: 12-14

> And that is the reason why I am going through these things I am going through. But I am not ashamed, for I know Him in whom my belief is fixed, and I am quite certain that He is able to keep safe what I have entrusted to Him until the last day comes. Hold fast the pattern of health-giving words you have received from me, never slackening in that faith and love which are in Christ Jesus. Guard the fine trust that has been given to you through the Holy Spirit who dwells in you.

THIS passage uses a very vivid Greek word in a most suggestive double way. Paul talks of that which he has entrusted to God; and he urges Timothy to safeguard the trust which has been reposed in him by God. In both cases the word is the Greek word *parathēkē*. *Parathēkē* means *a deposit committed to someone's trust*. A man might deposit something with a friend whom he could trust; he might deposit something with someone to be kept for his children or his loved ones; he might deposit his valuables in a temple for safe keeping, for the temples were the banks and safe deposits of the ancient world. In each case the thing entrusted and deposited was a *parathēkē*. In the ancient world there was no more sacred duty than the safe-guarding of such a deposit and the returning of it when in due time it was claimed. There was a famous Greek story which told just how sacred such a trust was (*Herodotus* 6: 89; Juvenal, *Satires*, 13: 199-208). The Spartans were famous for their strict honour and honesty. A certain man of Miletus came to a certain Glaucus of Sparta. He said that he had heard such great reports of the honesty of the Spartans that he had turned half his possessions into money, and he wished to deposit that money with Glaucus, until he or his heirs should claim it again. Certain symbols, tallies, were given and received which would identify the rightful claimant when he should make his claim. The years passed on; the man of Miletus died; his sons came to Sparta to see Glaucus, produced the identifying tallies, and asked for the return of the deposited money. But Glaucus claimed that he had no memory of ever receiving any such money. The sons from Miletus went sorrowfully away; but Glaucus went to the famous oracle at Delphi to see what he should do, to see whether he should admit the trust, or whether, as Greek law entitled him to do, he should swear that he knew nothing about it, for the Greeks accepted such an oath as true. The oracle answered:

" Best for the present it were, O Glaucus, to do as thou wishest,
Swearing an oath to prevail, and so to make prize of the money.
Swear then—death is the lot even of those who never swear falsely.
Yet hath the Oath-god a son who is nameless, footless and handless;
Mighty in strength he approaches to vengeance, and whelms in destruction
All who belong to the race, or the house of the man who is perjured.
But oath-keeping men leave behind them a flourishing offspring."

Glaucus understood; the oracle was telling him that if he wished for momentary profit, he should deny the trust; but such a denial would inevitably bring eternal loss.

Glaucus besought the oracle to pardon his question; but the answer was that to have tempted the god was as bad as to have done the deed. He sent for the sons of the man of Miletus and restored the money. Then Herodotus goes on: " Glaucus at this present time has not a single descendant; nor is there any family known as his; root and branch has he been removed from Sparta. It is a good thing therefore when a pledge has been left with one, not even in thought to doubt about restoring it." To the Greeks a trust, a deposit, a *parathēkē* was completely sacred.

Paul says that he has made his deposit with God Paul means that he has entrusted both his work and his life to God. It might seem that he had been cut off in mid-career. That he should end as a criminal in a Roman gaol might seem the undoing of all his work. But Paul had sowed his seed, and preached his gospel, and the result he left in the hands of God. It might seem that this was the end for Paul; but Paul had entrusted his life to God; and he was sure that in life and in death he was safe. Why was Paul so sure? Because he knew *whom* he had believed in. We must always note and remember that Paul does not say that he knew *what* he had believed. Paul's certainty did not come from the intellectual knowledge of a creed or a theology; it came from a personal knowledge of God. He knew God personally; he knew God intimately; he knew what God was like in love and in power; and to Paul it was incredible and inconceivable that God should fail him or let him down. If we have worked honestly, if we have done the best that we can do, we can take that work and take that effort, and leave the result and the outcome to God, however meagre they may seem to us to be. No matter whether we live or die, we can entrust life to God. With Him in this or any other world life is safe, for nothing can separate us from the love of God in Christ Jesus our Lord.

TRUST HUMAN AND DIVINE

2 Timothy 1: 12-14 *(continued)*

BUT there is another side to this matter of trust; there is another *parathēkē*. Paul urges Timothy to safeguard and to keep inviolate the trust that God has reposed in him. Not only do we put our trust in God; God also puts His trust in us. The idea of God's dependence on men is never far from New Testament thought. When God wants something done, He has to find a man to do it. If God wants a child taught, a message brought, a sermon preached, a wanderer found, a sorrowing one comforted, a sick one healed, he has to find some agent and some instrument to do His work.

The trust that God had particularly reposed in Timothy was the oversight and the edification of the Church. If Timothy was truly to discharge that trust, he had to do certain things.

(i) He had to hold fast to *the pattern of health-giving words*. That is to say, he had to see to it that Christian belief was maintained in all its purity, that false and misguided and misleading ideas were not allowed to enter in, that the great principles of the faith were preserved inviolate. That is not to say that in the Christian Church there must be no new thought, no new ideas, no development in doctrine and belief. But it does mean to say that there are certain great Christian verities which must always be preserved intact. And it may well be that the one Christian truth which must for ever stand is summed up in the creed of the early Church, " Jesus Christ is Lord " (*Philippians* 2: 11). Any theology which seeks to remove Christ from the topmost niche or to take from Him His unique place in the scheme of revelation and salvation is necessarily wrong. The Christian Church must ever be restating its faith—but the faith which is restated is faith in Christ.

(ii) He must never slacken in *faith*. Faith here has two ideas at the heart of it. (*a*) It has the idea of *fidelity* and *loyalty*. The Christian leader must be for ever true and loyal to Jesus Christ. He must never be ashamed to show whose he is and whom he serves. He must never fear to stand by the Master and the Saviour who accepted the Cross for him. Fidelity is the oldest and the most essential virtue in the world. (*b*) But faith also has in it the idea of *hope*. The Christian must never lose his confidence in God; he must never drift into a weary and resigned pessimism. He must never despair. As A. H. Clough wrote:

> " Say not, ' The struggle nought availeth;
> 　　The labour and the wounds are vain;
> The enemy faints not nor faileth,
> 　　And as things have been they remain.'
>
> For while the tired waves, vainly breaking,
> 　　Seem here no painful inch to gain,
> Far back, through creeks and inlets making,
> 　　Comes silent, flooding in, the main."

There must be no hopelessness, no pessimism, no despair, either for himself or for the world, in the heart of the Christian.

(iii) He must never slacken in *love*. To love men is to see men as God sees them. It is to refuse ever to do anything but to seek their highest good. It is to meet bitterness with forgiveness. It is to meet hatred with love. It is to meet indifference with a flaming passion which cannot be blunted or quenched or dulled. The Christian love insistently seeks to love men as God loves them, and to love others as God has first loved us.

THE FAITHLESS MANY AND THE FAITHFUL ONE

2 *Timothy* 1: 15-18

> You know this, that as a whole the people who live in Asia deserted me, and among the deserters are

Phygelus and Hermogenes. May the Lord give mercy to the family of Onesiphorus, because he often refreshed me, and was not ashamed of my chain. So far from that, when he arrived in Rome he eagerly sought me out and found me—may the Lord grant to him mercy from the Lord on that day—and you know better than I do the many services he rendered in Ephesus.

HERE is a passage in which pathos and joy are combined. In the end the same thing happened to Paul as happened to Jesus, his Master. His friends forsook him and fled. In the New Testament *Asia* is not the continent of Asia, but the Roman province of Asia which consisted of the western part of Asia Minor. Its capital was the city of Ephesus. When Paul was imprisoned his friends abandoned him. It is most likely that it was in fear that they abandoned him. The Romans would never have proceeded against Paul on a purely religious charge; the Jews must have persuaded the Romans that Paul was a dangerous trouble-maker and disturber of the public peace. There can be no doubt that in the end Paul would be held on a political charge. To be a friend of a man like that was dangerous; and in Paul's hour of need his friends from Asia abandoned him because they were afraid for their own safety.

But however others might fear and desert, one man was loyal to the end. His name was Onesiphorus, and the very name means *profitable*. Others might be ashamed and afraid to admit that they knew Paul, but not One-siphorus. P. N. Harrison draws a vivid picture of One-siphorus' search for Paul in Rome: " We seem to catch glimpses of one purposeful face in a drifting crowd, and follow with quickening interest this stranger from the far coasts of the Aegean, as he threads the maze of unfamiliar streets, knocking at many doors, following up every clue, warned of the risks he is taking but not to be turned from his quest; till in some obscure prison-house a known voice greets him, and he discovers Paul chained to a Roman soldier. Having once found his way Onesiphorus is not content with a single visit, but, true to his name, proves unwearied in his ministrations. Others have flinched from the menace and ignominy of that chain; but this visitor counts it the supreme privilege of his life to share with such a criminal the reproach of the Cross. One series of turnings in the vast labyrinth (of the streets of Rome) he comes to know as if it were his own Ephesus." There is no doubt that, when Onesiphorus sought out Paul and came to see him again and again, he took his life in his hands. It was a dangerous thing to keep asking where a certain criminal could be found; it was dangerous to visit him; it was still more dangerous to keep on visiting him; but that is what Onesiphorus did.

Again and again the Bible brings us face to face with a question which is a real question for every one of us. Again and again the Bible introduces and dismisses a man from the stage of history with one single sentence. Hermogenes and Phygelus—we know nothing whatever of them beyond their names and the fact that they were traitors and deserters to Paul. Onesiphorus—we know nothing of him except that in his loyalty to Paul he risked— and perhaps lost—his life. Hermogenes and Phygelus go down to history branded as deserters; Onesiphorus goes down to his history as the friend who stuck closer than a brother. If we were to be described in one sentence, what would that one sentence be? Would a one-sentence verdict on our lives be the verdict on a traitor, or the verdict on a disciple who was true?

Before we leave this passage we must note that in one particular connection it is a storm centre. Each one as he reads this passage must form his own opinion, but there are many who feel that the implication of the passage is that Onesiphorus is dead. It is for the family of Onesiphorus that Paul first prays. There are many who feel sure that this passage implies quite definitely that Onesiphorus was dead, and may indeed imply that it was his loyalty to Paul which cost him his life. Now if Onesiphorus was dead, this passage shows us Paul praying for the dead, for it shows us Paul praying that Onesiphorus may find mercy on the last and great day. Prayers for the dead are a much-disputed problem. We do not intend to discuss that matter here. But one thing we can say—to the Jews prayers for the dead were by no means unknown. In the days of the Maccabaean wars there was a battle between the troops of Judas Maccabaeus and the army of Gorgias, the governor of Idumaea. It ended in a victory for Judas Maccabaeus. After the battle the Jews were gathering the dead bodies of those who had fallen in battle. On each one of them they found " things conse-crated to the idols of the Jamnites, which is forbidden the Jews by the law." What is meant is that the dead Jewish soldiers were wearing heathen amulets in a super-stitious attempt to protect their lives. The story goes on to say that every man who had been slain was wearing such an amulet, and to say that it was because he had been wearing such an amulet that he was in fact slain. Seeing this, Judas and all the people prayed that the sin of these men " might be wholly put out of remembrance." Judas then collected money and made a sin-offering for those who had fallen because they believed that, since there was a resurrection, it was not superfluous " to pray and offer sacrifices for the dead." So the story ends with the saying of Judas Maccabaeus that " it was an holy and good thing to pray for the dead. Whereupon he made a reconciliation for the dead, that they might be delivered from sin " (2 Maccabees 12: 39-45). It is clear that Paul was brought up in a way of belief which saw in prayers for the dead, not a hateful, but a lovely thing. This is a subject on which there has often been long and bitter dispute; but this one thing we can and must say—if we love a person with all our hearts, and if the remem-brance of that person is never absent from our minds and memories, then, whatever the intellect of the theologian may say about it, the instinct of the heart is to remember such a one in prayer, whether they are in this or in any other world.

THE CHAIN OF TEACHING

2 *Timothy* 2: 1, 2

> As for you, my child, find your strength in the grace which is in Christ Jesus; and entrust the things which you have heard from me, and which are confirmed by many witnesses, to faithful men who will be competent to teach others too.

HERE we have in outline two things—the reception and the transmission of the Christian faith.

(i) The reception of the faith is founded on two things. It is founded on hearing. It was from Paul that Timothy heard the truth and the grace of the Christian faith. But the words he heard were confirmed by the witness of many. There were many who were prepared to say: " These words, these promises are true—and I know it, because I have found it so in my own life." It may be that there are many of us who have not the gift of expression, and who can neither teach nor explain and expound the Christian faith. But even he or she who has not the gift of teaching is able to witness to the living power of the Christian gospel, and to testify that all the promises are true.

(ii) But it is not only a privilege to receive the Christian faith; it is a duty to transmit it. Every Christian must look on himself as a link between two generations. Not only has he received the faith; he must also pass it on. E. K. Simpson writes on this passage: " The torch of heavenly light must be transmitted unquenched from one generation to another, and Timothy must count himself an intermediary between apostolic and later ages." Reception of the faith is the privilege of the Christian; transmission of the faith is the responsibility of the Christian.

(iii) The faith is to be transmitted to faithful men who in their turn will teach it to others. The Christian Church is dependent on an unbroken chain of teachers. When Clement was writing to the Church at Corinth, he sketched that chain. " Our apostles appointed the aforesaid persons (that is, the elders) and afterwards they provided a continuance, that, if these should fall asleep, other approved men should succeed to their ministry." The teacher is a link in the living chain which stretches unbroken from this present moment back to Jesus Christ. The glory of teaching is that it links the present with the earthly life of Jesus Christ.

These teachers are to be *faithful* men. The Greek word for faithful, *pistos*, is a word with a rich variety of closely connected meanings. A man who is a *pistos* is a man who is *believing*, a man who is *loyal*, a man who is *reliable* and *to be depended on*. All these meanings are there. Falconer said that these believing men are such " that they will yield neither to persecution or to error." The teacher's heart must be so stayed on Christ that no threat of danger will lure him from the path of loyalty, and no seduction of false teaching cause him to stray from the straight path of the truth. The Christian teacher must be steadfast alike in life and in thought.

THE SOLDIER OF CHRIST

2 *Timothy* 2: 3, 4

> Accept your share in suffering like a fine soldier of Christ Jesus. No soldier who is on active service entangles himself in ordinary civilian business; he lays aside such things, so that by good service he may please the commander who has enrolled him in his army.

THE picture of man as a soldier and life as a campaign is one which the Romans and the Greeks knew well. " To live," said Seneca, " is to be a soldier " (Seneca, *Epistles* 96: 5). " The life of every man," said Epictetus, " is a

kind of campaign, and a campaign which is long and varied "
(Epictetus, *Discourses*, 3, 24, 34). Paul took this picture
and applied it to all Christians, but very specially to the
leaders and outstanding servants of the Church. He
urges Timothy to fight a fine campaign (I *Timothy* I: 18).
He calls Archippus, in whose house a house Church met,
our fellow soldier (*Philemon* 2). He calls Epaphroditus,
the messenger of the Philippian Church, " my fellow soldier ",
(*Philippians* 2: 25). Clearly Paul saw in the life of the soldier a
picture of the life of the Christian and of the man who
would serve Christ. What then were the qualities of the
soldier which Paul would have repeated in the Christian life?

(i) The soldier's service must be a *concentrated service*.
Once a man has enlisted on a campaign he can no longer
entangle and involve himself in the ordinary daily business
of life and living. He must concentrate on his service
as a soldier. The Roman code of Theodosius said: " We
forbid men engaged on military service to engage in civilian
occupations." A soldier is a soldier and nothing else.
A Christian must concentrate on his Christianity. That
does not mean that he must engage on no worldly task
or business. He must still live in this world, and he must
still make a living; but it does mean that he must use
whatever task he is engaged upon to live out and to
demonstrate his Christianity.

(ii) The soldier is *conditioned to obedience*. The early
training of a soldier is designed to make him instinctively
and unquestioningly obey the word of command. There
may come a time when such prompt and instinctive
obedience may save his life, and save the life of others.
There is a sense in which it is true that it is no part of the
soldier's duty " to know the reason why." Involved as
he is in the midst of the battle, he cannot see the over-all
picture. The decisions he must leave to the commander
who sees the whole field of battle. The first Christian duty
is obedience to the voice of God, and acceptance even
of that which he cannot understand.

(iii) The soldier is conditioned to *sacrifice*. It most often happens that a soldier's duty is not so much to attack the enemy as it is to put his body a living wall between the enemy and those whom he loves. His task is self sacrifice for those whom he defends. A. J. Gossip tells how, as a chaplain in the 1914-18 war, he was going up the line for the first time. War, and blood, and wounds and death were new to him. As he went he saw by the roadside, left behind after the battle, the body of a young kilted Highlander. And somehow there flashed into his mind the words of Christ Himself: " This is my body broken for you." The essential condition of the soldier's life is willingness to lay down his life for his friend. The Christian must ever be ready to sacrifice himself, his wishes, his desires, his fortune, for God and for his fellow men.

(iv) The soldier is conditioned to *loyalty*. When the Roman soldier joined the army he took the *sacramentum*, the oath of loyalty to his emperor. Someone records a conversation between Marshal Foch and an officer in the 1914-18 war. " You must not retire," said Foch, " you must hold on at all costs." " Then," said the officer aghast, " that means we must all die." And Foch answered: " Precisely! " The supreme soldier's virtue is that he is faithful unto death. The Christian too must be loyal to Jesus Christ, through all the chances and the changes of life, down even to the gates of death.

THE ATHLETE OF CHRIST

2 *Timothy* 2: 5

> And if anyone engages in an athletic contest, he does not win the crown unless he observes the rules of the game.

PAUL has just used the picture of the soldier to represent the Christian, and now he uses two other pictures—the picture of the athlete, and the picture of the toiling husband-man. He uses the same three pictures close together in I *Corinthians* 9: 6, 7, 24-27.

Paul says that the athlete does not win the crown of victory unless he observes the rules of the contest. There is a very interesting point in the Greek here which is difficult to bring out in translation. The Authorised Version speaks of *striving lawfully*. The Greek is *athlein nomimōs*. In point of fact that is the Greek phrase which was used by the later writers to describe a *professional* as opposed to an *amateur* athlete. The man who strove *nomimōs* was the man who concentrated everything on his struggle. His struggle was not just a spare-time thing, as it might be for an amateur; it was a whole-time dedi-cation of his life to excellence in the contest which he had chosen. Here then we have the same idea as we came upon when we were thinking of Paul's picture of the Christian as a soldier. Once again we see that a Christian's life must be concentrated upon his Christianity just as a professional athlete's life is concentrated upon his chosen contest. The spare-time Christian is a contradiction in terms; a man's whole life should be one strenuous endea-vour to live out his Christianity in every moment and in every sphere of his life. What then are the characteristics of the athlete which are in Paul's mind?

(i) The athlete is a man under *discipline* and *self-denial*. He must keep to his schedule of training; he must let nothing interfere with it. There will be days when he would like to drop his training and relax his discipline ; but he must not do so. There will be pleasures and indul-gences which he would like to allow himself; but he must refuse them. There will be times when he is tired, and when he would like to stop; but a very great modern athlete, Puskas, the great Hungarian football player, gives it as his advice to the athlete that, when he thinks he can go on no longer, he must go on for another ten minutes. The athlete who would excel knows that he must let nothing interfere with that standard of physical fitness which he has set himself. There must be discipline in the Christian life. There are times when we do not wish to pray; there are times when the easy way is very attractive; there are times when the right thing is the hard thing; there are times when we would like to relax our standards. But the Christian is a man under discipline. He must train himself never to relax in the life-long attempt to make his soul pure and strong.

(ii) The athlete is a man who *observes the rules*. After the discipline and the rules of the training, there come the contest and the rules of the contest. An athlete cannot win unless he plays the game. The Christian too is often brought into contest with his fellow men. He must defend his faith; he must seek to convince and to persuade; he will have to argue and to debate; he will have to defend his own position and to attack the position of others. He must do it by the Christian rules. No matter how hot the argument, the Christian must never forget his courtesy. No matter how essential it is to win the argument, he must never be anything else but honest about his own position and fair to that of his opponent. The *odium theologicum*, the hatred of theologians, has become a byword and a proverb. There is often no bitterness like religious bitterness. But the real Christian knows that the supreme rule of the Christian life is love, and he will carry that love into every argument and every debate in which he is engaged.

THE TOILER OF CHRIST

2 *Timothy* 2: 6, 7

> It is the toiling husbandman who must be first to receive his share of the fruits. Think of what I am saying, for the Lord will give you understanding in all things.

To represent the Christian life Paul has used the picture of the soldier, and the picture of the athlete, and now he uses the picture of the husbandman. It is not the lazy husbandman, but the husbandman who toils, who must be the first to receive the share of the fruits of the harvest. It is his toil which gives him the right to reap and to enjoy. What then are the characteristics of the husbandman which Paul would wish to see in the life of the Christian?

(i) Often the husbandman must be content, first, to work, and, then, to wait. More than any other workman, the farmer has to learn that there are no such things as quick results. The Christian too must learn to work and to wait. Often he must sow the good seed of the word into the hearts and the minds of his hearers and see no immediate result. A teacher has often to teach, and see no difference in those he or she teaches. A parent has often to seek to train and to guide, and see no difference in the son or daughter. It is only when the years go by that the result is seen; for it often happens in the after-years that when that same young person, that same son or daughter has grown to manhood or womanhood, he or she is faced with some overmastering temptation, or some terrible decision, or some intolerable effort, and then back into his or her mind there comes some word of God, some flash of remembered teaching, some phrase dropped into the mind; and then after all the years of teaching, the guidance, the discipline bears its fruit, and brings honour where without it there would have been dishonour, and salvation where without it there would have been ruin. The husbandman has learned to wait with patience, and so must the Christian teacher and the Christian parent.

(ii) One special thing characterizes the work of the husbandman—he must be prepared to work at any hour. In the harvest time we can see farmers at work in their fields, even till midnight, so long as the last streak of light is left. The farmer knows no hours. Neither must the

Christian. No man can take time off from being a Christian. The trouble with so much Christianity is in fact that it is spasmodic. But from dawn to sunset the Christian must be for ever at his task of being a Christian.

One thing remains in all these three pictures. The soldier is upheld by the thought of final victory. The athlete is upheld by the vision of the crown. The husband-man is upheld by the hope of the harvest. Each of them submits to the discipline and the toil for the sake of the glory which shall be. It is so with the Christian. The Christian struggle is not a struggle without a goal; it is not a pointless effort. It is always going somewhere. And the Christian can be very certain that after the effort of the Christian life, there comes the joy of heaven; and the greater the struggle the greater the joy.

THE ESSENTIAL MEMORY

2 *Timothy* 2: 8-10

> Remember Jesus Christ, risen from the dead, born of the seed of David, as I preached the gospel to you; that gospel for which I suffer, even to the length of fetters, on the charge of being a criminal. But though I am fettered, the word of God is not bound. Therefore I endure everything for the sake of God's chosen ones, that they too may obtain the salvation which is in Christ Jesus, with eternal glory.

RIGHT from the beginning of this letter Paul has been trying to urge and to inspire Timothy to his task. He has reminded him of his own belief in him; he has reminded him of the godly parentage from which he has come; he has shown him the picture of the Christian soldier, the Christian athlete and the Christian toiler. And now he comes to the greatest appeal of all—*Remember Jesus Christ*. Falconer calls these words: " The heart of the Pauline gospel." Even if every other appeal to Timothy's gallantry should fail, surely the memory of Jesus Christ cannot fail. In the words which follow there are implied three things to remember.

(i) Remember Jesus Christ *risen from the dead*. The tense of the Greek verb which Paul uses does not imply one definite act in time, but a continued state which lasts for ever. Paul is not so much saying to Timothy: " Remember the actual resurrection of Jesus "; rather he is saying: " Remember Jesus for ever risen and for ever present; remember your risen and your ever-present Lord." Here is the great Christian inspiration. We do not depend on the inspiration of a memory, however great. We enjoy the power of a presence. When a Christian is summoned to a great task, a task that he cannot but feel is beyond him, he must go to it in the certainty that he does not go to it alone, but that there is with him for ever and for ever the presence and the power of his risen Lord. When fears threaten, when doubts assail, when inadequacy depresses, remember the presence of the risen Lord.

(ii) Remember Jesus Christ *born of the seed of David*. This is the other side of the question. " Remember," says Paul to Timothy, "the manhood of the Master." We do not remember one who is only a Spirit and a spiritual presence; we remember one who trod this road, and lived this life, and faced this struggle, and who therefore knows what we are going through. We have with us, not only the presence of the glorified Christ; we have with us also the presence of the Christ who knew the desperate struggle of being a man, who followed to the bitter end the will of God.

(iii) Finally, Paul says, remember the *gospel*. Remember the good news. Even when the gospel demands much, even when it leads to an effort which seems to be beyond human ability, and to a future which seems dark with every kind of threat, remember that it is a gospel, that it is good news; and remember that the world is waiting for that good news. However hard the task the gospel offers, that same gospel is the message of liberation from sin and victory over circumstances for us and for all mankind.

So Paul kindles Timothy to heroism by calling upon him to remember Jesus Christ, to remember the continual presence of the risen Lord, to remember the sympathy which comes from the manhood of the Master, to remember the glory of the gospel for himself and for the world which had never heard it, and which was waiting for it.

THE CRIMINAL OF CHRIST

2 Timothy 2: 8-10 (continued)

WHEN Paul wrote these words he was in a Roman prison, bound by a chain. This was literally true, for all the time he was in prison, night and day Paul would be bound by a length of chain to the arm of a Roman soldier. Rome took no risks that her prisoners should escape.

Paul was in prison on the charge of being a criminal. It seems strange that even a hostile government should be able to regard a Christian, and especially Paul, as a criminal. There were two possible ways in which Paul might appear a criminal to the Roman government.

First, Rome had an empire which was almost co-extensive with the then known world. It was obvious that such an empire was subject to stresses and to strains. The peace had to be kept and every possible centre of disaffection and rebellion had to be eliminated. One of the things about which Rome was very particular was the formation of associations. In the ancient world there were many associations. There were for instance dinner clubs who met at stated intervals to dine together. There were what we would call friendly societies designed for charity for the dependants of members who had died. There were burial societies to see that their members were decently buried. But so particular were the Roman authorities about associations that even these humble and harmless societies had to receive special permission from the emperor before they were allowed to meet. Now the Christians were in effect an illegal association; and that is one reason why Paul, as a leader of such an association, might well be in the very serious position of being a political criminal.

Second, there was another reason why Paul would be regarded as a criminal. The first persecution of the Christians was intimately connected with one of the greatest disasters which ever befell the city of Rome. On 19th July A.D. 64 the great fire of Rome broke out. It burned for six days and seven nights and devastated the city. The most sacred shrines and the most famous buildings perished in the flames. But worse—the homes of the common people were destroyed. By far the greater part of the population of Rome lived in great tenement buildings built largely of wood; they went up like tinder. People were burned alive, killed, injured; they lost their nearest and their dearest; they were left homeless and destitute. The population of Rome was reduced to what someone has called " a vast brotherhood of hopeless wretchedness." It was believed that none other than Nero, the emperor, himself was responsible for this fire. It was said that he had watched the fire from the Tower of Maecenas and that he had declared himself charmed with " the flower and loveliness of the flames." It was said that when the fire showed signs of dying down men were seen rekindling it with burning brands, and that these men were the servants and employees of Nero. Nero had a passion for building, and it was said that he had deliberately fired the city so that from the ruins he might build a new and a nobler Rome. Whether the story was true or not—the chances are that it was true—no man will ever know for sure. But one thing was certain—nothing would kill the rumour and the report. The homeless, destitute citizens of Rome were sure that Nero had been responsible. There was only one thing for the Roman government to do; they must find a scapegoat on whom to pin the responsibility and the blame. And a scapegoat was found. Let Tacitus, the Roman historian, tell how it was done: "But all human efforts, all the lavish gifts of the emperor, and the propitiations of the gods did not banish the sinister belief that the conflagration was the result of an order. Consequently, to get rid of the report, Nero fastened the guilt and inflicted the most exquisite tortures on a class hated for their abominations, called Christians by the populace" (Tacitus, *Annals*, 15: 44) Obviously slanders were already circulating regarding the Christians. No doubt the influential Jews were responsible for them. And the hated Christians were saddled with the blame for the disastrous fire of Rome. It was from that event and that charge that the first great persecution sprung. Paul was a Christian. Nay more, he was the great leader of the Christians. And it may well be that part of the charge against Paul was that he was one of those whose followers were responsible for the fire of Rome and the resulting misery of the populace.

So, then, Paul was in prison as a criminal, a political prisoner, member and leader of an illegal association, and as a member of that hated sect of incendiaries, on whom Nero had fastened the blame for the destruction of Rome. It can easily be seen how helpless Paul was in face of charges like that.

FREE YET IN FETTERS BOUND

2 Timothy 2: 8-10 (*continued*)

EVEN though he was in prison on charges which made release impossible, Paul was not dismayed, and was very far from despair. He had two great uplifting thoughts.

(i) He was certain that, though he might be bound, nothing could bind the word of God. Andrew Melville was one of the earliest heralds of the Scottish Reformation One day the Regent Morton sent for him and denounced his writings. " There will never be quietness in this country," he said, " till half a dozen of you be hanged or banished the country." " Tush! sir," answered Melville, " threaten your courtiers in that fashion. It is the same to me whether I rot in the air or in the ground. The earth is the Lord's; my fatherland is wherever well-doing is. I have been ready to give my life when it was not half as well worn, at the pleasure of my God. I lived out of your country ten years as well as in it. Yet God be glorified, it will not lie in your power to hang nor exile His truth! " You can exile a man, but you cannot exile the truth. You can imprison a preacher but you cannot imprison the word he preaches. The message is always greater than the man. The truth is always mightier than the bearer. Paul was quite certain that the Roman government might imprison him but could never find a prison whose bars and fetters could contain and restrain the word of God. One of the facts of history is the irresistible might of the word of God. If human effort could have obliterated Christianity, Christianity would have perished long ago. Men cannot kill that which is immortal.

(ii) Paul was certain that what he was going through would in the end be a help to other people. His suffering was not pointless and profitless. The fact that he was suffering would make it possible for others to believe. The blood of the martyrs has ever been the seed of the Church; and the lighting of the pyre where the Christians were burned has always been the lighting and relighting of a fire which can never be put out. When anyone has to suffer for his Christianity, let him remember that his suffering makes the road easier for someone else who is still to come. In suffering we bear our own small portion of the weight of the Cross of Christ, and we do our own small part in the bringing of God's salvation to men.

THE SONG OF THE MARTYR

1 *Timothy* 2: 11-13

> This is a saying which can be relied upon:
>> If we die with Him,
>>> We shall also live with Him.
>> If we endure,
>>> We shall also reign with Him.
>> If we deny Him,
>>> He too will deny us.
>> If we are faithless,
>>> He remains faithful
>> For He cannot deny Himself.

THIS is a peculiarly precious passage because in it there is enshrined one of the first hymns of the Christian Church. In the days of persecution the Christian Church put its faith into song. It may be that this is only a fragment of a longer hymn. *Polycarp* (5: 2) seems to give us a little more of it, when he writes: " If we please Christ in the present world, we shall inherit the world to come; as He has promised to raise us from the dead, and has said:

> ' If we walk worthily of Him,
>> So shall we reign with Him '."

There are two possible interpretations of the first two lines—" If we die with Him, we shall also live with Him." There are those who wish to take these lines as a reference to baptism. In *Romans* 6 baptism is likened to dying and rising with Christ. " Therefore we are buried with Him by baptism into death: that like as Christ was raised up from the dead by the glory of the Father, even so we also should walk in newness of life." " Now if we be dead with Christ, we believe that we shall also live with Him " (*Romans* 6: 4, 8). No doubt the language is the same; but the thought of baptism is quite irrelevant here; it is the thought of martyrdom that is in Paul's mind. Luther, in a great phrase, said: " *Ecclesia haeres crucis est*," " The Church is the heir of the Cross." The Christian inherits Christ's Cross, but he also inherits Christ's Resurrection.

The Christian is the partner both in the shame and in the glory of his Lord.

So the hymn goes on: " If we endure, we shall also reign with Him." It is he who endures to the end who will be saved. Without the Cross there cannot be the Crown.

Then there comes the other side of the matter: " If we deny Him, He too will deny us." That is what Jesus Himself said: " Whosoever shall confess me before men, him will I confess also before my Father who is in heaven. But whosoever shall deny me before men, him will I also deny before my Father who is in heaven " (*Matthew* 10: 32, 33). Jesus Christ cannot vouch in eternity for a man who has refused to have anything to do with Him in time; but Jesus Christ is for ever true to the man who, however much he has failed, has tried to be true to Him.

These things are true because they are part of the very nature of God. A man may deny himself, but God cannot deny Himself. " God is not a man that He should lie, neither the son of man that He should repent" (*Numbers* 23: 19). It is the great fact of life that God will never fail the man who has tried to be true to Him, but not even God can help the man who has refused to have anything to do with God.

Long ago Tertullian said: " The man who is afraid to suffer cannot belong to Him who suffered " (Tertullian, *De Fuga*, 14). Jesus died to be true to the will of God; and the Christian also must follow that same will of God, whatever light may shine or shadow fall.

THE DANGER OF WORDS

2 *Timothy* 2: 14

> Remind your people of these things; and charge them before the Lord not to engage in battles of words—a thing of no use at all, and a thing which can only result in the undoing of those who listen to it.

HERE once again Paul returns to the inadequacy of words. We must remember that the Pastoral Epistles were written against a background of those Gnostics who talked and speculated and produced their long words and their fantastic theories, and who tried to make Christianity into a recondite philosophy instead of an adventure of faith.

There is both a fascination and a peril in words. Words can become a substitute for deeds. There are people who are more concerned to talk about things than to do things. If the world could have been saved by talking, it would have been saved long before now; and if the world's problems could have been solved by discussion, they would have been solved long ago. But words cannot replace deeds. As Charles Kingsley wrote in *A Farewell*:

> " Be good, sweet maid, and let who can be clever;
>   Do lovely things, not dream them, all day long."

As Philip James Bailey wrote in *Festus*:

> " We live in deeds, not years, in thoughts, not breaths;
>   In feelings, not in figures on a dial.
>   We should count time by heart-throbs. He most lives
>   Who thinks most—feels the noblest—acts the best."

Dr. Johnson was one of the great talkers of all time; John Wesley was one of the great men of action of all time. They knew each other, and Johnson had only one complaint about Wesley: " John Wesley's conversation is good, but he is never at leisure. He is always obliged to go at a certain hour. This is very disagreeable to a man who loves to fold his legs and have his talk out, as I do." But the fact remains that Wesley, the man of action, wrote his name across England in a way in which Johnson, the man of talk, never did.

It is not even true that talk and discussion fully solve intellectual problems. One of the most suggestive things that Jesus ever said was: " If any man will do His will, he shall know of the doctrine " (*John* 7: 17). Often understanding comes not by talking, but by doing. In the old

Latin phrase, *solvitur ambulando*, the thing will solve itself as you go on. It often happens that the best way to understand the deep things of Christianity is to embark on the unmistakable duties of the Christian life.

There remains one further thing to be said. There are times when too much talk can be positively dangerous. Too much talk and too much discussion can have two dangerous effects. First, they may give the impression that Christianity is nothing but a collection of questions for discussion and problems for solution. The discussion circle is a characteristic phenomenon of this age. As G. K. Chesterton once said: "We have asked all the questions which can be asked. It is time we stopped looking for questions, and started looking for answers." In any society the discussion circle must be balanced by the action group. Second, discussion can be stimulating and invigorating for those whose approach to the Christian faith is intellectual, for those who have a background of knowledge and of culture, for those who are characteristically students, for those who have a real knowledge of, or interest in, theology. But it sometimes happens that a simple-minded person finds himself in a group which is tossing heresies about, and propounding unanswerable questions, and it may well be that the faith of that simple person, so far from being helped, is upset. It may well be that that is what Paul means when he says that wordy battles can undo those who listen to them. The normal word which is used for building a person up in the Christian faith, for *edification*, is the same word as is used for literally *building a house*; the word which Paul uses here for ruin (*katastrophē*) is the word which might well be used for the *demolition* of a house. And it may well happen that clever, subtle, speculative, destructive, intellectually reckless discussion may have the effect of demolishing, and not building up, the faith of some simple person who happens to become involved in it. As in all things, there is a time to discuss, and a time to be silent.

THE WAY OF TRUTH AND THE WAY OF ERROR

2 Timothy 2: 15-18

> Put out every effort to present yourself to God as one who has stood the test, as a workman who has no need to be ashamed, as one who rightly handles the word of truth.
>
> Avoid these godless chatterings, for the people who engage in them only progress further and further into ungodliness, and their talk eats its way into the Church like an ulcerous gangrene.
>
> Amongst such people are Hymenaeus and Philetus, who, as far as the truth is concerned, have lost the way, when they say that the resurrection has already happened, and who by such statements are upsetting the faith of some.

PAUL urges Timothy to present himself, amidst the false teachers, as a real teacher of the truth. The word which Paul uses for *to present* is the Greek word *parastēsai*, which characteristically means *to present oneself for service*. The following words and phrases all develop this idea of usefulness for and in service.

The Greek word for *one who has stood the test* is *dokimos*. *Dokimos* describes anything which has been tested and purified and which is fit for service. For instance, it describes gold or silver which has been purified and cleansed of all alloy in the fire. It is therefore the word for money which is genuine, or, as we would say, *sterling*. It is the word used for a stone which has been cut and tested and is fit to be fitted into its place in a building. A stone with a flaw in it was marked with a capital A, which stands for the Greek word *adokimastos*, which means *tested and found wanting*. So Timothy was to be purified and tested that he might be a fit weapon for the work of Christ, and therefore a workman who had no need to be ashamed.

Further, Timothy is urged in a famous phrase *rightly to divide* the word of truth. The Greek word which is translated *to divide rightly* is an interesting word. It is the word *orthotomein*, which literally means *to cut rightly*. It has many pictures in it. Calvin connected it with a father dividing out the food at a meal, and cutting it up so that each member of the family received the right and necessary and fitting portion. Beza connected it with the cutting up of sacrificial victims so that each part of the victim was correctly apportioned to the altar or to the priest. The Greeks themselves used the word, or the phrase, in three different connections. They used it for driving a straight road across country; they used it for ploughing a straight furrow across a field; they used it for the work of a mason in cutting and squaring a stone so that it fitted into its correct place in the structure of the building. So the man who rightly divides, rightly handles, the word of truth, drives a straight road through the truth and refuses to be lured down pleasant but irrelevant bypaths; he ploughs a straight furrow across the field of truth; he takes each section of the truth, and fits it into its correct position, as a mason does a stone, allowing no part to usurp an undue place or an undue emphasis, and so to knock the whole structure of truth out of balance.

On the other hand the false teacher engages on what Paul would call " godless chatterings." And then Paul uses a vivid phrase. The Greeks had a favourite word for making progress (*prokoptein*). It literally means *to cut down in front*; it means to remove the obstacles from a road so that straight and uninterrupted progress is possible. Paul says of these senseless talkers that they progress further and further into ungodliness. Their progress is progress in reverse. The more they talk, the farther they get from God. Here then is the test. If at the end of our talk and discussion, we are closer to one another and closer to God, then all is well. But if at the end of our discussion, we have erected barriers between each other and we have left God more distant and our view of Him befogged, then all is wrong. The aim of all Christian discussion and of all Christian action is to bring a man nearer to God.

THE LOST RESURRECTION

2 *Timothy* 2: 15-18 (*continued*)

AMONGST the false teachers Paul numbers especially Hymenaeus and Philetus. Who these men were we do not know. But we get a brief glimpse of their teaching in at least one of its aspects. They said that the resurrection had already happened. This of course does not refer to the Resurrection of Jesus; it refers to the resurrection of the Christian after death. We do know two false views of the resurrection of the Christian which had some influence in the early Church.

(i) It was claimed that the real resurrection of the Christian took place at baptism. It is true that in *Romans* 6 Paul had written vividly about how the Christian dies in the moment of baptism and rises to life anew. There were those who taught that the resurrection happened in that moment of baptism, and that it was resurrection to new life in Christ here and now, and not after death.

(ii) There were those who taught that the meaning of individual resurrection was nothing more than that a man lived on in his children, that he found his resurrection, his continuing life in the children who, as it were, carried on his life, and who came after him.

The trouble was that this kind of teaching found an answer and an echo in both the Jewish and the Greek side of the Church. On the Jewish side, the Pharisees did believe in the resurrection of the body, but the Sadducees did not. Any teaching which did away with the conception of life after death would have appealed to the Sadducees, and would have suited their beliefs. The trouble with the Pharisees was that they were wealthy, aristocratic materialists, who had so big a stake and so big an interest in this world that they were not interested in any world to come.

On the Greek side, the trouble was much more difficult In the early days of Christianity the Greeks, generally speaking, did believe in immortality, but they did not believe in the resurrection of the body. The highest belief was that of the Stoics. The Stoics believed that God was what might be called fiery spirit. The life in man was a spark of that fire spirit, a spark of God Himself, a *scintilla* of deity. But they believed that when a man died that spark went back to God and was reabsorbed in God. That is a noble belief but it clearly abolishes *personal* survival after death. Further, the Greeks believed that the body was entirely evil. They had their play on words as a watchword: "*Sōma Sēma*," "The body is a tomb." The last thing they desired or believed in was the resurrection of the body; and therefore they too were open to receive any teaching about the resurrection of each man which fitted their beliefs.

It is obvious that the Christian does not believe in the resurrection of *this* body. No one could conceive of someone smashed in an accident or dying of cancer reawakening in heaven with the same body; but the Christian does believe with all his heart in the survival of personal identity; he believes most strenuously that after death you will still be you and I will still be I. And any teaching which removes that certainty of the personal survival of each individual man strikes at the very root of Christian belief.

When Hymenaeus and Philetus and their like taught that the resurrection had already happened, either at the moment of baptism, or in a man's children, they were teaching something which Sadducean Jews and philosophic Greeks would be by no means averse to accepting; but they were also teaching something which undermined one of the central and essential beliefs of the Christian faith.

THE FIRM FOUNDATION

2 *Timothy* 2: 19

But the firm foundation of God stands fast with this inscription: " The Lord knows those who are His," and, " Let every one who names the name of the Lord depart from unrighteousness."

IN English we use the word *foundation* in a double sense. We use it to mean the basis on which a building is erected; and we also use it in the sense of an association, a society, a college, a city which has been *founded* by someone. We talk about the *foundation* of a house; and we also say that King's College, Cambridge, is a *foundation* of Henry the Sixth. Greek used the word *themelios* in the same two ways; and the *foundation* of God here means the Church. The Church is the society, the association which God has founded; the Church is God's foundation.

Paul goes on to say that the Church has a certain *inscription* on it. The word he uses is *sphragis*. The usual meaning of *sphragis* is *seal*. The *sphragis* is the seal which proves genuineness or ownership. The seal on a sack of goods proved that the contents were genuine and had not been interfered with; and it also indicated the ownership and the source of the goods. But *sphragis* had other uses. It was used to denote the *brandmark*, what we would call the *trademark*. Galen, the Greek doctor, speaks of the *sphragis* on a certain phial of eyesalve, meaning the mark or sign which showed what brand of eyesalve the phial contained. Still further, the *sphragis* was the *architect's mark* on a building. Always on a monument or a statue or a building the architect put his mark, to show that he was responsible for its design and for its erection. The *sphragis* can also be the sign or inscription which indicates the purpose for which a building has been built and exists.

The Church has a *sphragis*, a seal, an inscription which shows at once what it is and what it is designed to be. The sign on the Church Paul gives in two quotations. But the way in which these two quotations are made is very illuminating in regard to the way in which Paul and the preachers and thinkers of the early Church used scripture. The two quotations are: " The Lord knows those who are His," and "Let every one who names the name of the Lord depart from unrighteousness." The interesting thing is that neither of these sentences is a literal and an accurate quotation from any part of scripture. The first—"The Lord knows those who are His"—is a reminiscence of a saying of Moses to the rebellious friends and associates of Korah in the wilderness days. When they gathered themselves together against Moses, Moses said: "The Lord will show who are His" (*Numbers* 16: 5). But that Old Testament text was read and listened to and heard in the light and sound of the saying of Jesus in *Matthew* 7: 22: "Many will say to me in that day, 'Lord, Lord have we not prophesied in Thy name? and in Thy name have cast out devils? and in Thy name done many wonderful works?' And then will I profess unto them, I never knew you: depart from me ye that work iniquity." The Old Testament text is, as it were, retranslated into the words of Jesus. The second—"Let every one who names the name of the Lord depart from iniquity "— is another reminiscence of the Korah story. It was Moses' command to the people: "Depart, I pray you, from the tents of these wicked men, and touch nothing of theirs" (*Numbers* 16: 26). But that Old Testament text is again read in the light of the words of Jesus in *Luke* 13: 27, where Jesus says to those who falsely claim to be His followers: "Depart from me, all ye workers of iniquity." The interesting thing is twofold; it is that the New Testament writers always read the Old Testament in the light of the New Testament, and especially in the light of the words of Jesus; and that they were not interested in verdal accuracies and verbal niceties, but that to any problem they brought the general sense of the whole range of scripture. And these two principles are still excellent principles, in the light of which to read and to use scripture.

The two texts give us two broad principles about the Church.

The first one tells us that the Church consists of those who belong to God, of those who have given themselves to God in such a way that they no longer possess themselves, and the world no longer possesses them, but God possesses them. The Church consists of those who have given themselves to God to do with as He likes.

The second one tells us that the Church consists of those who have departed from unrighteousness. That is not to say that the Church consists of perfect people. If that were so, there would be no Church. It has been said that the great interest of God is not so much in where a man has reached as in the direction in which a man is facing. And the Church consists of those whose faces are turned to holiness and righteousness. They may often fail and they may often fall, and the goal may sometimes seem tragically and distressingly far away, but their faces are ever towards the goal and their desires are ever towards righteousness.

The Church consists of those who belong to God and of those who have dedicated themselves to the struggle for righteousness.

VESSELS OF HONOUR AND OF DISHONOUR

2 *Timothy* 2: 20, 21

> In any great house there are not only gold and silver vessels; there are also vessels of wood and earthenware. And some are put to a noble use and some to an ignoble use. If anyone purifies himself from these things, he will be a vessel fit to be put to a noble use, ready for any good work.

THE connection between this passage and the passage which immediately precedes it is very practical. Paul had just given a very great and high definition of the Church. The Church consists of those who belong to God, and of those who are on the way to righteousness. The obvious answer to that is: If that is so, how do you explain the existence of these chattering heretics in the Church? How do you explain the existence of Hymenaeus and Philetus in the Church? Paul's reply is that in any great house there are all kinds of vessels and utensils; there are things of precious metal and things of base metal; there are things which have a dishonourable use and things which have an honourable use. There are things of every kind. It must be so in the Church. So long as the Church is an earthly institution the Church must be a mixture. So long as the Church consists of men and women the Church must remain a cross-section of humanity. Just as it takes all kinds of people to make a world, so it takes all kinds of people to make a Church.

That is a practical truth which Jesus had stated long before this. He stated it in the Parable of the Wheat and the Tares (*Matthew* 13: 24-30, 36-43). The point of that parable is that the wheat and the tares grow together, and, in the early stages, the wheat and the tares are so like each other that it is impossible to separate them without uprooting the wheat as well as the tares. He stated it again in the Parable of the Drag-net (*Matthew* 13: 47, 48). The drag-net gathered *of every kind*. In both parables Jesus teaches that the Church is necessarily a mixture, that human judgment must be suspended, but that God's judgment is in the end certain, and in the end the necessary separations will be made.

Those who criticize the Church because there are imperfect and unsatisfactory people in it are criticizing the Church because it is composed of men and women. It is not given to us to judge; the judgment belongs to God.

But it is the duty of a Christian to keep himself free from all the polluting influences. And if he does, what is his reward? His reward is that he will be *used in service*. His reward is not special honour and special privilege and special exaltation; his reward is special service.

Here is the very essence of the Christian faith. A really good man does not regard his goodness as entitling him to special honour and special respect; his goodness does not make him stand on a little eminence and look down. If he is good, his one desire will be to have more and more work to do, for his work will be his greatest privilege. If he is good, the last thing he will do will be to seek to stand apart and aloof from and above his fellow men. He will rather seek to be down among them, at their worst, serving God by serving them. His glory will not be in exemption from service; his glory will be in a still harder and a still more demanding service from God. No Christian should ever think of fitting himself for honour; every Christian must always think of himself as fitting himself for service.

ADVICE TO A CHRISTIAN LEADER

2 *Timothy* 2: 22-26

> Flee from youthful passions; run in pursuit of righteousness in the company of those who call on the Lord from a clean conscience. Have nothing to do with foolish and stupid arguments, for you know that they only breed quarrels. The servant of the Lord must not fight, rather he must be kindly to all, apt to teach, forbearing, disciplining his opponents by gentleness. It may be that God will enable them to repent, so that they will come to know the truth, and so that they will escape from the snare of the devil, when they are captured alive by God's servant that they may do God's will.

HERE is a passage of most practical advice for the Christian leader and teacher.

He must flee from youthful lusts. Many commentators have made many suggestions as to what these youthful lusts and passions are. They are far more than the lusts and passions of the flesh. They include that *impatience*, which has never learned to hasten slowly, and which has still to discover that too much hurry can do far more harm than good; that *self-assertion*, which is intolerant in its opinions, and arrogant in its expression of them, and which has not yet learned to sympathize with and to see the good in points of view other than its own; that *love of disputation*, which tends to argue long and to act little, which is in love with mental acrobatics, and which will talk the night away and be left with nothing but a litter of unsolved problems; that *love of novelty*, which tends to condemn a thing simply because it is old, and to desire a thing simply because it is new, which underrates the value of experience, and brands as old-fashioned that in which a former generation believed. One thing is to be noted—the faults of youth are the faults of idealism. It is simply the newness and the freshness and the intensity of the vision which makes youth run into these mistakes. Such faults are not matters for austere condemnation, but for sympathetic correction, for every one of them is a fault which has a virtue hidden beneath it.

The Christian teacher and leader is to aim at *righteousness*, which means giving both to men and to God their due; at *faith*, which means loyalty and reliability which both come from trust in God; at *love*, which is the utter determination never to seek anything but the highest good of our fellow men, no matter what they do to us, and which has for ever put away all bitterness and all desire for vengeance and revenge; at *peace*, which is the right relationship of loving fellowship with God and with men. And all these things are to be sought *in the company of those who call upon the Lord*. The Christian must never seek to live alone, detached and aloof from his fellow men. He must find his strength, his joy, his support in the Christian fellowship. As John Wesley said: " A man must have friends or make friends; for no one ever went to heaven alone."

The Christian leader must not get involved in senseless controversies. It is precisely such arguments that are the curse of the Christian Church. The curse of the modern Church is that Christian arguments are usually doubly senseless, for they are seldom about the great matters of life and doctrine and faith, but almost always they are about little unimportant things like teacups and the like. Once a leader is involved in senseless and unchristian controversy he has forfeited all right to lead.

The Christian leader must be *kindly* to all; even when he has to criticize and point out a fault, it must be done with the gentleness which never seeks to hurt. He must be *apt to teach*; he must not only know the truth, but he must also be able to communicate the truth; and he will do that, not so much by talking about the truth, as by living in such a way that he shows men Christ. He must be *forbearing*; like his Master, if he is reviled, he must not revile again; he must be able to accept insult and injury, slights and humiliations as Jesus accepted them. There may be greater sins than touchiness, but there is none which does greater damage in the Christian Church. He must discipline his opponents in *gentleness*; his hand must be like the hand of a surgeon, unerring to find the diseased spot, yet never for a moment causing unnecessary pain. He must melt the frigidity of opposition with the warmth of love. He must love men, not batter men, into submission to the truth.

The last sentence of this passage is in very involved Greek, but it seems to be a hope that God will awaken repentance and the desire for the truth in the hearts of men, so that those who are caught in the snare and the trap of the devil may be rescued while their souls are still alive, and brought into obedience to the will of God, by the work of the servant of God. It is God who awakes the repentance; it is the Christian leader who opens the door of the Church to the penitent heart.

TIMES OF TERROR

2 Timothy 3: I

You must realize this—that in the last days difficult times will set in.

THE early Church lived in an age when the time was waxing late. They expected the Second Coming at any moment. Now Christianity was cradled in Judaism, and very naturally it thought very largely in Jewish terms and pictures. Jewish thought had one basic conception. The Jews divided all time into *this present age* and *the age to come*. This present age was altogether evil; and the age to come would be the golden age of God. In between the two ages there was *The Day of the Lord*. That day would be a day when God would definitely and personally intervene and would shatter the world in order to remake it. That Day of the Lord was to be preceded by a time of terror; a time when evil would gather itself for its last and final assault; a time when the world would be shaken to its moral and physical foundations. It is in terms of these last times that Paul is thinking in this passage.

He says that in these last days *difficult* times would set in. The word *difficult* is the Greek word *chalepos*. It is the normal Greek word for *difficult*, but it has certain usages which explain its meaning here. It is used in *Matthew* 8: 28 to describe the two Gergesene demoniacs who met Jesus among the tombs. They were violent and dangerous maniacs. It is used in Plutarch to describe what we would call an *ugly* wound. It is used by ancient writers on astrology to describe what we would call a *threatening* conjunction of the heavenly bodies. There is the idea of threat, of menace, of danger in it. In the last days there would come threatening times which would menace the very existence of the Christian Church and of goodness itself; there would come a kind of last tremendous assault of evil before its final defeat.

In the Jewish pictures of these last terrible times we get exactly the same kind of picture as we get here. There would come a kind of terrible flowering of evil, when the moral foundations seemed to be shaken. In the *Testament of Issachar*, one of the books written between the Old and the New Testaments, we get a picture like this:

> " Know ye, therefore, my children, that in the last
> times
> Your sons will forsake singleness
> And will cleave unto insatiable desire;
> And leaving guilelessness, will draw near to malice;
> And forsaking the commandments of the Lord,
> They will cleave unto Beliar.
> And leaving husbandry,
> They will follow after their own wicked devices,
> And they shall be dispersed among the Gentiles,
> And shall serve their enemies."
>
> *(Testament of Issachar, 6: 1, 2).*

In 2 *Baruch* we get an even more vivid picture of the
moral chaos of these last times:

> " And honour shall be turned into shame,
> And strength humiliated into contempt,
> And probity destroyed,
> And beauty shall become ugliness . . .
> And envy shall rise in those who had not thought
> aught of themselves,
> And passion shall seize him that is peaceful,
> And many shall be stirred up in anger to injure many,
> And they shall rouse up armies in order to shed
> blood,
> And in the end they shall perish together with them."
>
> *(2 Baruch 27).*

In this picture which Paul draws here he is thinking in
terms familiar to the Jews. If we may use a modern
colloquialism, there was to be a final show-down with
the forces of evil. As E. K. Simpson put it: " The world
will wax worldlier." As we often say, things had to become
a great deal worse before they could become better.

Nowadays we have to take and restate these old pictures
in modern terms. They were never meant to be anything
else but pictures and visions; we do violence to Jewish
and to early Christian thought if we take them with a
crude literalness. But they do enshrine this permanent
truth that some time there must come the consummation,
when evil meets God in a kind of head-on collision, and
when there comes the final triumph of God, which will

precede the day when the kingdoms of the world become
the Kingdom of God.

THE QUALITIES OF GODLESSNESS

2 Timothy 3: 2-5

> For men will live a life that is centred in self; they
> will be lovers of money, braggarts, arrogant, lovers
> of insult, disobedient to their parents, thankless,
> regardless even of the ultimate decencies of life,
> without human affection, implacable in hatred,
> revelling in slander, ungovernable in their passions,
> savage, not knowing what the love of good is, treacher-
> ous, headlong in word and action, inflated with pride,
> lovers of pleasure rather than lovers of God. They
> will maintain the outward form of religion, but they
> will deny its power. Avoid such people.

HERE is one of the most terrible pictures in the New
Testament of what a godless world would be like. Here
are the terrible qualities of godlessness set out in a ghastly
series. Let us look at them one by one.

It is no accident that the first of these qualities will
be *a life that is centred in self*. The adjective which is used
is *philautos*, which means *self-loving*. Love of self is the
basic sin, from which all other sins flow. The moment
a man makes his own will and his own desires the centre
of life, divine and human relationships are destroyed.
Once a man erects himself as his god, obedience to God
and charity to men both become impossible. If self is
the centre of life, then Christ is banished from life. The
essence of Christianity is not the enthronement, but the
obliteration of self. All sin begins in selfishness.

Men would become *lovers of money* (*philarguros*). We
must remember that Timothy's work lay in Ephesus.
Ephesus was perhaps the greatest market in the ancient
world. In those days trade tended to flow down river
valleys; Ephesus was at the mouth of the River Cayster,
and commanded the trade of one of the richest hinterlands
in all Asia Minor. At Ephesus some of the greatest roads

in the world met. There was the great trade route from the Euphrates valley which came by way of Colosse and Laodicaea and poured the wealth of the east into the lap of Ephesus. There was the road from north Asia Minor and from Galatia which came in via Sardis. There was the road from the south which centred the trade of the Maeander valley in Ephesus. Ephesus was called " The Treasure-house of the ancient world," " The Vanity Fair of Asia Minor." It has been pointed out that the John who wrote the *Revelation* may well have been thinking of Ephesus, when he wrote that haunting passage which describes the merchandise of men: " The merchandise of gold, and silver, and precious stones, and of pearls and fine linen and purple and silk and scarlet and all thyine wood and all manner of vessels of ivory, and all manner of vessels of most precious wood, and of brass and iron and marble and cinnamon and odours and ointments and frankincense and wine and oil and fine flour and wheat and beasts and sheep and horses and chariots and slaves and souls of men " (*Revelation* 18: 12, 13). Ephesus was the town of a prosperous, worldly, materialistic civilization; it was the kind of town where a man could so easily lose his soul. There is peril here. There is peril when men assess prosperity by material things, when civilization is assessed in terms of money and material goods. It is to be remembered that it is always true that a man may lose his soul far more easily in prosperity than in adversity; and he is on the way to losing his soul when he assesses the value of life by the number of things which he possesses.

THE QUALITIES OF GODLESSNESS
2 *Timothy* 3: 2-5 (*continued*)

IN these terrible days men would be *braggarts* and *arrogant*. In Greek writings these two words often went together; and they are both picturesque words.

The word *braggart* has an interesting derivation. It is the word *alazōn*, and it was derived from the word *alē*, which means *a wandering about*. Originally the *alazōn* was a wandering quack or mountebank. Plutarch uses the word to describe a quack doctor. The *alazōn* was one of these quacks and cheapjacks who wandered the country with medicines and spells and methods of exorcism which, they claimed, were panaceas and cure-alls for all diseases. We can still see these kind of men in fairs and market-places shouting the virtues of a patent medicine or pill or powder which will act like magic. Then the word went on to widen its meaning until it meant any *braggart* or *boaster*. The Greek moralists wrote much about this word. The Platonic Definitions defined the corresponding noun (*alazoneia*) as: " The claim to good things which a man does not really possess." Aristotle (*Nicomachean Ethics*, 7: 2) defined the *alazōn* as " the man who pretends to creditable qualities that he does not possess, or possesses in a lesser degree than he makes out." Xenophon tells us how Cyrus, the Persian king, defined the *alazōn*: " The name *alazōn* seems to apply to those who pretend that they are richer than they are or braver than they are, and to those who promise to do what they cannot do, and that, too, when it is evident that they do this only for the sake of getting something or making some gain " (Xenophon, *Cyropoedia*, 2, 2, 12). Xenophon in the *Memorabilia* tells how Socrates utterly condemned such imposters. Socrates said that they were to be found in every walk of life, but they were worst of all in politics. " Much the greatest rogue of all is the man who has gulled his city into the belief that he is fit to direct it." The world is full of these braggarts to this day; the clever know-alls who deceive people into thinking that they are wise; the politicians who claim that their parties have a programme which will bring in the Utopia and that they alone are born to be leaders of men; the people who crowd the advertisement columns with claims to give beauty, knowledge, health by their system; the people in the Church who have a kind of swaggering and ostentatious goodness. The trouble is that in any competitive society there will be these braggarts whose one desire is to stand out amongst their fellow men, by fair means or by foul.

Closely allied with the *braggart*, but—as we shall see —even worse is the man who is *arrogant*. The word is *huperēphanos*. It is derived from two Greek words which mean *to show oneself above*. The man who is *huperēphanos*, said Theophrastus, has a kind of contempt for everyone except himself. He is the man who is guilty of the " sin of the high heart." He is the man whom God resists, for it is repeatedly said in scripture, that God receives the humble, but he resists the man who is proud, *huperēphanos* (*James* 4: 6; I *Peter* 5: 5; *Proverbs* 3: 24). Theophylact called this kind of pride *akropolis kakōn*, the citadel of evils, the peak of evils.

The difference between the braggart and the man who is arrogant is this. The braggart is a swaggering creature, who shouts his claims to the four winds of heaven, and tries to boast and bluster his way into power and eminence. No one can possibly mistake him or fail to see him. But the sin of the man who is *arrogant*, in this sense, is in his heart. He might even seem to be humble; he might even seem to be quiet and inoffensive; but in his secret heart there is this contempt for everyone else. He nourishes an all-consuming, all-pervading pride. In his heart there is a little altar where he bows down before himself, and in his eyes there is something which looks at all men with a silent contempt.

THE QUALITIES OF GODLESSNESS

2 *Timothy* 3: 2-5 (*continued*)

THESE twin qualities of the braggart and the arrogant man inevitably result in *love of insult* (*blasphēmia*). *Blas-*

phēmia is the word which is transliterated into English
as *blasphemy*; in English we usually associate that word
with insult against God; but in Greek it means insult
against man and God alike. Pride always begets insult. It
begets disobedience to and disregard of God, in the pride
that thinks that it does not need God and that it knows
better than God. It begets contempt of men, a contempt
which can issue in hurting actions and in wounding words.
The Jewish Rabbis ranked high in the list of sins what
they called *the sin of insult*. The insult which comes
from anger is bad, but it is forgivable, for it is launched
in the heat of the moment; but the cold insult which comes
from arrogant and contemptuous pride is an ugly and an
unforgivable thing.

Men will be *disobedient to their parents*. The ancient
world set duty to parents very high. The oldest Greek
laws disfranchised the man who struck his parents; to
strike a father was in Roman law as bad as murder; in
the Jewish law honour for father and mother comes high
in the list of the Ten Commandments. It is the sign of
a supremely decadent civilization when youth loses all
respect for age, and fails to recognize the unpayable debt
and the basic duty it owes to those who gave it life.

Men will be *thankless* (*acharistos*). They will refuse to
recognize the debt they owe both to God and to men.
The strange characteristic of ingratitude is that it is the
most hurting of all sins, because it is the blindest of all
sins. Lear's words remain true:

" How sharper than a serpent's tooth it is
   To have a thankless child! "

It is the sign of a man of honour that he pays his debts;
and for every man there is a debt to God, and there are
debts to his fellow men, which as a man of honour he must
remember and repay.

Men will *refuse to recognize even the ultimate decencies
of life*. The Greek word is that men will become *anosios*.
Anosios does not so much mean that men will break the

written laws; it means that they will offend against the unwritten laws, which are part and parcel of the very essence of life. To the Greek it was *anosios* to refuse burial to the dead; it was *anosios* for a brother to marry a sister, or a son a mother. The man who is *anosios* offends against the fundamental decencies of life. Such offence can happen yet, and does happen yet. The man who is mastered by his lower passions will gratify them in the most shameless way, as the streets of any great city will show when the night is late. The man who has exhausted the normal pleasures of life, and who is still unsated, will seek his thrill in the pleasures which are abnormal and which are shame even to name. Once again, in a decadent and debased civilization, the ultimate decencies can be forgotten.

Men will be *without human affection* (*astorgos*). The Greek word *storgē* is the word which is used especially of *family love*, the love of child for parent and parent for child. If there is no human affection then the family cannot exist. In the terrible times men will be so set on self that even the closest ties will be nothing to them. In their selfish quest for the pleasures of life they will refuse to acknowledge even the fundamental duties and ties upon which life is built.

Men will be *implacable in their hatreds* (*aspondos*). *Spondē* is the word for a truce, a treaty or an agreement. *Aspondos* can mean two things. It can mean that a man is so bitter and truculent and unappeasable in his hatred that he will never come to terms with the man with whom he has quarrelled. Or it can mean that a man is so dishonourable that he breaks and disregards the terms of the agreements that he has made. In either case the word describes a certain harshness and hardness of mind which separates a man from his fellow men in unrelenting bitterness. It may be that, since we are only human, we cannot live entirely without differences with our fellow men, but to perpetuate these differences is one of the worst—and also one of the commonest—of all sins. When we are tempted

to do so we should hear again the voice of our blessed
Lord saying, even on the Cross: " Father, forgive them."

THE QUALITIES OF GODLESSNESS

2 *Timothy* 3: 2-5 (*continued*)

IN these terrible days men will be *slanderers*. The Greek
word for *slanderer* is *diabolos* which is precisely the English
word *devil*. The devil is the patron saint of all slanderers,
and of all slanderers he is chief. There is a sense in which
slander is the most cruel of all sins. If a man's goods
are stolen, he can set to and build up his fortunes again;
but if a man's good name is taken away, irreparable
damage has been done to him. It is one thing to start
an evil and untrue report on its malicious way; it is
entirely another thing to stop it. As Shakespeare had it:

" Good name in man and woman, dear my lord,
　Is the immediate jewel of their souls;
　Who steals my purse steals trash; 'tis something,
　　　nothing;
　'Twas mine, 'tis his, and has been slave to thousands;
　But he that filches from me my good name
　Robs me of that which not enriches him,
　And makes me poor indeed."

Many a man, and many a woman, who would never dream
of putting his or her hand in other peoples' pockets
and stealing their money or their belongings, thinks nothing
—even finds a pleasure—in passing on a story which ruins
someone else's good name, without even trying to find
out whether or not the story is true. There is slander
enough in every village, and not infrequently in many a
Church, to make the recording angel weep as he records
these cruel words.

Men will be *ungovernable in their desires* (*akratēs*). The
Greek verb *kratein* means *to control*, to have power over.
A man can reach a stage when, so far from controlling it,
he can become a slave to some habit or desire. That way

is the inevitable way to ruin, for no man can master anything unless he first masters himself.

Men will be *savage*. The word is *anēmeros*, and it is a
word which would be more fittingly applied to a wild beast
than to a human being. It denotes a savagery which
has neither sensitiveness nor sympathy. Men can be
savage in rebuke; men can be savage in pitiless action.
Even a dog is sorry when he has hurt his master, but
there are people who, in their treatment of others, can
be lost to human sympathy and feeling.

THE QUALITIES OF GODLESSNESS

2 Timothy 3: 2-5 (continued)

IN these last terrible days men will come *to have no love
for good things or good persons* (*aphilagathos*). There can
come a time in a man's life when the company of good
people and the presence of good things is to him simply
an embarrassment. He finds that he has nothing to say
to them. The devotee of cheap music has no pleasure in
listening to good music. He who feeds his mind on cheap
literature can in the end find nothing in the great master-
pieces. His mental palate loses its taste. A man has sunk
very far when he finds the company, the conversation,
even the presence of good people something which he
would only wish to avoid.

Men will be *treacherous*. The Greek word (*prodotēs*)
means nothing less than a *traitor*. We must remember
when this was written. It was written just at the beginning
of the years of persecution, just at the beginning of the
time when it was becoming a crime to be a Christian.
At this particular time in other things than Christianity,
in the ordinary matters of politics, one of the curses of
Rome was the existence of *informers* (*delatores*). Things
were so bad that Tacitus could say: " He who had no
foe was betrayed by his friend." There were those who

would gratify an old grudge, and revenge themselves on an enemy by informing against him. What Paul is thinking of here is more than faithlessness in friendship—although that in all truth is wounding enough—he is thinking of those who to pay back an old score, to satisfy an old hatred, to gratify an old spite, to win a moment's cheap reward, would inform against the Christians to the Roman government.

Men would be *headlong* in words and action. The word is *propetēs*; it means reckless, precipitate. It describes the man who is swept on by passion and impulse and desire to such an extent that he is totally unable to think wisely and sensibly. Far more harm is done from want of thought than almost anything else. Many and many a time we would be saved from hurting ourselves and from wounding other people, if we would only stop to think.

Men will be *inflated with conceit* (*tetuphōmenos*). The word is almost exactly the English word *swelled-headed*. They will be bumptious, inflated with a sense of their own importance. There are still Church dignitaries whose main thought is their own dignity. The Christian is the follower and the disciple of Him who was meek and lowly in heart.

They will be *lovers of pleasure rather than lovers of God*. Here we come back to where we started; such men place their own wishes and desires in the centre of life. They worship self instead of God.

The final condemnation of these people is that they retain the outward form of religion, but they deny its power. That is to say, they recite the orthodox creeds, they go through the movements of a correct and dignified ritual and liturgy and worship; they maintain all the external forms of religion; but they know nothing of religion as a dynamic power which changes the lives of men. It is said that, after hearing an evangelical sermon, Lord Melbourne once remarked: " Things have come to a pretty pass when religion is allowed to invade the sphere of private life." It may well be that the greatest handicap to religion is not the scarlet sinner, but the sleek devotee of an unimpeachable orthodoxy and a dignified convention, who is horrified when it is suggested that real religion is a dynamic power which changes a man's personal life. No one need even approach Christianity unless he is prepared to undergo a personal revolution through the changing power of Jesus Christ.

SEDUCTION IN THE NAME OF RELIGION

2 *Timothy* 3: 6, 7

> For from among these there come those who enter into houses, and take captive foolish women, laden with sins and driven by varied desires, ready to listen to any teacher but never able to come to a knowledge of the truth.

THE Christian emancipation of women inevitably brought its problems. We have already seen how secluded the life of the respectable Greek woman was, how she was brought up under the strictest supervision, how she was not allowed " to see anything, to hear anything, or to ask any questions," how she never appeared, even on a shopping expedition alone on the streets, how she was never allowed even to appear at a public meeting. Inevitably Christianity changed all that, and inevitably a new set of problems arose. It was only to be expected, it could not have been otherwise, that there were certain women who did not know how to use their new emancipation and their new liberty. There were false teachers who were quick to take advantage of that.

Irenaeus draws a vivid picture of the methods of just such a teacher in his own day. True, Irenaeus is telling of something which happened later than this, but the wretched story would be the same (Irenaeus, *Against Heresies*, I, 13, 3). There was a certain heretic called

Marcus who dealt in magic and spells. " He devotes himself specially to women, and those such as are well-bred, and elegantly attired, and of great wealth." He tells such women that by his spells and his incantations he can enable them to prophesy. The woman protests that she has never done so, and that she cannot do so. He says: " Open thy mouth, speak whatsoever occurs to thee, and thou shalt prophesy." The woman, thrilled to the heart, does so, and is deluded into thinking that she can prophesy. " She then makes the effort to reward Marcus, not only by the gift of her possessions (in which way he has collected a very large fortune), but also by yielding up to him her person, desiring in every way to be united to him, that she may become altogether one with him." The technique would be the same in the days of Timothy as it was in the later days of Irenaeus.

There would be two ways in which these heretics in the days of Timothy could exert an evil influence. We must remember that they were Gnostics; and we must remember that the basic principle of Gnosticism was that spirit was altogether good and that matter was altogether evil. We have already seen that that teaching issued in one of two things. The Gnostic heretics taught, either, that, since matter is altogether evil, a rigid asceticism must be practised, and the body and all the things of the body must be as far as possible destroyed and eliminated, or, that, since the body is altogether evil, it does not matter what we do with it, and that therefore the desires of the body can be sated and indulged in to the limit because they do not matter. The Gnostic insinuators would teach these doctrines to impressionable women. The result would either be that the woman would break off all married relationships with her husband, in order to live the ascetic life, or that she would give the lower instincts full play, and abandon herself to promiscuous relationships with men. In either case the home and the family life would be destroyed.

It is still possible for a teacher or leader to gain an undue and an unhealthy influence over other people, especially when such people are impressionable and easily influenced and emotional and unstable. No teaching can ever be right which breaks through and interrupts the sacred ties of home and family life.

It is Paul's charge that such people are "willing to learn from anyone, and yet never able to come to a knowledge of the truth." E. F. Brown has pointed out the danger of what he calls "intellectual curiosity without moral earnestness." There is a type of person who is eager to discuss every new theory, who is always to be found deeply involved in the latest fashionable religious movement or society, but who is quite unwilling to accept the day-to-day discipline—and even drudgery—of living the Christian life. No amount of intellectual curiosity can ever take the place of moral earnestness. We are not meant to titillate our minds with the latest intellectual crazes; we are meant to purify and strengthen our lives in the moral battle to live the Christian life.

THE OPPONENTS OF GOD

2 *Timothy* 3: 8, 9

In the same way as Jannes and Jambres opposed Moses, so these also oppose the truth, men whose minds are corrupt, and whose faith is counterfeit. But they will not get much further, for their folly will be as clear to all as that of those ancient impostors.

IN the days between the Old and the New Testaments many Jewish books were written which expanded the Old Testament stories, and which added new material and new details to them. In certain of these books Jannes and Jambres figured largely. Jannes and Jambres were the names given to the court magicians of Pharaoh who opposed Moses and Aaron, when Moses was leading the children of Israel out of their slavery in Egypt. At first these magicians were able to match the wonders which Moses and Aaron did, but in the end they were defeated and discredited. In the Old Testament itself they are not named, but they are referred to in *Exodus* 7: 11; 8: 7; 9: 11. A whole collection of stories and legends gathered round their names. They were said to be the two servants who accompanied Balaam when he was disobedient to God (*Numbers* 22: 22); they were said to have been part of the great mixed multitude who accompanied the children of Israel out of Egypt (*Exodus* 12: 38); some said that they perished at the crossing of the Red Sea; other stories said that it was Jannes and Jambres who were behind the making of the golden calf and that they perished among those who were killed for that sin (*Exodus* 32: 28); still other stories said that in the end they became proselytes to Judaism. Amidst all the stories one fact stands out—Jannes and Jambres became legendary figures typifying all those who opposed and sought to frustrate the purposes of God, and the work of the true leaders of God.

The Christian leader will never lack his opponents. There will always be those who prefer their ideas to God's ideas. There will always be those who wish to exercise power and influence over people and who will stoop to any means to do so. There will always be those who have their own twisted ideas of the Christian faith, and who wish to win others to their mistaken beliefs. But of one thing Paul was sure—the days of the deceivers were numbered. Their falsity would be demonstrated; and they would receive their own appropriate place and reward.

The history of the Christian Church teaches us one thing—falsity cannot live. It may flourish for a time, but when it is exposed to the light of truth it is bound to shrivel and die. There is only one test for falsity— " By their fruits ye shall know them." The best way to overcome and to banish the false is to live in such a

223

way that the beauty and the loveliness and the graciousness of the truth is plain for all to see. The defeat of error depends, not on skill in controversy, but in the demonstration in life of the more excellent way.

THE DUTIES AND THE QUALITIES OF AN APOSTLE

2 *Timothy* 3: 10-13

> But you have been my disciple in my teaching, my training, my aim in life, my faith, my patience, my love, my endurance, my persecutions, my sufferings, in what happened to me at Antioch, at Iconium, at Lystra, in the persecutions which I underwent; and the Lord rescued me from them all. And those who wish to live a godly life in Christ Jesus will be persecuted; while evil men and impostors will go from bad to worse, deceived themselves and deceiving others.

HERE Paul contrasts the conduct of Timothy, his loyal disciple, with the conduct of the heretics who were doing their utmost to wreck the Church. The word which we have translated *to be a disciple* is a word which includes so much that it is beyond translation in any single English word. It is the Greek word *parakolouthein*; it literally means *to follow alongside*; but in Greek it is used with a magnificent width of meaning. It means to follow a person *physically*, to stick by him through thick and thin, to be by his side in fair weather and in foul. It means to follow a person *mentally*, to attend diligently to his teaching, and fully to understand the meaning and the significance of what he says. It means to follow a person *spiritually*, not only to understand what he says, but also to carry out his ideas, and to be the kind of person that he wishes us to be. *Paraklouthein* is indeed the word for the disciple, for it includes the unwavering loyalty to the true comrade, the full understanding of the true scholar, and the complete obedience of the dedicated servant.

Then Paul goes on to list in a series the things in which Timothy has been his follower and his disciple; and the interest of that list is that it consists of the strands and threads out of which the life and the work of an apostle are woven. In it we find the *duties*, the *qualities*, and the *experiences* of an apostle.

First, then, there are the *duties* of an apostle. There is *teaching*. No man can teach what he does not know, and therefore before a man can teach Christ to others he must know Christ himself. When Carlyle's father was discussing the kind of minister his parish needed, he said: "What this parish needs is a man who knows Christ other than at secondhand." Real teaching is always born of real experience. There was *training*. The Christian life does not consist only in knowing something; it consists even more in being something. The task of the apostle is not only to tell men the truth; it is also to help men to do the truth. The training which the true leader gives is training in living and in life.

Second, there are the *qualities* of the apostle. First and foremost the apostle has an *aim in life*. Two men were talking of a great satirist who had been filled with moral earnestness. "He kicked the world about," said one, "as if it had been a football." "True," said the other, "but he kicked it to a goal." As individuals, we should sometimes pause and ask ourselves: what is our aim in life? Have we got one at all? As teachers we should sometimes ask ourselves: what am I trying to do with these people whom I teach? Once Agesilaus, the Sparta king, was asked, "What shall we teach our boys?" His answer was: "That which will be most useful to them when they are men." Is it knowledge, or is it life, that we are trying to transmit? As members of the Church, we should sometimes ask ourselves: what are we trying to do in the Church? It is not enough to be satisfied when a Church is humming like a dynamo, and when every night in the week has its own crowded organisation.

Sometimes we should be asking: what, if anything, is the unifying purpose which binds all this activity together? We must always remember that in all life there is nothing so creative of really productive effort as a clear consciousness of a purpose and a goal.

So Paul goes on to the other qualities of an apostle. There is *faith*, complete trust in God, complete belief that God's commands are binding and that God's promises are true. There is *patience*. The word here is *makrothumia*; and *makrothumia*, as the Greeks used it, usually meant *patience with people*. It is the ability not to lose patience when people are foolish, not to grow irritable when people seem unteachable. It is the ability to suffer fools gladly, to accept the folly, the perversity, the blindness, the ingratitude of men, and still to remain gracious, and still to toil on. There is *love*. Love is God's attitude to men. Love is the attitude to men which bears with everything that men can do, and which refuses to be either angry or embittered, and which will never seek anything but their highest good. To love men is to forgive them and to care for them as God forgave and God cares—and it is only God who can enable us to do that.

THE EXPERIENCES OF AN APOSTLE

2 Timothy 3: 10-13 (*continued*)

PAUL completes the story of the things in which Timothy has shared, and must share, with him, by speaking of the *experiences* of an apostle, and he prefaces that list of experiences by setting down the quality of *endurance*. The Greek word is *hupomonē*, which does not mean a passive sitting down and bearing things; it means a triumphant facing of things, so that out of even evil things there can come good. *Hupomonē* describes, not the spirit which *accepts* life, but the spirit which *masters* life.

And that quality of conquering endurance is necessary, because persecution is an essential part of the experience of an apostle. Paul cites three instances when he had to suffer things for Christ. He was driven from Antioch in Pisidia (*Acts* 13: 50); he had to flee from Iconium to avoid lynching (*Acts* 14: 5, 6); in Lystra he was stoned and left for dead (*Acts* 14: 19). It is true that these things happened before the young Timothy had definitely entered on the Christian way, but they all happened in the district of which Timothy was a native; and Timothy may well have been an eye-witness of them. It may well be a proof of Timothy's courage and consecration that he had seen very clearly what could and did happen to an apostle, and had yet not hesitated to cast in his lot with Paul.

It is Paul's conviction that the real follower of Christ, the man who sets out to live a godly life, cannot escape persecution. When trouble fell on the Thessalonians, Paul wrote to them: " When we were with you, we told you before that we should suffer tribulation; even as it came to pass, and ye know " (I *Thessalonians* 3: 4). It is as if he said to them: " You have been well warned." When Paul made his return journey after the first missionary journey, he visited the Churches he had founded, " confirming the souls of the disciples, and exhorting them to continue in the faith, and that we must through much tribulation enter into the kingdom of God " (*Acts* 14: 22). The Kingdom had its price. And Jesus Himself had said: " Blessed are they which are persecuted for righteousness' sake " (*Matthew* 5: 10). If anyone proposes to accept a set of standards which are quite different from the world's standards, then he is bound to encounter trouble. If anyone proposes to introduce into his life a loyalty which surpasses all earthly loyalties, then there are bound to be clashes and collisions. And that is precisely what Christianity demands that a man should do, and what the Christian pledges himself to do.

Persecution and difficulty and problems and hardships will come, but of two things Paul is sure.

He is sure that God will rescue the man who puts his faith in Him. He is sure that in the long run it is better to suffer with God and the right than to prosper with men and the wrong. Even if Paul is certain of the temporary persecution, he is equally certain of the ultimate glory.

He is sure that the evil and the ungodly man will go from bad to worse. To put it in modern language, Paul is very sure that there is literally no future for the man who refuses to accept the way of God.

THE VALUE OF SCRIPTURE

2 *Timothy* 3: 14-17

> But as for you, remain loyal to the things which you have learned, and in which your belief has been confirmed, for you know from whom you learned them, and you know that from childhood you have known the sacred writings which are able to give you the wisdom that will bring you salvation through the faith which is in Christ Jesus. All God-inspired scripture is useful for teaching, for the conviction of error, for correction, and for training in righteousness, that the man of God may be complete, fully equipped for every good work.

PAUL concludes this section with an appeal to Timothy to remain loyal to all the teaching which he had received. On his mother's side Timothy was a Jew, although his father had been a Greek (*Acts* 16: 1). And it is clear that it was his mother who had the bringing up of Timothy. It was the glory of the Jews that their children from their earliest days were taught and trained in the law. The Jews claimed that their children learned the law even from their swaddling clothes, and that they drank it in with their mother's milk. They claimed that the law was so imprinted on the heart and mind of a Jewish child that he would sooner forget his own name than he would forget the law. So from his earliest childhood Timothy had known the word of God. We must remember that the scripture of which Paul is writing is the Old Testament, for of course as yet the New Testament had not come into being. And if what Paul claims for scripture is true of the Old Testament, how much truer it is of the still more precious words of the New Testament.

We must note that Paul here makes a distinction. He speaks of " all God-inspired scripture." The Gnostics had their own fanciful and fantastic books; the heretics all produced their own literature to support and to expound their own claims; Paul regarded these things as man-made things. It is not books like that which help a man; the great books for a man's soul are the God-inspired books which time and tradition and the experience of men had consecrated and sanctified.

Let us then see what Paul says of the usefulness of scripture.

(i) Paul says that the Scriptures bring *the wisdom which will bring salvation*. A. M. Chirgwin in *The Bible in World Evangelism* tells the story of a Ward Sister in a children's hospital in England. She had been finding life, as she herself said, futile and meaningless. She had waded through book after book, and laboured with philosophy after philosophy in an attempt to find satisfaction. She had never even tried the Bible, for a friend had convinced her by subtle arguments that the Bible was not true, and could not be true. One day a visitor came to the ward and left a gift of a supply of gospels. The Sister was persuaded to take and to read a copy of *John*. "It shone and glowed with truth," she said, " and my whole being responded to it. The words that finally decided me were those in *John* 18: 37: ' To this end was I born and for this cause came I into the world, that I should bear witness unto the truth. Everyone that is of the truth heareth my voice.' So I listened to that voice, and heard the truth, and found my Saviour." Again and again Scripture has opened for men and women the way to God. In simple fairness no man who is seeking for the truth has any right to neglect the reading of the Bible. A book with a record such as the Bible has cannot be disregarded. Even an unbeliever is acting unfairly unless he tries to read it. The most amazing things may happen if he tries, for there is a saving wisdom there that is not in any other book.

(ii) The Scriptures are of use in *teaching*. It is the simple truth that only in the New Testament have we any picture of Jesus, any account of His life, and any record of His teaching. For that very reason it is unanswerable that, whatever a man might argue about the rest of the Bible, it is impossible for the Church ever to do without the Gospels. It is perfectly true—as we have so often and so emphatically said—that Christianity is not founded on a printed book, but on a living person, but the fact remains that the only place in all the world where we get a first-hand account of that person and of His teaching is in the New Testament. That is the reason why the Church which has no Bible Class is a Church in whose work an essential and irreplaceable element is missing.

(iii) The Scriptures are valuable for *reproof*. It is not meant that the Scriptures are valuable for *finding fault*; what is meant is that they are valuable for *conviction*, for convincing a man of the error of his ways, and for pointing him on the right way. A. M. Chirgwin has story after story of how the Scriptures came by chance into the hands of men and changed their lives. In Brazil Signor Antonio of Minas bought a New Testament which he took home to burn. He went home and found the fire was out. Deliberately he lit it. He flung the New Testament on it. It would not burn. He opened out the pages to make it burn more easily. It opened at the Sermon on the Mount. He glanced at it as he consigned it to the flames. His mind was caught; he took it back. " He read on, forgetful of time, through the hours of the night, and just as the dawn was breaking, he stood up and declared, ' I believe'."

Vincente Quiroga of Chile found a few pages of a book washed up on the seashore by a tidal wave following an earthquake. He read them. He never rested until he obtained the rest of the Bible. Not only did he become a Christian, but he even devoted the rest of his life to the distribution of the Scriptures in the forgotten villages of northern Chile.

A colporteur was caught one dark night by brigands in a forest in Sicily. He was held up at the point of the revolver. He was ordered to light a bonfire and to burn his books. He lit the fire, and then he asked if he might read a little from each book before he dropped it in the flames. He read the twenty-third psalm from one; the story of the Good Samaritan from another; from another the Sermon on the Mount; from another I *Corinthians* 13. At the end of each reading, the brigand said: "That's a good book; we won't burn that one; give it to me." In the end not a book was burned; the brigand left the colporteur and went off into the darkness with the books. Years later that same brigand turned up again. *This time he was a Christian minister*, and it was to the reading of the books that he attributed his change.

It is beyond doubt and beyond argument that the Scriptures can convict a man of his error, and convince him of the power of Christ.

(iv) The Scriptures are of use for *correction*. The real meaning of this is that all theories, all theologies, all ethical teaching, are to be tested against the teaching of the Bible. If they contradict the teaching of the Bible, they are to be refused. It is a bounden duty to use our minds; it is our responsibility to set them adventuring; speculation and thought is a Christian necessity. But the test must ever be agreement with the teaching of Jesus Christ as the Scriptures present it to us.

(v) But Paul makes one final point. The study of the Scriptures trains a man in righteousness until he is equipped for every good work. Here is the essential conclusion. The study of the Scriptures must never be selfish; it must never be simply for the good of a man's own soul. Any change, any conversion which makes a man think of nothing but of the fact that *he* has been saved is no true change and no true conversion. He must study the Scriptures to make himself useful to God and useful to his fellow men. He must study, not simply and solely to save his own soul, but that he may make himself such that God will use him to help to save the souls and comfort the lives of others. No man is saved unless he is on fire to save his fellow men.

PAUL'S GROUNDS OF APPEAL

2 Timothy 4: 1-6

> I charge you before God and Christ Jesus, who is going to judge the living and the dead—I charge you by His appearing and by His Kingdom—herald forth the word; be urgent in season and out of season; convict, rebuke, exhort, and do it all with a patience and a teaching which never fail. For there will come a time when men will refuse to listen to sound teaching, but, because they have ears which have to be continually titillated with novelties, they will bury themselves under a mound of teachers, whose teaching suits their own lusts after forbidden things. They will avert their ears from the truth, and they will turn to extravagant tales. As for you, be steady in all things; accept the suffering which will come upon you; do the work of an evangelist; leave no act of your service unfulfilled.

As Paul comes to the end of his letter, he wishes to nerve and to challenge Timothy to his task. To do so ne reminds him of three things concerning Jesus.

(i) Jesus is the judge of the living and the dead. Some day Timothy's work will be tested, and that test will be carried out by none other than Jesus Christ Himself. A Christian's work must be good enough, not to satisfy men, but to satisfy Jesus. He must do every task in such a way that he can take it and offer it to Christ. He is not concerned with either the criticism or the verdict of men. The one thing he covets is the " Well done! " of Jesus Christ. If we all within the Church and within the world did our work in that spirit, the difference in life would be incalculable. It would save us from the touchy spirit which is offended by the criticisms of men; it would save us from the self-important spirit which is concerned with matters of personal rights and personal prestige; it would save us from the self-centred spirit which demands thanks and praise from men for its every act; it would even save us from being hurt by the ingratitude of men. The Christian concentration is on Christ.

(ii) Jesus is the returning conqueror. " I charge you," says Paul, " by His *appearing*." The word he uses is *epiphaneia*. *Epiphaneia* is used in two special ways. It is used for the manifest intervention of some god. And it is specially used in connection with the Roman Emperor. His accession to the throne of the Empire was his *epiphaneia*; and in particular—and this is the background of Paul's thought here—it was used of a visit by the Emperor to any province or town. The Emperor's appearance in any place was his *epiphaneia*. Obviously when the Emperor was due to visit any place, everything was put in perfect order. The streets were swept and garnished; all work was up-to-date. The town was scoured and decorated to be fit for the *epiphaneia* of the Emperor. So Paul says to Timothy: " You know what happens when any town is expecting the *epiphaneia* of the Emperor; *you* are expecting the *epiphaneia* of Jesus Christ. Do your work in such a way that all things will be ready whenever He appears." The Christian so orders life that at any moment he is ready for the coming of Christ.

(iii) Jesus is King. Paul urges Timothy to action by the

remembrance of the Kingdom of Jesus Christ. The day comes when the kingdoms of the world will be the Kingdom of the Lord. In any kingdom the citizen who obeys the laws and honours the king himself walks in honour. So Paul says to Timothy: " So live and so work that you will rank high in the roll of citizens of the Kingdom when the Kingdom comes."

Here is our Christian motive for work and service. Our work must be such that it will stand the scrutiny of Christ. Our lives must be such that they will welcome the appearance of the King. Our service must be such that it will demonstrate the reality of our citizenship of the Kingdom of God.

THE CHRISTIAN'S DUTY

2 Timothy 4: 1-6 (*continued*)

THERE can be few New Testament passages where the duties of the Christian preacher and teacher and evangelist are more clearly set out than here.

The Christian teacher is to be *urgent*. The message he brings is literally a matter of life and death. The teacher and the preacher who really get their message across to people are those who have the tone of earnestness in their voice. Spurgeon had a real admiration for Martineau. Now Martineau was a Unitarian, and therefore denied the divinity of Jesus Christ, while Spurgeon believed in that divinity with a passionate intensity. And yet more than once Spurgeon expressed real admiration for Martineau. Someone said to Spurgeon: " How can you possibly say that you admire Martineau? You don't believe what he preaches." " No," said Spurgeon, " *but he does.*" Any man with the note of urgency in his voice demands, and will receive, a hearing from other men.

The Christian teacher is to be *persistent*. He is to urge the claims of Christ " in season and out of season." As someone has put it: " Take or make your opportunity."

As Theodore of Mospeuestia put it: " The Christian must count every time an opportunity to speak for Christ." It was said of George Morrison of Wellington Church in Glasgow that with him wherever the conversation started, it went straight across country to Christ. This does not mean that we will not choose our time to speak, for there is a courtesy in evangelism as there is in every other human contact; but it does mean that it may well be that we are far too shy in speaking to others about Jesus Christ.

Paul goes on to speak of the effect the Christian teacher and preacher and witness must produce.

He must *convict*. He must make the sinner aware of his sin. Walter Bagehot once said: " The road to perfection lies through a series of disgusts." Somehow or other the sinner must be made to feel disgusted with himself and his sin. Epictetus draws a contrast between the false philosopher, who is out for popularity, and the real philosopher, whose one aim is the good of his hearers. The false philosopher tells his hearer that he is a man of great ability, and sincerity, and genuineness. He deals in flattery; he panders to self-esteem. The invitation of the real philosopher is: " I invite you to come and be told that you are in a bad way—that you care for everything except what you should care for—that you do not know what things are good and what are evil—that you are unhappy and unfortunate." " The philosopher's lecture," he said, " is a surgery; when you go away you ought to have felt not pleasure, but pain." It was Alcibiades, the brilliant but spoiled darling of Athens, who used to say to Socrates: " Socrates, I hate you, because every time I meet you, you make me see what I am." The first essential is to compel a man to see himself as he is.

He must *rebuke*. In the great days of the Church there was an utter fearlessness in the voice of the Church. And because the Church was fearless things happened. E. F. Brown tells of an incident from India. There was a certain young nobleman in the Viceroy's suite in Calcutta who became notorious for his profligacy and bad habits. Bishop Wilson one day put on his robes, drove to Government House, and said to the Viceroy: "Your excellency, if Lord ——— does not leave Calcutta before next Sunday, I shall denounce him from the pulpit in the Cathedral." Before that Sunday came that young man was gone. Ambrose of Milan was one of the great figures of the early Church. He was an intimate friend of Theodosius, the Emperor, who was a Christian, but a man of violent and ungovernable temper. Ambrose never hesitated to tell the Emperor the truth. "Who," he demanded, "will dare to tell you the truth if a priest does not dare?" Theodosius had appointed one of his close friends, Botherich, as governor of Thessalonica. Botherich was a good governor. He had occasion to imprison a famous charioteer for infamous conduct. The popularity of these charioteers was incredible. The populace rose in a riot and murdered Botherich. Theodosius was mad with anger. Ambrose pled with him for discrimination in punishment, but Rufinus, his minister of state, still further deliberately inflamed his anger. Theodosius sent out orders for a massacre of vengeance in Thessalonica. Later he countermanded the order, but he countermanded it too late for the new order to reach Thessalonica in time. The theatre of Thessalonica was crammed to capacity; the doors were shut; and the soldiers of Theodosius went to and fro slaughtering men, women and children for three hours. More than seven thousand people were killed. News of the massacre came back to Milan. Theodosius presented himself at the Church service the next Sunday. Ambrose refused him admission. The Emperor pled for pardon. Eight months passed and again he came to Church. Again Ambrose refused him entry. In the end the Emperor of Rome had to lie prostrate on the ground with the penitents before he was allowed to worship with the Church again. In its great days the Church was fearless in rebuke.

In our personal relationships a word of warning and rebuke

would often save a brother from many a sin and many a shipwreck. But, as someone has said, that word must always be spoken as " brother setting brother right." It must be spoken with a consciousness of our common guilt. It is not our place to set ourselves up as the moral judge of anyone; nonetheless it is our duty to speak that warning word when it needs to be spoken.

He must *exhort*. Here is the other side of the matter. No rebuke, no conviction should ever be such that it drives a man to despair and takes the heart and the hope out of him. Not only must men be rebuked, they must also be encouraged. Encouragement is at least as much a Christian duty as rebuke.

Still further, the Christian duty of conviction, of rebuke, of encouragement, must be carried out with unwearied *patience*. The word is *makrothumia*, and it describes the spirit which never grows irritated, never grows annoyed, never grows weary, never despairs; it describes the spirit which never loses its faith in human nature, and never regards any man as hopeless and beyond salvation. The Christian patiently believes in men because he unconquerably believes in the changing power of Christ.

FOOLISH LISTENERS

2 Timothy 4: 1-6 (*continued*)

THEN Paul goes on to describe the foolish listeners. He warns Timothy that the day is coming when men will refuse to listen to sound teaching, and when they will collect teachers who will titillate their ears with their pleasant and flattering and novel teachings, and who will tell them precisely the easy-going, comfortable things which they want to hear.

In Timothy's day it was tragically easy to find such teachers. They were called *sophists*. They wandered from city to city, offering to teach anything for pay. Isocrates said of them: " They try to attract pupils by low fees and big promises." They were prepared to teach the whole of virtue for £15 or £20. They would teach a man to argue subtly and to use words cleverly until he could make the worse appear the better reason. Plato described them savagely: " Hunters after young men of wealth and position, with sham education as their bait, and a fee for their object, making money by a scientific use of quibbles in private conversation, while quite aware that what they are teaching is wrong."

They competed for customers. Dio Chrysostom wrote of them: " You might hear many poor wretches of sophists shouting and abusing one another, and their disciples, as they call them, squabbling, and many writers of books reading their stupid compositions, and many poets singing their poems, and many jugglers exhibiting their marvels, and many soothsayers giving the meaning of prodigies, and ten thousand rhetoricians twisting law-suits, and no small number of traders driving their several trades."

Men in the days of Timothy were beset by false teachers hawking round a sham knowledge. Their deliberate policy was to find arguments and teaching whereby a man could justify himself for doing what he wanted to do. Any teacher, to this day, whose teaching tends to make men think less of sin is a menace to Christianity and a menace to mankind.

In contradistinction to that, certain duties are to be laid on Timothy.

He is to be *steady in all things*. The word (*nēphein*) means that he is to be sober and self-contained, like an athlete who has his passions and his appetites and his nerves under self-control. Hort says that the word describes " a mental state free from all perturbations or stupefactions . . . every faculty at full command, to look all facts and all considerations deliberately in the face." The Christian is not the victim of crazes. Stability is the badge of the Christian in an unbalanced and often insane world.

238

He is to *accept whatever suffering comes upon him*. Christianity will cost something, and the Christian is to pay the price of it without grumbling and without regret.

He is to do *the work of an evangelist*. In spite of the conviction, the rebuke, the warning, the Christian is essentially *the bringer of good news*. If the Christian insists on discipline and self-denial, it is that an even greater happiness may be attained than ever the cheap pleasures of the world can bring.

He is to leave *no act of service unfulfilled*. The Christian has only one ambition—to be of use to the Church of which he is a part, and to the society in which he lives. The chance he dare not miss is not the chance of a cheap profit; it is the chance of being of service to his God, his Church and his fellow men.

PAUL COMES TO THE END

2 Timothy 4: 7, 8

> For my life has reached the point when it must be sacrificed, and the time of my departure has come. I have fought the good fight: I have completed the course: I have kept the faith. As for what remains, there is laid up for me the crown of righteousness which on that day the Lord, the righteous judge, will give to me—and not only to me, but also to all who have loved His appearing.

FOR Paul the end was very near now, and he knew it When Erasmus was growing old, he said: " I am a veteran, and have earned my discharge, and must leave the fighting to younger men." Paul, the aged warrior, is laying down his arms that Timothy may take them up.

There is no passage in the New Testament which is more full of vivid pictures than this passage is.

" My life," said Paul, " has reached the point where it must be sacrificed." The word that Paul here uses for *sacrifice* is the verb *spendesthai*. *Spendesthai* literally means *to pour out as a libation to the gods.* Every Roman meal ended with a kind of sacrifice. A cup of wine was taken and was poured out (*spendesthai*) to the gods. It is as if Paul said: " The day is ended; it is time to rise and go; and my life must be poured out as a sacrifice to God." Paul did not think of himself as going to be executed; he thought of himself as going to offer his life to God. His life was not being taken from him; he was laying it down. Ever since his conversion Paul had offered everything to God—his money, his scholarship, his strength, his time, the vigour of his body, the acuteness of his mind, the devotion of his passionate heart. Only life itself was left to offer, and gladly Paul was going to lay life down.

He goes on to say: " The time of my departure is at hand." The word he uses for departure is a vivid word; it is the word *analusis,* and it has many a picture in it, and each picture tells us something about leaving this life. (*a*) It is the word for unyoking an animal from the shafts of the cart or the plough. Death to Paul was rest from toil. He would be glad to lay the burden down. As Spenser had it, ease after toil, port after stormy seas, death after life, are lovely things. After life's fitful fever, he would sleep well. (*b*) It is the word for loosening bonds or fetters. Death for Paul was a liberation and a release. He was to exchange the confines of a Roman prison for the glorious liberty of the courts of heaven. (*c*) It is the word for loosening the ropes of a tent. For Paul it was time to strike camp again. Many a journey he had made across the roads of Asia Minor and of Europe. Now he was setting out on his last and his greatest journey; he was taking the road that led to God. (*d*) It is the word for loosening the mooring-ropes of a ship. Many a time Paul had sailed the Mediterranean, and had felt the ship leave the harbour for the deep waters. Now he is to launch out into the greatest deep of all; he is setting sail to cross the waters of death to arrive in the haven of eternity.

So then, for the Christian, death is laying down the burden

in order to rest. Death is laying aside the shackles in order to be free. Death is striking camp to take up residence in the heavenly places. Death is casting off the ropes which bind us to this world to set sail on the voyage which ends in the presence of God. Who then shall fear this death?

THE JOY OF THE WELL-FOUGHT CONTEST

2 Timothy 4: 7, 8 (continued)

So, then, Paul goes on, still speaking in these vivid pictures of which he was such a master: " I have fought the good fight: I have completed the race: I have kept the faith." It is likely that Paul here is not using three different pictures from three different spheres of life, but that he is using one picture from one sphere of life—from the games.

(i) First, he says: " I have fought the good fight." The word he uses for fight is *agōn*, which is the word for a contest in the arena. When an athlete can really say that he has done his best, when he comes off the field conscious that he has put his last ounce of energy into the contest, when it has been a good fight and a fair contest, then, win or lose, there is a deep satisfaction in his heart. Paul has come to the end, and he is quite certain that he has put up a good show. When Sir James Barrie's mother died, Barrie made a great claim. " I can look back," he said, " and I cannot see the smallest thing undone." There is no satisfaction in all the world like knowing that we have done our best.

(ii) Second, Paul says: " I have finished the race." That is precisely the difficulty in life. It is easy to begin; it is hard to finish. The one thing necessary for life is staying-power, and that is what so many people lack. It was suggested to a certain very famous man that his biography should be written while he was still alive. He absolutely refused to give permission, and his reason for his refusal was: " I have seen so many men fall out on the last lap." It is easy to wreck a noble life by some closing folly; it is easy to spoil a fine record, in our work both in the world and in the Church, by something which spoils it all. But it was Paul's claim that he had finished the race. There is a deep satisfaction in reaching the goal. Perhaps the world's most famous race is the Marathon race. The Battle of Marathon was one of the decisive battles of the world. In it the Greeks met the Persians, and, if the Persians had conquered, the glory that was Greece would never have flowered upon the world. Against fearful odds the Greeks won the victory, and, after the battle, a Greek soldier ran all the way day and night to Athens with the news. Straight to the magistrates of Athens he ran. " Rejoice," he gasped, " we have conquered," and even as he delivered his message he fell dead. He had completed his course and done his work, and there is no finer way for any man to die.

(iii) Third, Paul says: " I have kept the faith." This phrase can have more than one meaning and background. If we are to keep the background of the games, the background is this. The great games in Greece were the Olympic Games. To these games there came all the greatest athletes in the world. On the day before the games all the competitors met, and they took a solemn oath before the gods that they had done not less than ten months training, and that they would not resort to any trickery to win. They swore and pledged themselves to keep the rules of honour in their contest. So Paul may well be saying: " I have kept the rules: I have played the game." It would be a great thing to die knowing that we had never in our lives transgressed the rules of honour and of honesty in the race of life.

But we have said that this phrase may have other meanings. It is also a business phrase. It was the regular Greek phrase for: " I have kept the conditions of the contract; I have been true to my engagement." If Paul used it in that way, he meant that he had engaged himself to serve

Christ and he had stood by that engagement, and had never let his Master down. Still further, it could mean: " I have kept my faith: I have never lost my confidence and my hope." If Paul used it in that way, he meant that through thick and thin, in freedom and in imprisonment, in all his perils by land and sea, and now in the very face of death, he had never lost his perfect confidence and trust in Jesus Christ. Within his heart there was a hope which never flickered, but which burned throughout all life, and finally in face of death.

So, then, Paul goes on to say there is laid up for him the crown. In the games in Greece the greatest prize was the laurel wreath. With it the victor was crowned; and to wear it was the greatest honour which could come to any athlete. They strove for the crown which in a few short days would wither and shrivel, but Paul knew that there awaited him the crown which would never fade and never wither.

In this moment Paul is turning from the verdict of men to the verdict of God. Paul knew that in a very short time he would stand before the Roman judgement seat, and that his trial could only have one end. He knew what Nero's verdict would be, but he also knew what God's verdict would be. The man whose life is dedicated to Jesus Christ is indifferent to the verdict of men. He cares not if they condemn him so long as he hears his Master's " Well done! "

And then Paul sounds still another note—this crown awaits not only him; it awaits all those who wait with expectation for the coming of the King. It is as if Paul said to the young Timothy: " Timothy, my end is near: and I know that I go to my reward. If you follow in my steps, you will feel the same confidence and the same joy when the end comes to you." The joy of Paul is open to every man who fights the same fight, who also finishes the race, and who also keeps the faith.

A ROLL OF HONOUR AND DISHONOUR

2 *Timothy* 4: 9-15

> Do your best to come and see me soon. Demas has deserted me, because he loved this present world, and has gone to Thessalonica. Crescens has gone to Galatia, Titus to Dalmatia. Luke alone is with me. Take Mark and bring him with you, for he is very useful in service. I have sent Tychichus to Ephesus.
>
> When you come bring with you the cloak which I left behind at Troas at Carpus' house, and bring the books, especially the parchments.
>
> Alexander, the coppersmith, did me a great deal of harm. The Lord will reward him according to his deeds. You yourself must be on your guard against him, for he hotly opposed our words.

HERE Paul draws up a kind of roll of honour and roll of dishonour of his friends. Some of them are only names to us. Of some, as we read the *Acts* and the *Epistles*, we get little revealing glimpses. Some of the stories, if we are allowed to use our imagination, we can reconstruct. Let us then look at some of the men on this list.

THE SPIRITUAL PILGRIMAGE OF DEMAS

First on the list there comes Demas. There are three mentions of Demas in Paul's letters; and it may well be that the three references have in them the story of a tragedy. (i) In *Philemon* 24 Demas is listed amongst a group of men whom Paul calls his *fellow-labourers*. (ii) In *Colossians* 4: 14 Demas is mentioned without any comment at all. (iii) Here Demas is Demas who has forsaken Paul because he loved this present world. First, Demas is Demas the fellow-labourer; second, Demas is just Demas; third, Demas is the deserter who loved the world. There is the history of a spiritual degeneration there. Bit by bit the fellow-labourer has become the deserter; the title of honour has become the name of shame.

What happened to Demas? That we cannot tell for sure, but we can guess.

(i) It may be that Demas had begun to follow Christ without first counting the cost. It may be that Demas was one of these people who came to Christ in a kind of moment of spiritual glow. It may be that he was swept into the Church in a moment of emotion, without ever having thought out and faced the cost of being a Christian. And it may be that Demas was not altogether to blame. There is a kind of evangelism which proclaims: " Accept Christ and you will have rest and peace and joy." There is a sense, the deepest of all senses, in which that is profoundly and blessedly true. But it is also true that it is when we accept Christ that our troubles begin. Up to that time we have lived in conformity with the world and with the world's standards. Because of that life was easy, because inevitably we followed the line of least resistance and went with the crowd. But once a man accepts Christ, he has accepted an entirely new set of standards; he is committed to an entirely new kind of life at his work, in his personal relationships, in his pleasure, in his conduct, in his speech, in the things which he allows himself to do. And there are bound to be collisions. It may be that Demas was swept into the Church in a moment of emotion without ever thinking things out; and then when unpopularity, persecution, the necessity of sacrifice, loneliness, imprisonment came, Demas quit because Demas had never bargained for anything like that. When a man undertakes to follow Christ, the first essential is that he should know what he is doing.

(ii) It may be that there came to Demas the inevitable weariness of the years. The years have a way of taking our ideals away, of making us satisfied with less and less, of lowering our standards, of accustoming us to defeat. Halliday Sutherland tells how he felt when he first qualified as a doctor. If on the street or in any company there came the call: " Is there a doctor here? " he thrilled to it, proud and eager to step forward and to help. But as the years went on, a request and a summons like that became a nuisance. The thrill was gone. W. H. Davies, the tramp who was also one of the greatest poets, has a revealing passage about himself: he had walked to see Tintern Abbey, and the last time that he had seen it was twenty seven years ago. He says: " As I stood there now, twenty-seven years after, and compared that young boy's enthusiasm with my present lukewarm feelings, I was not very well pleased with myself. For instance, at that time I would sacrifice both food and sleep to see anything wonderful; but now in my prime I did not go seeking things of beauty, and only sang of things that came my way by chance."

Dean Inge had a sermon on *Psalm* 91: 6—" The destruction that wasteth at noonday." He called it " The Peril of Middle Age." There is no threat so dangerous and so insidious as the threat of the years to a man's ideals. And that threat can only be kept at bay and defeated by living constantly in the thrill of the presence of Jesus Christ.

(iii) Paul said of Demas that " he loved this present world." The trouble of Demas may have been quite simple, and yet very terrible. It may simply have been that he loved comfort more than he loved Christ, that he loved the easy way more than he loved the way which led first to a cross and then to the stars. It may be that Demas preferred to be a prosperous man of the world than a Christian. He preferred a flabby prosperity to the athletic heroism of the Christian way.

We think of Demas, not to condemn, but to sympathize, for so many of us are like him.

But it is just barely possible that this is neither the beginning nor the end of the story of Demas. The name *Demas* is exactly the same name as the name *Demetrius*; *Demas* is a shortened and familiar form of Demetrius. Now Demetrius and Demas were not uncommon names and what we are about to suggest now need not be historical fact—but it may be so in the mercy of God.

Twice we come upon a Demetrius in the New Testament story. There was a Demetrius who led the riot of the silversmiths at Ephesus, and who wished to lynch Paul because he had taken their temple trade away (*Acts* 19: 25). There was a Demetrius of whom John wrote that he had a good report of all and of the truth itself, a fact to which John bore willing and decisive witness (3 *John* 12). Is this the beginning and the end of the story? Did Demetrius the silversmith find something about Paul and Christ which twined itself round his heart? Did the hostile leader of the riot become the convert to Christ? It could have happened. Did he then follow the Christian way, and then for a time fall away from the Christian way, and become Demas, the deserter, who loved this present world? And then did the grace of God lay hands on him again, and bring him back, and recreate and redeem him, and make him the Demetrius of Ephesus of whom John wrote that he was a servant of the truth of whom all spoke well? That we will never know, but it is a lovely thing to think that the charge of being a deserter was not the final verdict on the life of Demas.

A ROLL OF HONOUR AND DISHONOUR

2 *Timothy* 4: 9-15 (*continued*)

LET us continue our way through this roll of honour and dishonour.

THE GENTILE OF WHOM ALL SPOKE WELL

After Paul has spoken of the man who was the deserter he goes on to speak of the man who was faithful unto death. " Luke alone is with me," he says. We know very little about Luke, and yet from the little that we do know he emerges one of the loveliest characters in the New Testament.

(i) One thing we know by implication—Luke accompanied Paul on his last journey to Rome and to prison. Luke was the writer of the *Book of Acts*. Now there are certain passages of *Acts* which are written in the first person plural. There are passages where it is said: " We did this; we did that." We can be quite sure that when Luke writes in the first person, he is describing incidents and occasions on which he himself was actually present. *Acts* 27 describes Paul setting out under arrest for Rome, and the story is told in the first person. Therefore we can be sure that Luke was there. But from that we can deduce something else. It may well have been true that when an arrested prisoner was on his way to trial at Rome, he was allowed to be accompanied by only two slaves. It is therefore highly probable that Luke enrolled himself as Paul's slave in order to be allowed to accompany him to Rome and to prison. Little wonder that Paul speaks of Luke with a thrill of love in his voice. Surely devotion could go no farther. Rather than be separated from him, Luke became Paul's slave.

(ii) There are only two other definite references to Luke in the New Testament. In *Colossians* 4: 14 he is described as *the beloved physician*. Paul owed much to Luke. All his life Paul had the torturing thorn in his flesh; and Luke must have been the man who nursed him, and cared for him and tended him, and used his skill to ease his pain, and to enable him to go on. Luke was essentially a man who was kind. He does not seem to have been a great preacher or a great evangelist; Luke was the man who made his contribution in terms of personal service. God had given him healing skill in his hands, and it was that skill that Luke gave back to God. Kindness is the quality and the virtue which lifts a man out of the ruck of ordinary men. Eloquence will be forgotten; mental cleverness may live on the printed page; but kindness lives on enthroned in the hearts of men. Dr. Johnson had certain contacts with a young man called Harry Hervey. Hervey was rich and Hervey was more than something of a rake. But Hervey had a London house, and at that house Johnson was always welcome. Years later Harry Hervey was being discussed, and unkindly discussed. Johnson said seriously: " Harry Hervey, he was a vicious man, but very kind to me. If you call a dog Hervey, I shall love him." Kindness covered a multitude of sins. Luke was loyal and Luke was kind.

(iii) The other reference to Luke is in *Philemon* 24; and there Paul calls him his *fellow-labourer*. Luke was the man who shared in the work. Luke was not content only to write; he was not content to confine himself to his job as a doctor; Luke was the man who set his hand to the work. The Church is full of talkers; the Church is full of people who are there far more for what they can get than for what they can give; Luke was one of these priceless people—one of the workers of the Church.

(iv) There is one other possible reference to Luke in the New Testament. *2 Corinthians* 8: 18 speaks of " the brother whose praise is throughout all the Churches." From the earliest times that brother has been identified with Luke. Luke was the man of whom all men spoke well. He was the friend who was loyal unto death; he was the man who was essentially kind; he was the man who was dedicated to the work. Such a man will always be a man of whom all men speak well.

A ROLL OF HONOUR AND DISHONOUR

2 Timothy 4: 9-15 (*continued*)

THERE is still another name with an untold, yet a thrilling, story behind it in this roll of names.

THE MAN WHO REDEEMED HIMSELF

Paul urges Timothy to bring Mark with him " for he is profitable to me for the ministry." The word *ministry* is not used in its narrower sense of the ministry of the Church. It is used in its wider sense, the sense of *service*. " Bring Mark," says Paul, " for he is very useful in service." As E. F. Scott puts it; " Bring Mark, for he can turn his hand to anything." Or, as we might put it in our own everyday language: " Bring Mark, for he is a useful man to have about the place."

Mark had a curiously chequered career. He was very young when the Church began, but he lived at the very centre of the Church's life. It was to the house of Mary, Mark's mother, that Peter turned his steps when he escaped from prison, and we may therefore take it that Mark's mother's house was the central meeting place of the Jerusalem Church (*Acts* 12: 12).

When Paul and Barnabas set out on their first missionary journey they took Mark with them—John Mark was his full name—to be their helper and their assistant (*Acts* 13: 5). It looked as if Mark was earmarked for a great career in the company of Paul and in the service of the Church. And then something happened. When Paul and Barnabas left Pamphylia and struck inland on the hard and dangerous road that led to the central plateau of Asia Minor, Mark left them and went home (*Acts* 13: 13). His nerve and his courage failed him, and he turned back.

Paul took that defection very hard. When Paul and Barnabas set out on their second missionary journey, Barnabas—he was related to Mark (*Colossians* 4: 10)— planned to take Mark with them again. But Paul absolutely refused to have that quitter with them a second time; and so fierce was the argument and so acute the difference that Paul and Barnabas split company and never, so far as we know, worked together again (*Acts* 15: 36-40). So then, there was a time when Paul had no use for Mark, when he looked on him as a spineless deserter, and when he completely refused to have him on his staff.

What happened to Mark after that we do not know. Tradition has it that he went to Egypt and that he was the founder of the Christian Church in that country. But, whatever Mark did, he certainly redeemed himself. When Paul came to write *Colossians* from his Roman prison, Mark is with him, and Paul commends him to the Colossian Church and charges them to receive him. And now, when the end is near, the one man Paul wants, besides his beloved Timothy, is Mark, for he was a useful man to have about. Mark the quitter had become Mark the man who can turn his hand to anything in the service of Paul and in the service of the gospel.

Fosdick has a sermon with the great and the uplifting title, " No man need stay the way he is." Mark was the living proof of that. Mark is our encouragement and our inspiration, for Mark was the man who failed and who yet made good. Still to this day Jesus Christ can make the coward spirit brave and nerve the feeble arm for fight. He can release the sleeping hero in the soul of every man. He can turn the shame of failure into the joy of triumphant service.

A ROLL OF HONOUR AND DISHONOUR

2 *Timothy* 4: 9-15 (*continued*)

HELPERS AND A HINDERER AND A LAST REQUEST

So the list of names goes on. Of Crescens we know nothing at all. Titus was another of Paul's most faithful lieutenants. " Mine own son," Paul calls him (*Titus* 1: 4). When the trouble with the Church at Corinth had been worrying him, Titus had been one of Paul's emissaries in the struggle to mend things (2 *Corinthians* 2: 13; 7: 6, 13; 12: 18). Tychicus had been entrusted with the delivery of the letter to the Colossians (*Colossians* 4: 7), and of the letter to the Ephesians (*Ephesians* 6: 21). The little group of helpers was being dispersed throughout the Church, for even if Paul was in prison the work had still to go on, and Paul must go lonely that his scattered people might be strengthened and guided and comforted.

Then there comes the mention of a man who had hindered instead of helping: " Alexander the coppersmith did me a great deal of harm." We do not know what Alexander had done; but perhaps we can deduce what harm he did. The word that Paul uses for *did* me much evil is the Greek verb *endeiknumi*. That verb literally means *to display*; and it was in fact often used for *the laying of information* against a man. Informers were one of the great curses of Rome at this time. They sought to curry favour for themselves and to receive rewards by laying information. And it may well be that Alexander was a renegade Christian, who went to the magistrates with false and slanderous information against Paul. It may be that Alexander turned against Paul and sought to ruin him in the most dishonourable way.

Paul has certain personal requests to make. He wants the cloak he had left behind at the house of Carpus in Troas. The cloak (*phainolē*) was a great circular rug-like garment. It had a hole for the head in the middle, and when it was put on it covered a man like a little tent, reaching right down to the ground. It was a garment for the winter time and no doubt Paul was feeling a Roman prison cold.

He wants the *books*; the word is *biblia*, which literally means papyrus rolls; and it may well be that these rolls contained the earliest forms of the gospels. He wanted the *parchments*. The parchments could be one of two things. They might be Paul's necessary legal documents, especially his certificate of Roman citizenship. More likely they were copies of the Hebrew Scriptures, the Old Testament, for the Hebrews wrote the rolls of their sacred books on parchment made from the skins of animals. It was the word of Jesus and the word of God that Paul wanted most of all, when he lay in prison awaiting death.

Sometimes history has a strange way of repeating itself. Fifteen hundred years later William Tyndale was lying in prison in Vilvorde, arrested, waiting for death, because he had dared to give the people the Bible in their own language. It is a cold damp winter, and he writes to a friend: " Send me, for Jesus' sake, a warmer cap, something to patch my

leggings, a woollen shirt, and *above all my Hebrew Bible.*"
When they were up against it, and when the chill breath of
death was on them, the great ones wanted more than anything else the word of God to put strength and courage
into their souls.

LAST WORDS AND GREETINGS

2 Timothy 4: 16-22

> At my first defence no one was there to stand by me,
> but all forsook me. May it not be reckoned against
> them! But the Lord stood beside me, and He streng-
> thened me, so that through me the proclamation of
> the gospel was fully made so that the Gentiles might
> hear it. So I was rescued from the mouth of the lion.
> The Lord will rescue me from every evil, and will save
> me for His heavenly kingdom. Glory be to Him for
> ever and ever. Amen.
> Greet Prisca and Aquila, and the family of Onesi-
> phorus. Erastus stayed in Corinth. I left Trophimus
> at Miletus. Eubulus sends greetings to you, as do
> Pudens, Linus and Claudia, and all the brothers.
> The Lord be with your spirit.
> Grace be with you.

A ROMAN trial began with a preliminary examination to
formulate the precise charge with which the prisoner was to
be charged. When Paul was brought to that preliminary
examination, not one of his friends stood by him. It was too
dangerous to proclaim oneself the friend of a man on trial
for his life.

One of the curious things about this passage is the number
of reminiscences of Psalm 22. " Why hast Thou forsaken
me? " " All men forsook me." " There is none to help."
" No one was there to stand by me." " Save me from the
lion's mouth." " I was rescued from the mouth of the lion."
" All the ends of the earth shall turn unto the Lord."
" That the Gentiles might hear it." " The kingdom is the
Lord's." " He will save me for his heavenly kingdom." It
seems certain that the words of this psalm were running in

Paul's mind. And the lovely thing is that this was the psalm which was in the mind of Jesus when He hung upon His Cross, for this is the psalm which begins: " My God, my God, why hast Thou forsaken me? " and which ends in triumph (*Psalm* 22: 1; *Matthew* 27: 46). As Paul faced death, he comforted and encouraged his heart with the same Psalm as His Lord did in the same circumstances.

Three things brought Paul courage in that lonely hour.

(i) All men had forsaken him, but the Lord was with him. Jesus had said that he would never leave His own or forsake them; He had said that He would be with them to the end of the world, and Paul is a witness that Jesus kept His promise. If to do the right means to be alone, as Joan of Arc said, " It is better to be alone with God."

(ii) Paul never forgot the task of proclaiming Christ. He would use even a Roman court to proclaim the message of Christ. He obeyed his own commandment; in season and out of season he pressed the claims of Christ on men. He was so busy thinking of the task of preaching that he forgot the danger. A man who is lost and immersed in his task has conquered fear.

(iii) He was quite certain of the ultimate rescue. In time Paul might seem to be the victim of circumstances, and a criminal condemned at the bar of Roman justice; but Paul saw beyond time and he knew that his eternal safety was assured. It is always better to be in danger for a moment and safe for eternity, than to be in safety for a moment and to jeopardize eternity.

A HIDDEN ROMANCE?

2 *Timothy* 4: 16-22 (*continued*)

FINALLY there come greetings sent and given. There is a greeting to Priscilla and Aquila, that husband and wife whose home was ever a Church, wherever it might be, and who had at some time risked their lives for Paul's sake (*Acts* 18: 2;

Romans 16: 3; I *Corinthians* 16: 19). There is a greeting to the
gallant Onesiphorus, who had sought Paul out in prison in
Rome (2 *Timothy* I: 16) and who, it may be, had paid for
his loyalty with his life. There is a greeting to Erastus, whom
once Paul sent as his emissary to Macedonia (*Acts* 19: 22),
and whom, it may be, was afterwards within the Church at
Rome (*Romans* 16: 23). There is a greeting to Trophimus,
whom Paul had been accused of bringing into the Temple
precincts in Jerusalem, although he was a Gentile, an
incident for which Paul's last imprisonment began
(*Acts* 20: 4; 21: 29). Finally there are greetings from
Linus, Pudens and Claudia. In the later lists Linus stands
as the first bishop of Rome.

Around the names of Pudens and Claudia a romance has
been woven. It may be that the story is impossible, or at
least improbable, but it is too interesting not to quote.
There was a famous Roman poet, a writer of epigrams, called
Martial, who flourished in Rome from A.D. 66 to A.D. 100.
Two of his epigrams celebrate the marriage of a highborn
and distinguished Roman called Pudens to a lady called
Claudia. In the second of them Claudia is called a stranger
in Rome, and it is said that she came from Britain. Now
Tacitus tells us that in A.D. 52, in the reign of the Emperor
Claudius, certain territories in south-east Britain were
given to a British king called Cogidubnus, for his loyalty to
Rome. Still further, in 1723, a marble tablet was dug up in
the city of Chichester in England, which commemorates
the erection of a heathen temple by Cogidubnus, the king,
and by Pudens, his son. As we shall see, that may mean his
son-in-law. In the inscription the full name of the king
is given and, no doubt in honour of the Roman Emperor, we
find that the British king had taken the name of Tiberius
Claudius Cogidubnus. If that king had a daughter her
name must have been Claudia, for that is the name that
she would take from her father. We can carry the story
still further. It may be that Cogidubnus would send his
daughter Claudia to stay in Rome. That he should do so

was almost certain, for when a foreign king entered into an alliance with Rome, as Cogidubnus had done, some members of his family were always sent to Rome as hostages and pledges for keeping of the agreement. If Claudia went to Rome she would certainly stay in the house of a Roman called Aulus Plautius, who had been the Roman governor in Britain from A.D. 43-52, and to whom Cogidubnus had rendered his faithful service. The wife of Aulus Plautius was a lady called Pomponia, and we learn from Tacitus that Pomponia had been arraigned before the Roman courts in A.D. 57 because she was " tainted with a foreign superstition." That " foreign superstition " may well have been nothing else than Christianity. Pomponia may have been a Christian, and from her Claudia, the British princess, may have learned of Jesus also.

We cannot say whether the guesses and deductions in that story are true. But it would be a wonderful thing to think that this Claudia was actually a British princess, who had come to stay in Rome and who had become a Christian, and that Pudens was her husband.

So Paul comes to the end by commending his friends to the presence and the Spirit of His Lord and theirs, and, as always, his last word is grace.

THE LETTER TO TITUS

TITUS

THE MAINSPRINGS OF APOSTLESHIP

Titus I: 1-4

This is a letter from Paul, the slave of God and the envoy of Jesus Christ, whose task it is to awaken faith in God's chosen ones, and to equip them with a fuller knowledge of that truth, which enables a man to live a really religious life, and whose whole work is founded on the hope of eternal life, which God, who cannot lie, promised before time began. In His own good time God set forth His message plain for all to see in the proclamation with which I have been entrusted by the royal command of God our Saviour. This letter is to Titus, his true son in the faith they both share. Grace be to you and peace from God the Father and from Christ Jesus our Saviour.

WHEN Paul summoned one of his henchmen to a task, he always began by setting forth his own right to speak, and by, as it were, laying again the foundations of the gospel. So Paul begins here by saying certain things about his own apostleship.

(i) His apostleship set him in *a great succession*. Right at the beginning Paul calls himself " the slave (*doulos*) of God." That was a title of mingled humility and legitimate pride. It meant that Paul was the undisputed possession of God; it meant that Paul had no will and no time of his own; it meant that Paul's life was totally submitted to God. But there is pride here too; for this very title, *slave of God, doulos theou*, was the one title that was given to the prophets and the great ones of the past. Moses was the slave of God (*Joshua* I: 2); and Joshua, his successor, would have claimed no higher title (*Joshua* 24: 29). It was to the prophets, the slaves of God, that God revealed all His will and all His intentions (*Amos* 3: 7); it was His slaves the prophets whom God had repeatedly sent to Israel all throughout the history of the nation (*Jeremiah* 7: 25). The title *slave of God* was a title which gave Paul the right to walk in a great succession. When anyone enters the Church, he does not enter an institution which began yesterday; the Church has centuries of human history behind her, and goes back before the eternities in the mind and the intention of God. When anyone takes upon himself anything of the preaching, or the teaching, or the serving work of the Church, he does not enter on a service which is without traditions. He walks where the saints have trod. To be within the Church of God is to be within a great succession.

(ii) His apostleship gave him *a great authority*. He was the envoy of Jesus Christ. Paul never thought of his authority as coming to him from his own mental excellence, still less from his own moral goodness. It was in the authority and with the authority of Christ that he spoke. An envoy always bears upon himself a delegated authority. The man who preaches the gospel of Christ or teaches the truth of Christ, if he is a truly dedicated soul, does not talk about his own opinions, or offer his own conclusions; he comes with the message of Christ and with the word of God. The true envoy of Christ has reached past the stage of *perhapses* and *maybes* and *possiblys*, and speaks with the accent of the certainty and the authority of one who knows.

AN APOSTLE'S GOSPEL

Titus I: I-4 (*continued*)

STILL further, in this passage we can see the essence of an apostle's gospel, and the central things in an apostle's task.

(i) The whole message of the apostle is founded on *the hope of eternal life*. The Christian offer is the offer of nothing less than a new kind of life. Again and again the phrase *eternal life* recurs in the pages of the New Testament. The word for *eternal* is *aiōnios*. Strictly and properly there is only one person in the whole universe to whom that word may correctly be applied, and that one person is God. The Christian offer is nothing less than the offer of a share in the life of God. The Christian offer is the offer of God's power for our frustration, of God's serenity for our dispeace, of God's truth for our guessing, of God's goodness for our moral failure, of God's joy for our sorrow. The Christian gospel does not in the first place offer men an intellectual creed or a moral code; it offers them life, the very life of God.

(ii) To enable a man to enter into that life, two things are necessary. It is the apostle's duty to awaken *faith* in men. With Paul, faith always means one thing—total and absolute trust in God. The first step in the Christian life is to realize that we can do nothing except receive. In every sphere of life, no matter how great and precious an offer may be, that offer remains inoperative until it is received. The first duty of the Christian is to persuade others to accept the offer of God. In the last analysis, we can never argue a man into Christianity. All we can say is, " Try it, and see! "

(iii) But, secondly, it is the apostle's duty to equip others with *knowledge*. Christian evangelism and Christian education must go hand in hand. The Christian preacher and the Christian teacher must be one and the same person. Faith may begin by being a response of the heart, but it must go on to be the possession of the mind. The Christian gospel must be thought out in order to be tired out. No man can live for ever on the crest of a wave of emotion. The Christian life must be a daily loving Christ more and understanding Him better.

(iv) The result of faith and knowledge must be *a truly religious life*. Faith must always issue in life. Christian knowledge is not merely intellectual knowledge; it is knowledge *how to live*. There have been many people who have been great scholars and whose shoulders have been heavy with the weight of their academic distinctions, and who have been completely inefficient in the ordinary

261

things of life, and total failures in their personal relationships. A truly religious life is a life in which a man is on the right terms with God, with himself and with his fellow men. It is a life in which a man can cope alike with the great moments and the everyday duties. It is a life in which Jesus Christ lives again.

It is the duty of the Christian to offer to men the very life of God Himself; to awaken faith in men's hearts and to deepen knowledge in their minds; to enable men to live in such a way that others will see the reflection of the Master in their daily walk and conversation.

GOD'S PURPOSE AND GOD'S GOOD TIME

Titus I: 1-4 (*continued*)

THIS passage tells us of God's purpose and plan for man, and of God's way of working that purpose out.

(i) God's purpose for man was always a purpose of salvation. God's promise of eternal life was there before the world began. It is very important to note that in this passage Paul applies the word *Saviour* both to God and to Jesus. We sometimes hear the gospel presented in such a way that it seems to draw a distinction between a gentle, loving, and gracious Jesus, and a hard, stern, and severe God. Sometimes it almost sounds as if there was a contrast between Jesus, the lover of the souls of men, and God, the judge of the souls of men. Sometimes it sounds as if Jesus had done something to change the attitude of God to men, and had persuaded God to lay aside His wrath and not to punish men. There is no justification for that in the New Testament. At the back of the whole process of salvation is the eternal and unchanging love of God, and it was of that love that Jesus came to tell men. God is characteristically the Saviour God, the God whose last desire is to condemn men, and whose first desire is to save them. God is the Father who desires only that His children should come home, not that He may smash them, but that He may gather them to His breast.

(ii) But this passage does more than speak of God's eternal purpose; it also speaks of God's method. It tells us that God sent His message in *His own good time*. That means to say that all history was a preparation for the coming of Jesus. We cannot teach any kind of knowledge to any man until he is fit to receive it. Anyone who has to learn has to go through the lower stages of knowledge before he can come to the higher stages. In all human knowledge we have to start at the beginning. So men had to be prepared for the coming of Jesus. All the history of the Old Testament, all the searchings and the seekings of the Greek philosophers, were preparations for the coming of Jesus. God's Spirit was moving both amongst the Jews, the chosen people, and amongst all other peoples, that they should be ready to receive His Son when He came. The teaching of the prophets, the search for the truth of the minds of men in every nation, were a divinely inspired process which was meant to culminate in the coming of Jesus with God's perfect truth to men. As a child is led in his schooling from stage to stage, so all the world was being educated to receive God's truth in His Son, when Jesus Christ should come. We must look on all history as God's education of men.

(iii) Still further, Christianity came into this world at a time when it was uniquely possible for its message to spread. It is the simple truth to say that there never was a time in history when it was easier for a message to spread itself across all Europe. There were five elements in the world situation which facilitated the spread of Christianity. (*a*) Practically all the world spoke Greek. That is not to say that the nations had forgotten their own language; but nearly all men spoke Greek as well as their own language. Greek was the language of trade, of commerce, of literature. If a man was going to take any part in public life and activity he had to know Greek.

People were bilingual, just as they are in the western Highlands of Scotland to-day. Just as there men speak Gaelic at home, and in the private and intimate occasions of life, and English in public, so the ancient world used its own languages for its private affairs and Greek for the activities of public life. The first age of Christianity was one of the very few ages in history when the missionary had no language problem to solve. (*b*) There were to all intents and purposes no frontiers. The Roman Empire was co-extensive with the known world. Wherever the traveller might go, he was within that Empire. Nowadays, if a man intended to cross Europe, he would need a passport; he would be held up at frontiers; he would find iron curtains, behind which he would not be able to penetrate. But in the first age of Christianity a missionary could move without let or hindrance from one end of the known world to the other. (*c*) Travel was comparatively easy. True, it was slow because there was no mechanized travel, and most journeys had to be done on foot, with the baggage carried by slow-moving animals. But the Romans had built their great roads from land to land and continent to continent; they had, for the most part, cleared the land of brigands and the sea of pirates, and travel was easier than it had ever been before. (*d*) The first age of Christianity was one of the few ages when the world was very largely at peace. If there had been wars raging all over Europe, the progress of the missionary would have been rendered impossible. But the *pax Romana*, the Roman peace, held sway; and the traveller could move within the Roman Empire in safety and in peace. (*e*) It was a world which was conscious of its needs. The old faiths and the old religions had broken down; the new philosophies were beyond the reach of the mind of simple people. Men were looking, as Seneca said, *ad salutem*, towards salvation. They were increasingly conscious of " their weakness in necessary things." They were searching for " a hand let down to lift them up." They were searching for " a peace, not of Caesar's proclamation, but of God's." There never was a time when the hearts of men were more open to receive the message of salvation which the Christian missionaries brought.

It was no accident that Christianity came when it did come. It came in God's own time. All history had been a preparation and an education for it; and the circumstances of the time were such that the way was open for the tide to spread.

A FAITHFUL HENCHMAN

Titus I: I-4 (*continued*)

WE do not know a great deal about Titus, to whom this letter was written, but from the scattered references to him, there emerges a picture of one who was one of the most trusted and most valuable helpers of Paul. Paul calls him " my true son," so it is most likely that Paul himself converted him, perhaps at Iconium.

Titus was the companion for an awkward and a difficult time. When Paul paid his visit to Jerusalem, to a Church which suspected him and which was prepared to mistrust and to dislike him, it was Titus whom he took with him along with Barnabas (*Galatians* 2: I). It was said of Dundas, the famous Scotsman, by one of his friends, " Dundas is no orator; but Dundas will go out with you in any kind of weather." Titus was like that. When Paul was up against it, Titus was by his side.

Titus was the man for a tough assignment. When the trouble at Corinth was at its peak, it was Titus who was sent to Corinth with one of the severest letters that Paul ever wrote (2 *Corinthians* 8: 16). Titus clearly had the strength of mind and the toughness of fibre which enabled him to face and to handle a difficult situation. There are two kinds of people. There are the people who can make a bad situation worse, and there are the people who can bring order out of chaos and peace out of strife. Titus was the man to send to the place where there was trouble.

Titus had a gift for practical administration. It was Titus whom Paul chose to organize the collection for the poor members of the Church at Jerusalem (2 *Corinthians* 8: 6, 10). It is clear that Titus had no great gifts of speech, but Titus was the man for practical administration. The Church ought to thank God for the people to whom we turn whenever we want a practical job well done.

Paul has certain great titles by which he calls Titus.

He calls him his *true child*. That must mean that Titus was Paul's convert, and child in the faith (*Titus* 1: 4). Nothing in this world gives a preacher and teacher more joy than to see someone whom he has taught and trained rise to usefulness within the Church. Titus was the son who brought joy to the heart of Paul, his father in the faith.

He calls him his *brother* (2 *Corinthians* 2: 13) and his *sharer in work and toil* (2 *Corinthians* 8: 23). The great day for a preacher or a teacher is the day when his child in the faith becomes his brother in the faith, when the one whom he has taught and trained and nurtured is able to take his place in the work of the Church, no longer as a junior, but as an equal.

He says that *Titus walked in the same spirit* (2 *Corinthians* 12: 18). Paul knew that Titus would deal with things as he would have dealt with them himself. Happy is the man who has a lieutenant to whom he can commit his work, certain that it will be done in the way in which he himself would have wished to do it.

Paul gives to Titus a great task. He sends him to Crete to be a *pattern* to the Christians who are there (*Titus* 2: 7). The greatest compliment that Paul paid Titus was that he sent him to Crete, not to *talk* to them about what a Christian should be, but to *show* them what a Christian should be. There could be no greater responsibility and no higher compliment than that.

One very interesting suggestion has been made. 2 *Corinthians* 8: 18 and 2 *Corinthians* 12: 18 both say that when Titus was sent to Corinth another brother was sent with him. In the former passage that brother is described as " the brother whose praise is in all the Churches." That brother is commonly identified with Luke; and it has been suggested that Titus was Luke's brother. It is rather an odd fact that Titus is never mentioned in *Acts*; but we know that Luke wrote *Acts*, and that often he tells the story in the first person plural, saying: " We did this," or, " We did that," and it has been suggested that in such passages he includes Titus with himself. Whether that suggestion is true we cannot tell for sure, but certainly Titus and Luke have a family resemblance in that they were both men of practical service.

In the Western Church Titus is commemorated on 4th January, and in the Eastern Church on 25th August.

THE ELDER OF THE CHURCH

Titus 1: 5-7

> The reason why I left you in Crete was that any deficiencies in the organization of the Church should be rectified, and that you might appoint elders in each city as I instructed you. An elder is a man whose conduct must be beyond reproach, the husband of one wife, with children who are also believers, who cannot be accused of profligacy, and who are not undisciplined. For he who oversees the Church of God must be beyond reproach, as befits a steward of God.

WE have already studied in detail the qualifications of the elder as they are set out by Paul in 1 *Timothy* 3: 1-7. It is therefore not necessary to examine them all in detail again.

It was always Paul's custom to ordain elders as soon as a Church had been founded (*Acts* 14: 23). Crete was an

267

island of many cities. " Crete of the hundred cities," Homer called it. The Christian Church needs its organization and its leaders. It was Paul's principle that his little Churches should be encouraged and trained to stand on their own feet as soon as possible.

In this repeated list of the qualifications of the elder, one thing is specially stressed. The elder must be a man who has taught and trained his own family in the faith. The Council of Carthage later laid it down: " Bishops, elders and deacons shall not be ordained to office before they have made all in their own households members of the Catholic Church." Christianity begins at home. It is no virtue for any man or for any woman to be so engaged in public work that he or she neglects his or her own home. All the Church service in the world will not atone for neglect of a man's own family.

Paul uses one very vivid word. The family of the elder must be such that they cannot be accused of *profligacy*. The Greek word is *asōtia*. The man who is *asōtos* (the adjective) is the man who is incapable of saving; he is the man who is wasteful and extravagant and who pours out his substance on personal pleasure. It is the word which is used in *Luke* 15: 13 for the *riotous* living of the prodigal son. The man who is *asōtos* destroys his substance, and in the end ruins himself. One who is *asōtos* is in the old English word a *scatterling*, in the Scots term *a ne'er-do-well*, in the modern word a *waster*. Aristotle, the greatest of the Greek ethical teachers, always described a virtue as the mean between two extremes; virtue to him was always the happy medium. He deals with this word *asōtia*. The correct mean is liberality; on the one hand there is stinginess, on the other hand there is *asōtia*, reckless and selfish extravagance. The household of the elder must never be guilty of the bad example of reckless and prodigal spending on personal pleasure.

Further, the family of the elder must not be *undisciplined*. Nothing can make up for the lack of parental control.

The training of children is ultimately in the hands of the parent, and there is no substitute for the training which only the parent can give. Falconer quotes a saying about the household of Sir Thomas More: " He controls his family with the same easy hand: no tragedies, no quarrels. If a dispute begins, it is promptly settled. His whole house breathes happiness, and no one enters it who is not the better for the visit." The true training ground for the eldership is at least as much in the home as it is in the Church.

WHAT THE ELDER MUST NOT BE

Titus 1: 7

> He must not be obstinately self-willed; he must not be an angry man; he must not be given to drunken and outrageous conduct; he must not be a man ready to come to blows; he must not be a seeker of gain in disgraceful ways.

HERE is a summary of the qualities which the elder of the Church must not possess, and from which his life must be free. Every one of the words which are used here is a vivid word. Let us look at them one by one.

(i) He must not be *obstinately self-willed*. The Greek word is *authadēs*, which literally means *pleasing himself*. The man who is *authadēs* has been described as the man who is so pleased with himself that nothing else pleases him, and he cares to please nobody. R. C. Trench said of such a man that, " he obstinately maintains his own opinion, or asserts his own rights, while he is reckless of the rights, opinions and interests of others." The Greek ethical writers had much to say about this fault of *authadeia*. Aristotle, who always defined every virtue as the mean between two extremes, set on the one extreme the man who pleases everybody (*areskos*), and on the other extreme the man who pleases nobody (*authadēs*), and between them the man who had in his life a true and proper dignity (*semnos*). He said of the *authadēs* that he is the man who will not converse or associate with any man. Eudemus said that the *authadēs* was the man who "regulates his life with no respect to others, but who is contemptuous." Euripides said of him that he was "harsh to his fellow citizens through want of culture." Philodemus said that his character was compounded in equal parts of conceit, arrogance and contemptuousness. His conceit made him think too highly of himself; his contemptuousness made him think too meanly of others; and his arrogance made him act on his estimate of himself and others. Clearly the man who is *authadēs* is an unpleasant character. He is the man who is intolerant, who condemns everything that he cannot understand, who thinks that there is no way of doing anything except his way, who believes that there is no way to heaven except his way, who is careless of the feelings of others and contemptuous of the beliefs of others. Such a quality, as Lock said, "is fatal to the rule of free men." No man in whose character there is contemptuous and arrogant intolerance is fit to be an office-bearer of the Church.

(ii) He must not be *an angry man*. The Greek word is *orgilos*. There are two Greek words for anger. There is *thumos*, which comes from a root which means *to boil*. *Thumos* is the anger which quickly blazes up, and just as quickly subsides, like a fire in straw. There is *orgē*, which is the noun which is connected with the adjective *orgilos*. *Orgē* means inveterate anger. It is not the anger of the sudden blaze, but the wrath which a man nurses to keep it warm. A blaze of anger is an unhappy thing; but this long-lived, deliberately nurtured, purposely maintained anger is still worse. The man who nourishes within his heart a long-lasting anger against any man is not fit to be an office-bearer of the Church.

(iii) He must not be *given to drunken and outrageous conduct*. The word in Greek is *paroinos*, which literally means *given to over-indulgence in wine*. But the word widened its meaning until it came to describe all conduct which is outrageous. The Jews, for instance, used it of the conduct of Jews who married Midianite women; the Christians used it of the conduct of those who crucified Christ. The word describes the character of the man who, even in his sober moments, acts with the lack of self-control and the outrageousness of a drunken man.

(iv) He must not be a man *ready to come to blows*. The word is *plēktēs*, which literally means *a striker*. It would seem that in the early Church there were over-zealous bishops of the Church who chastised erring members of their flock with physical violence, for the *Apostolic Canons* lay it down: " We order that the bishop who strikes an erring believer should be deposed." Pelagius says: " He cannot strike anyone who is the disciple of that Christ who, being struck, returned no answering blow." The Greeks themselves widened the meaning of this word to include, not only violence in action, but also violence in speech. The word came to mean one who *browbeats* his fellow men, and it may well be that it should be so translated here. The man who abandons love and who resorts to violence of action or of speech is not fit to be an office-bearer of the Christian Church.

(v) He must not be *a seeker of gain in disgraceful ways*. The word is *aischrokerdēs*, and it describes a man who does not care how he makes money so long as he makes it. It so happens that this was a fault for which the Cretans were notorious. Polybius said: " They are so given to making gain in disgraceful and acquisitive ways that among the Cretans alone of all men no gain is counted disgraceful." Plutarch said of them that they stuck to money like bees to honey. The Cretans counted material gain far above honesty and honour; they did not care how much their money cost them. The Christian knows that there are some things which cost too much. The man whose only aim in life is to amass material things, irrespective of how he does so, is not fit to be an office-bearer of the Christian Church.

WHAT THE ELDER MUST BE

Titus 1: 8, 9

> Rather he must be hospitable, a lover of all good things and all good people, prudent, just, pious, self-controlled, with a strong grip on the truly reliable message which Christian teaching gave to him, that he may be well able to encourage the members of the Church with health-giving teaching, and to convict the opponents of the faith.

THE previous passage set out the things which the elder of the Church must not be, and this passage goes on to set out what he must be. These necessary qualities group themselves into three sections.

(i) First, there are the qualities which the elder of the Church must display *to other people*. He must be *hospitable*. The Greek word is *philoxenos*, which literally means *a lover of strangers*. In the ancient world there were always many who were on the move. Ancient inns were notoriously expensive, dirty and immoral. It was essential that the wayfaring Christian should find an open door within the homes of the Christian community. To this day there is no one who needs Christian fellowship more than the stranger in a strange place. The second word which is used is the word *philagathos*, which means either a lover of good things, or a lover of good people, and which Aristotle uses in the sense of *unselfish*, that is, a lover of good actions. We do not have to choose between these three meanings; they are all included in the word. The Christian office-bearer must be a man whose heart answers to the good in whatever person, in whatever place and in whatever action he finds it.

(ii) Second, there comes a group of terms which tell us the qualities which the Christian office-bearer must have *within himself*. He must be *prudent* (*sōphrōn*). Euripides called this prudence " the fairest gift the gods have given to men." Socrates called it " the foundation stone of virtue." Xenophon said that it was that spirit which shunned evil, not only when evil could be seen, but even when no one would ever see it. Trench defined it as " entire command over the passions and desires, so that they receive no further allowance than that which the law and right reason admit and approve." It is the adjective to be applied to the man, as the Greeks said themselves, " whose thoughts are saving thoughts." The Christian office-bearer must be a man who wisely uses and controls every instinct and every passion of his being. He must be *dikaios*, which is *just*. The Greeks defined the just man as the man who gives both to men and to the gods what is due to them. The Christian office-bearer must be such that he gives to man the respect, and to God the reverence, which are their due. He must be *pious* (*hosios*). The Greek word is hard to translate, for it describes the man who reverences the fundamental decencies of life, the things which go back beyond any man-made law or regulation. He must be *self-controlled*. The Greek word is *egkratēs*, which describes the man who has achieved complete self-mastery. Any man who would serve others must first be master of himself.

(iii) Finally, there comes a description of the qualities of the Christian office-bearer *within the Church*. He must be able *to encourage* the members of the Church. The navy has a rule which says that no officer shall speak discouragingly to any other officer in the performance of his duties. There is always something wrong with a religion and with a preaching or a teaching the effect of which is to discourage others. The function of the true Christian teacher and preacher is, not to drive a man to despair, but to lift him up to hope. He must be able *to convict* the opponents of the faith. The Greek word is *elegchein* and it is a most meaningful word. It means to rebuke a man in such a way that he is compelled to see and to admit the error of his ways. Trench says that it means " to rebuke another, with such an effectual wielding of the victorious arms of the truth, as to bring him, if not always to a confession, yet at least to a conviction, of his sin." Demosthenes said that it describes the situation in which a man unanswerably demonstrates the truth of the things that he has said. Aristotle said that it means to prove that things cannot be otherwise than as we have stated them. Christian rebuke means far more than " giving a man a row." It means far more than merely flinging angry and condemning words at him. It means speaking to him in such a way that he sees the error of his ways and accepts the truth. The aim of Christian rebuke is not to humiliate a man, but to enable him to see and recognize and admit the duty and the truth to which he has been either blind or disobedient.

THE FALSE TEACHERS OF CRETE

Titus I: 10, 11

> For there are many who are undisciplined, empty talkers, deceivers. Those of the circumcision are especially so. They are the kind of people who upset whole households, by teaching things which should not be taught in order to acquire a shameful gain.

HERE we have a picture of the false teachers who were troubling Crete. The worst were apparently Jews. These Jews would try to persuade the Cretan converts of two things. They would try to persuade them that the simple story of Jesus and the Cross was not sufficient, but that, to be really wise, they needed all the subtle stories, and the long genealogies, and the elaborate allegories of the Rabbis. Further, they would try to teach them that grace is not enough, but that, to be really good, they would need to take upon themselves all the rules and regulations about foods and washings which were so characteristic of

Judaism. The peril of the false teachers was that they were seeking to persuade men that they needed more than Christ and more than grace in order to be saved. They were intellectualists for whom the truth of God was too simple and too good to be true.

One by one the characteristics of these false teachers pass before us.

They were *undisciplined*; they were like disloyal soldiers who refused to obey the word of command. They refused to accept the guidance of the Church; they refused to accept the creed of the Church; they refused to accept the control of the Church. It is perfectly true that the Church does not seek to impose upon men a flat uniformity of belief, nor does it ask men to abandon their own minds and to let the Church do their thinking for them; but there are certain things which a man must believe to be a Christian, and the greatest of these things is the all-sufficiency of Christ. When a man tampers with that, he must be silenced within the Church. Even in the Protestant Church discipline is not eliminated.

They were *empty talkers*; the word is *mataiologoi*, and the adjective *mataios, vain, empty, profitless*, was the adjective which was applied to heathen worship. The main idea of it is that it is a worship which produces no goodness in life. These people in Crete could talk glibly and speciously, but all their talk was ineffective in bringing anyone one step nearer goodness. The Cynics used to say that all knowledge which is not profitable for virtue is empty and vain. The teacher who simply provides his pupils with a forum for pleasant intellectual and speculative discussion teaches in vain.

They were *deceivers*. Instead of leading men to the truth they led men away from the truth. Instead of establishing men in the faith they slowly eroded away their faith.

Their teaching *upset whole households*. There are two things to notice there. First, their teaching was fundamentally upsetting. It is true that truth must often make

275

a man rethink his ideas. It is true that Christianity does not run away from doubts and questions, but faces them fairly and squarely. It is true that the truth often mentally takes a man by the scruff of the neck and shakes him; but it is also true that teaching which ends in nothing but doubts and questionings is bad teaching. In true teaching, out of the mental disturbance there should come in the end a new and greater certainty than ever. Second, they upset households. That is to say, they had an ill effect on family life. Any teaching which tends to disrupt the family is false teaching. The Christian Church is always built on the basis of the Christian family.

Their teaching was designed for *gain*. They were more concerned with what they could get out of the people they were teaching than with what they could put into them. Parry has said that this is indeed the besetting temptation of the professional teacher. When a teacher or a preacher looks on his teaching or preaching as a career designed for personal advancement and personal profit and gain, he is in a perilous condition.

One final thing we must notice in this passage. These men are to be *muzzled*. That does not imply that they are to be silenced by violence or by persecution. The Greek word which is used (*epistomizein*) does mean *to muzzle*, but it became the normal word for *to silence a person by reason*. The way to combat false teaching is to offer true teaching, and the only truly unanswerable teaching is the teaching of a Christian life.

A BAD REPUTATION

Titus I: 12

> One of themselves, a prophet of their own, has said:
> " The Cretans are always liars, wild and evil
> beasts, lazy gluttons."
> His testimony is true!

No people ever had a worse reputation in the ancient world than the Cretans. The ancient world spoke of the three most evil C's—the Cretans, the Cilicians, and the Cappadocians. The Cretans were famed as a drunken, insolent, untrustworthy, lying, gluttonous people.

Their avarice was proverbial. " The Cretans," said Polybius, " on account of their innate avarice, live in a perpetual state of private quarrel and public feud and civil strife . . . and you will hardly find anywhere characters more tricky and deceitful than those of Crete." He writes of them: " Money is so highly valued among them, that its possession is not only thought to be necessary, but highly creditable; and in fact greed and avarice are so native to the soil in Crete, that they are the only people in the world among whom no stigma attaches to any sort of gain whatever."

Polybius tells of a certain compact that a traitor called Bolis made with a leader called Cambylus, who was also a Cretan. Bolis approached Cambylus " with all the subtlety of a Cretan." " This was now made the subject of discussion between them in a truly Cretan spirit. They never took into consideration the saving of the person in danger, or their obligations of honour to those who had entrusted them with the undertaking, but confined the discussion entirely to questions of their own safety and their own advantage. As they were both Cretans they were not long in coming to a unanimous agreement." The contempt of the Greek historian for these Cretans breathes through this passage.

So notorious were the Cretans that the Greeks actually formed a verb *krētizein, to Cretize,* which meant *to lie and to cheat*; and they had a proverbial phrase, *krētizein pros Krēta,* to Cretize against a Cretan, which meant *to match lies with lies,* as diamond cuts diamond.

The quotation which Paul makes is actually from a Greek poet called Epimenides. He lived about 600 B.C. and was ranked as one of the seven wise men of Greece.

The first phrase, " The Cretans are chronic liars," had been made famous by a later and equally well-known poet called Callimachus. In Crete there was shown a monument which was called *The Tomb of Zeus*. Obviously the greatest of the gods cannot die and be buried in a tomb, and Callimachus quoted this as a perfect example of Cretan lying. In his *Hymn to Zeus* he writes:

> " Cretans are chronic liars,
> For they built a tomb, O King,
> And called it thine; but you die not;
> Your life is everlasting."

The Cretans were notorious liars and cheats and gluttons and traitors.

Here precisely is the wonderful thing. Knowing that, and actually experiencing it, Paul does not say to Timothy: " Leave them alone. They are hopeless and all men know it." He says: " They are bad and all men know it. *Go and convert them*." There are few passages which so demonstrate the divine optimism of the Christian missionary and evangelist, who refuses to regard any man as hopeless. The greater the evil, the greater the challenge. It is the Christian conviction that there is no sin which is too great for the grace of Jesus Christ to encounter and to conquer.

THE PURE IN HEART

Titus I: 13-16

> For that very reason correct them with severity, that they may grow healthy in the faith, and that they may pay not attention to Jewish fables and to rules and regulations made by men who persist in turning their backs on the truth.
>
> " To the pure all things are pure."
>
> But to those who are defiled and who do not believe, nothing is pure, because their mind and conscience are defiled. They profess to know God, but they deny their profession by their deeds, because they are repulsive and disobedient and useless for any good work.

278

THE great characteristic of the Jewish faith was its thousands of rules and regulations. This, that and the next thing was branded and listed as unclean; this, that and the next food was held to be tabu; when Judaism and Gnosticism joined hands even the body became unclean, and marriage and the natural instincts of the body were held to be evil. The inevitable result of this was that long lists of sins were constantly being created. It became a sin to touch this or that; it became a sin to eat this or that food; it even became a sin to marry and to beget children. Things which were either good in themselves or quite natural became defiled and polluted. This type of mind simply succeeded in turning harmless things into sins, for the more rules and regulations which were worked out, the longer the possible list of sins became.

So Paul strikes out the great principle—To the pure all things are pure. He had already said that even more definitely in *Romans* 14: 20. To those who were constantly involved in questions about clean and unclean foods, he said: " All things are pure." It may well be that this phrase is not only a proverb; it may actually be a saying of Jesus. When Jesus was speaking about these countless Jewish rules and regulations, He said: " There is nothing from without a man, that entering into him can defile him; but the things which come out of him, those are they that defile the man " (*Mark* 7: 15).

It is a man's inner mind and heart which make all the difference. If he is pure in heart, all things are pure to him. If he is unclean in heart, then he makes unclean everything he thinks about or speaks about or touches. This was indeed a principle which the great classical writers had often stated. " Unless the vessel is pure," said Horace, " everything you pour into it grows bitter." Seneca said: " Just as a diseased stomach alters all the food which it receives, so the darkened mind turns everything you commit to it to its own burden and ruin. Nothing can come to evil men which is of any good to them, nay nothing can come to them which does not actually harm them. They change whatever touches them into their own nature. And even things which would be of profit to others become pernicious to them." The man with a dirty mind makes all things dirty. He can take the loveliest things and cover them with a smutted uncleanness. He can see an unclean jest where there is no uncleanness. But the man whose mind is pure finds all things pure. It is a terrible thing to have that film of uncleanness and impurity in the mind.

It is said of these men that both their *mind* and *conscience* are defiled. A man comes to his decisions and forms his conclusions by using two faculties. He uses his *intellect* to think things out; he uses *conscience* to listen to the voice of God. But if his intellect is twisted and warped in such a way that it can see the unclean thing anywhere, and if his conscience is darkened and numbed by his continual consent to evil, then he can take no good decision at all.

A man must keep the white shield of his innocence unstained. If he lets impurity infect his mind, he sees all things through a mist of uncleanness. His mind soils every thought that enteres into it; his imagination turns to lust every picture which it forms; he misinterprets every motive; he gives a double meaning to every statement; he cannot see the world except through the uncleanness of his own mind. To escape that uncleanness we must ever walk in the cleansing presence of Jesus Christ.

THE UGLY AND THE USELESS LIFE

Titus I: 13-16 (*continued*)

WHEN a man gets into this state of impurity, he may know God intellectually, but his life is a denial of his knowledge of God. Three things are singled out here about such a man.

(i) He is *repulsive*. The word is *bdeluktos*. It is the word which is particularly used of heathen idols and images. It is the word from which the noun *bdelugma*, an *abomination*, comes. There is something repulsive about a man with curious, prying, obscene mind, the kind of person who makes sniggering jests, and who is a master of the suggestive and unclean innuendo. There is always a simple and essential beauty in sheer cleanliness; and there is always a disgust in the presence of that which is soiled, and filthy and unclean.

(ii) He is *disobedient*. Such a man cannot obey the will of God. His conscience is darkened. He has made himself such that he can hardly hear the voice of God, let alone obey it. He has made himself unfit for any task. A man like that cannot be anything else but an evil and a soiling influence, and is therefore unfit to be an instrument in the hand and the purpose of God.

(iii) That is just another way of saying that he has become *useless* to God and to his fellow men. The word which is used for *useless* is interesting. It is the word *adokimos*. This word is used to describe a counterfeit coin which is below standard weight. It is used to describe a cowardly soldier who fails in the testing hour of battle. It is used of a rejected candidate for office, a man whom the citizens regarded as useless and of no value. It is used of a stone which the builders rejected. If a stone had a flaw in it, it was marked with a capital A, for *adokimos*, and left aside, as being unfit to have any place in the building. The ultimate test of life is usefulness, and the man whose influence is ever towards that which is unclean is of no use to God and of no use to his fellow men. Instead of helping God's work in the world, he hinders it; and uselessness always invites disaster.

THE LETTER TO TITUS

THE CHRISTIAN CHARACTER

Titus 2: 1, 2

(i) *The Senior Men*

You must speak what befits sound teaching. You must charge the senior men to be sober, serious, prudent, healthy in Christian faith and love and fortitude.

THIS whole chapter deals with what might be called *The Christian Character in Action*. It takes people by their various ages and stations and lays down what they ought to be within the world. It begins with the *senior men*.

They must be *sober*. The word is *nēphalios*, and it literally means *sober* in contradistinction to *given to over-indulgence in wine*. The point is that when a man has reached years of seniority, he ought to have learned what are, and what are not, real and true pleasures. He ought to have got his values right, and he ought to be able to assess his pleasures at their true worth. The senior men should have learned by their time of life that the pleasures of self-indulgence cost far more than they are worth.

They must be *serious*. The word is *semnos*, and it describes the behaviour which is grave and serious in the right way. It does not describe the demeanour of a person who is a gloomy killjoy, but it does describe the conduct of the man who knows that he lives in the light of eternity, and that before so very long he will leave the society of men for the society of God. The man who is the *semnos* is the man who lives in the constant memory that " Thou God seest me."

They must be *prudent*. The word is *sōphrōn*, and it describes the man with the mind which has everything under control. Over the years the senior men must have acquired that cleansing, saving strength of mind which has learned to govern every instinct and every passion, until each has its proper place, and no more than its proper place.

The three words taken together mean that the senior man must have learned what can only be called *the gravity of life*. A certain amount of instability, of recklessness, of unthinkingness may be pardonable in youth, but the years should have brought their wisdom. One of the most tragic sights in life is a man who has learned nothing from the years.

Further, there are three great qualities in which the senior man must be healthy.

He must be healthy in *faith*. If a man lives really close to Christ, the passing of the years and all the experiences of life, so far from taking his faith away, make his faith even stronger yet. The years must teach us, not to trust God less, but to trust God more.

He must be healthy in *love*. It may well be that the greatest danger of age is that it should drift into censoriousness, and criticism, and fault-finding. Sometimes the years take kindly sympathy away. It is so fatally possible for a man to become so settled in his ways that he comes to a stage when unconsciously he resents all new thoughts and all new ways. But the years ought to bring, not an increasing intolerance, but an increasing tolerance and sympathy for the views and with the mistakes of others.

He must be healthy in *fortitude*. The years should temper a man like steel, so that he can bear more and more and emerge more and more the conqueror over life. In the nature of things we must grow weaker in body, but in the divine nature of things we must grow ever stronger in the faith which can endure the slings and arrows of life, and not fail.

THE CHRISTIAN CHARACTER

Titus 2: 3-5

(ii) *The Older Women*

In the same way you must charge the older women to be in demeanour such as befits those who are engaged in sacred things. You must charge them not to spread slanderous stories, not to be enslaved by over indulgence in wine, to be teachers of fine things, in order that they may train the young women to be devoted to their husbands and their children, to be prudent, to be chaste, to be home-keepers and home-minders, to be kindly, to be obedient to their own husbands, so that no one will have any opportunity to speak evil of the word of God.

IT is clear that in the early Church a most honoured and responsible position was given to the older women in the Church. E. F. Brown, who was himself a missionary in India, and who knew much about Anglo-Indian society in the old days, relates a most interesting thing. A friend of his was on furlough in England, and was asked: " What is it you most want in India? " And his surprising answer was: " Grandmothers." In the old days in India there were few older women in Anglo-Indian society, because those who were engaged in the government and administration of the country almost invariably came to the end of their service and returned to Britain while they were still fairly young; and the result was that there were very few older women in that society, and the lack of them was a serious want. E. F. Brown goes on to say: " Old women play a very important part in society— how large a part one does not realize, till one witnesses a social life from which they are almost absent. Kindly grandmothers and sweet charitable old maids are the natural advisers of the young of both sexes." It is indeed true that the older women to whom the years have brought serenity and sympathy and understanding have a part to play in the life of the Church and of the community which is peculiarly their own.

Here the qualities which characterize them are laid down. Their demeanour must be such as befits those who are engaged in sacred things. As it has been said: " They must carry into daily life the demeanour of priestesses in a temple." As Clement of Alexandria had it: " The

Christian must live as if all life was a sacred assembly." It is easy to see what a difference it would make to the peace and to the fellowship of the Church, if it was always remembered, at every committee meeting, and at every activity of the Church, that we are engaged in sacred things. Much of the embittered argument and the touchiness and the intolerance which all too frequently characterize such activities would vanish overnight.

They must not spread slanderous stories. There is a thoughtless cruelty in malicious gossip. It is a curious trait of human nature that most people would rather repeat and hear a malicious tale than a tale to someone's credit. It is no bad resolution to make up our minds to say nothing about people when we cannot find anything good to say.

The older women must teach and train the younger. There are those who use their experience to discourage others. Sometimes it would seem that the only gift which experience gives to some people is the gift of pouring cold water on the schemes and plans and dreams of others; and that all they have learned from experience is the vast number of things which are impossible. It is a Christian duty ever to use experience to guide and to encourage, and not to daunton and to discourage.

THE CHRISTIAN CHARACTER

Titus 2: 3-5 (continued)

(iii) *The Younger Women*

THE younger women are bidden to be devoted to their husbands and to their children, to be prudent and chaste, to manage their households well, to be kindly to their servants, and to be obedient to their husbands; and the object of such conduct is that no one will be able to speak evil of the word of God.

In this passage there is something that is temporary and something which is permanent.

In the ancient Greek world the respectable woman lived a completely secluded life. In the house she had her own quarters, and she seldom left them, not even to sit at meals with the menfolk of the family; and into them came no man, except only her husband. She never attended any public assemblies or meetings; she seldom appeared on the streets, and if she did appear on the streets, she never appeared alone. In fact it has been said that there was no honest and honourable way in which a Greek woman could make a living. No trade and no profession was open to her; and if she tried to earn a living, she was driven to prostitution. If the women of the ancient Church had suddenly burst every barrier and limitation which the centuries had imposed upon them, the only result would have been to bring discredit on the Church, and to cause people to say that Christianity corrupted womanhood. The life that is laid down here seems a life that is narrow and circumscribed, but it is to be read against its own background, and is to be understood in the light of life in any great city. In that sense this passage is temporary.

But there is also a sense in which it is permanent. It is the simple fact that there is no greater task and responsibility and privilege in this world than to make a home. It may well be that when people, especially women, are involved in the hundred and one wearing duties which children and a home bring with them, they may say: " If only I could be done with all this, so that I could live a truly religious life." There is in fact nowhere where a truly religious life can better be lived than within the home. As John Keble had it:

> " We need not bid, for cloistered cell,
> Our neighbour and our work farewell,
> Nor strive to wind ourselves too high
> For sinful man beneath the sky;

The trivial round, the common task,
Will furnish all we need to ask—
Room to deny ourselves, a road
To bring us daily nearer God."

In the last analysis there can be no greater career than the career of homemaking. How many a man, who has set his mark upon the world, has been enabled to do so simply because there was someone at home who cared for him and loved him and tended him. It is infinitely more important that a mother should be at home to put her children to bed and to hear them say their prayers than that she should attend all the public and Church meetings in the world.

It has been said that consecration is that which makes drudgery divine; and there is no place where consecration can be more necessarily and beautifully shown than within the four walls of the place which we call home. The world can do without its committee meetings; it cannot do without its homes; and a home is not a home when the mistress of the home is absent from it.

THE CHRISTIAN CHARACTER

Titus 2: 6

(iv) The Younger Men

In the same way urge on the younger men the duty of prudence.

THE duty of the younger men is summed up in one sentence, but it is a pregnant sentence. They are bidden to remember the duty of prudence. As we have already seen, the man who is *prudent*, *sōphrōn*, has that quality of mind which keeps life safe. He has the security which comes from having all things under control.

The time of youth is necessarily the time of danger.

(i) In youth there are temptations which are stronger. The blood runs hotter and the passions speak more commandingly. The tide of life runs strongest in youth and it is a tide which sometimes threatens to sweep a young person away.

(ii) In youth there are more opportunities for going wrong. Young people are thrown into company where temptation can speak with a most compelling voice. Often young people have to study or to work away from home, and away from the influences which would keep them right. The young person is much more of an individual than the older person. The young person has not yet taken upon himself the responsibility of a home and of a family; he has not yet given hostages to fortune; and he does not yet possess the anchors which hold an older person in the right way through a sheer sense of obligation. In youth there are far more opportunities to make shipwreck of life.

(iii) In youth there is often that confidence which comes from lack of experience. In almost every sphere of life a young person will approach life more recklessly than an older person, for the simple reason that he has not yet discovered all the things which can go wrong. A young person, to take a simple example, will often drive a motor car much faster than an older person because he has not yet discovered how easily an accident can take place, and on how slender a piece of metal the safety of a car depends. A young man will often shoulder a responsibility in a much more carefree spirit than an older person, because he has not known the difficulties and has not experienced how easily shipwreck may be made. No one can buy experience; that is something for which only the years can pay. There is a risk, as there is a glory, in being young.

For that very reason, the first thing at which any young person must aim is self-mastery. No one can ever serve others until he has mastered himself. " He that ruleth his spirit is greater than he that taketh a city " (*Proverbs* 16: 32).

Self-mastery, self-discipline, self-control are not among the more glamorous and romantic of the virtues, but they are the very stuff of the foundation of life. When the eagerness of youth is buttressed by the solidity of self-mastery, then something really great comes into life.

THE CHRISTIAN CHARACTER

Titus 2: 7, 8

(v) *The Christian Teacher*

And all the time you are doing this you must offer yourself as a pattern of fine conduct; and in your teaching you must display absolute purity of motive, dignity, a sound message, which no one could condemn, so that your opponent may be turned to shame, because he can find nothing bad to say about us.

IF Titus' teaching is to be effective, it must be backed by the witness of his own life. He is himself to be the demonstration of all that he teaches. He is to provide men, not only with a pattern of conduct in words, but also with a pattern of conduct in life.

(i) It must be clear that his motives are absolutely pure. The Christian teacher and preacher is always faced with certain temptations. There is always the danger of self-display. There is always the temptation to demonstrate one's own cleverness and knowledge and wisdom. There is always the temptation to seek to attract notice to oneself instead of to God's message. There is always the temptation to power. The teacher, the preacher, the pastor, the minister is always confronted with the temptation to be a dictator. Leader he must be, but dictator never. He will find that men can be led, but that they will never be driven. The teacher is always confronted with the temptation of turning his vocation into a career. If there is one danger which confronts the Christian teacher and preacher more than another, it is to set before himself the wrong standards of success. It can often happen that the man who has never been heard of outside his own sphere of work is in God's eyes a far greater success than the man whose name is on every lip.

(ii) He must have dignity. Dignity is not aloofness, or arrogance, or pride. Dignity is the consciousness of having the terrible responsibility of being the ambassador of Christ. Other men may stoop to pettiness; he must be above it. Other men may bear their grudges; he must have no bitterness. Other men may take offence, or be touchy about their place and prestige; he must have a humility which has forgotten that it has a place. Other men may grow irritable or blaze into anger in an argument; he must have a serenity which cannot be provoked. There is nothing so injures the cause of Christ as for the leaders of the Church and the pastors of the people to descend to conduct and to words which are unbefitting an envoy of Christ.

(iii) He must have a sound message. The Christian teacher and preacher must be certain to propagate the truths of the gospel and not his own ideas. There is nothing easier for a preacher and teacher than to spend his time on side-issues. The man who teaches and preaches might well have one prayer: " God, give me a sense of proportion." The central things of the faith will last a man a life-time. As soon as a man becomes a propagandist either for his own ideas or for some sectional interest, he ceases to be an effective preacher or teacher of the word of God.

The duty which is laid on Titus is the tremendous task, not of talking to men about Christ, but of showing men Christ. It must be true of him as it was of Chaucer's saintly parson:

> " But Cristes love, and his apostles tweive
> He taught, but first he folwed it him-selve."

The greatest compliment that can be paid a teacher is to say of him: " First he wrought, and then he taught."

THE CHRISTIAN CHARACTER

Titus 2: 9, 10

(vi) The Christian Workman

> Impress upon slaves the duty of obeying their own
> masters. Urge them to seek to give satisfaction in
> every task, not to answer back, not to pilfer, but to
> display all fidelity with hearty good-will, that they
> may in all things adorn the teaching which God our
> Saviour gave to them.

IN the early Church the problem of the Christian workman
was acute. It was a problem which could operate in two
directions.

If the master was a heathen, then the responsibility
which was laid upon the servant was heavy indeed, for
it was only through the conduct of the workman that the
master could ever come to see what Christianity was. It
was the task of the workman to show the master what a
Christian could be. That responsibility still lies upon
the Christian layman and the Christian workman. Quite
clearly there are a large number of people who will never
willingly darken a Church door. The Church cannot
tell them what Christianity is, for the Church cannot
get at them at all. A minister of the Church will seldom
get a chance to speak to them, for they will not listen to
him. How then is Christianity ever to make contact with
these people at all? The only possible way is for their
fellow workman to *show* them what Christianity is. The
only possible way to commend Christianity to such people
is to show them Christianity in action in actual life and
conduct. There is a famous story of St. Francis. One
day Francis said to one of his young friars: " Let us go
down to the village and preach to the people." So they
went. They stopped to talk to this man and to that. They
begged a crust at this door and that. Francis stopped to
play with the children, and exchanged a greeting with
the passers-by. Then they turned to go home. " But
father," said the novice, " when do we preach? " " Preach?"

291

smiled Francis. "Every step we took, every word we spoke, every action we did, has been a sermon." The only possible sermon to those who will not come near the Church is the Christian life of the Christian workman at his daily job.

But there was another problem. If the master was a Christian, then a new temptation came into the life of the Christian workman. He might attempt to trade on his Christianity. He might think that, because he was a Christian, special allowances would be made for him. He might expect discipline to be easier for him. He might expect to "get away" with things because both he and the master were members of the same Church. He might, consciously or unconsciously, attempt to make his Christianity an excuse for inefficiency. It is perfectly possible for a man to trade on his Christianity—and there is no worse advertisement for Christianity than a man who does that.

So Paul lists the qualities of the Christian workman.

He is *obedient*. The Christian is never a man who is above taking orders. His Christianity teaches him how to serve. He is *efficient*. He is determined to give satisfaction. The Christian workman can never put less than his best into any task that is given him to do. He is *respectful*. He does not think that his Christianity gives him a special right to be undisciplined and to answer back. Christianity does not obliterate the necessary lines of authority in the world of industry and of commerce and of work. He is *honest*. Other may stoop to the petty dishonesties of which the world is full. His hands are clean. He is *faithful*. His master can rely and depend upon his loyalty and service.

It may well be that the man who takes his Christianity to his work with him will run into trouble; but, if he sticks to it, he will end by winning the respect of all men.

E. F. Brown tells of a thing which happened in India. "A Christian servant in India was once sent by his master with a verbal message which he knew to be untrue. He refused to deliver it. Though his master was very angry at the time, he respected the servant all the more afterwards and knew that he could always trust him in his own matters."

The truth is that in the end the world comes to see that the Christian workman is the only workman worth having. In one sense, it is hard to be a Christian at our work; in another sense, if we would try it, it is much easier than we think, for there is not a master under the sun who is not desperately looking for workmen on whose loyalty and efficiency he can rely.

THE MORAL POWER OF THE INCARNATION

Titus 2: 11-14

> For the grace of God, which brings salvation to all men, has appeared, schooling us to renounce godlessness and worldly desires for forbidden things, and to live in this world prudently, justly and reverently, because we expectantly await the realization of our blessed hope—I mean the glorious appearing of our great God and Saviour Jesus Christ, who gave Himself for us to redeem us from the power of all lawlessness, and to purify us as a special people for Himself, a people eager for all fine works.

THERE are few passages in the New Testament which so vividly set out the moral power of the Incarnation as this passage does. Its whole stress is the moral effect of the Incarnation on men, the moral miracle of change which Jesus Christ can work.

This moral miracle is repeatedly here expressed in the most interesting and significant way. Isaiah once exhorted his people: " Cease to do evil; learn to do well " (*Isaiah* 1: 16, 17). First, there is the negative side of goodness, the giving up of that which is evil, the liberation from that which is low; second, there is the positive side of goodness,

293

the acquisition of the great, shining virtues which mark the Christian life.

First, there is the renunciation of all godlessness and of all worldly desires. What did Paul mean by worldly desires? Chrysostom said that worldly things are things which do not pass over with us into heaven, but are dissolved together with this present world. Surely a man is very short-sighted if he sets all his heart and expends all his labour on things which he must leave behind him when he quits this world. If a man has spent all his life amassing nothing but material things, then he has nothing at all to take with him when this world ends. But there is an even simpler interpretation of the meaning of this phrase *worldly desires*. Worldly desires are for things we could not show to God. The work of Christ is to cleanse us from desires which we are ashamed that God should see. It is only Christ who can make, not only our outward life, but also our inward heart, fit for God to see.

That was the negative side of the moral power of the Incarnation; now comes the positive side. Jesus Christ makes us able to live with the *prudence* which has everything under perfect control, and which allows no passion or desire more than its proper place; with the *justice* which enables us to give both to God and to men that which is their due; with the *reverence* which makes us live in the awareness that this world is nothing other than the temple of God.

The dynamic of this new life is the expectation of the coming of Jesus Christ. When a royal visit is expected, everything is cleansed and decorated, and made fit for the royal eye to see. The Christian is the man who is always prepared for the coming of the King of kings.

Finally Paul goes on to sum up what Jesus Christ has done, and once again he does it in the same way, first negatively, and then positively.

Jesus has redeemed us from the power of lawlessness. He rescues us from that power which makes us sin.

Jesus can purify us until we are fit to be the special
people of God. The word we have translated *special*
(*periousios*) is an interesting word. It means *set apart,
reserved for*; and it was specially used for that part of the
spoils of a battle or a campaign which the king who had
conquered set apart specially for himself. Through the
work of Jesus Christ the Christian becomes fit to be the
special possession of God; he becomes good enough to
belong to God.

The moral power of the Incarnation is a tremendous
thought. Christ not only liberated us from the power and
the penalty of past sin; He can enable us to live the
perfect life within this world of space and time; and He
can so cleanse us that we can become fit in the life to come
to be the special possession of God Himself.

THE THREEFOLD TASK

Titus 2: 15

> Let these things be the substance of your message.
> Deal out encouragement and rebuke with all the
> authority which your royal commission confers
> upon you. Let no one regard your authority as cheap

HERE Paul succinctly lays before Titus the threefold task
of the Christian preacher and teacher and leader.

It is a task of *proclamation*. There is a message to be
proclaimed. There are some things about which argument
is not possible, and on which discussion is not relevant.
There are times when the preacher and the teacher must
say: " Thus saith the Lord."

It is a task of *encouragement*. Any preacher who reduces
his audience to bleak despair has failed in his task. Men
must be convicted of their sin, not that they may feel
that their case is hopeless, but that they may be led to
the grace which is greater than all their sin.

It is a task of *conviction*. The eyes of the sinner must

be opened to his sin. The mind of the misguided must be led to realize its mistake. The heart of the heedless must be stabbed broad awake. The Christian message is no opiate to send men to sleep; it is no comfortable assurance that everything will be all right. It is rather the blinding light which shows men themselves as they are and God as He is.

THE CHRISTIAN CITIZEN

Titus 3: 1, 2

> Remind them to be duly subject to those who are in power and authority, to obey each several command, to be ready for every work so long as it is good, to slander no one, not to be aggressive, to be kindly, to show all gentleness to all men.

HERE there is laid down the public duty of the Christian; and it is advice which was particularly relevant to the people of Crete. The Cretans were notoriously turbulent and quarrelsome and impatient of all authority. Polybius, the Greek historian, said of them that they were constantly involved in " insurrections, murders and internecine wars." This passage lays down six qualifications for the good citizen.

The good citizen is *law-abiding*. He recognizes that unless the laws are kept life becomes a chaos. He gives a proper respect to those who are set in authority, and carries out whatever command is given to him. Christianity does not insist that a man should cease to be an individual, but it does insist that a man must always remember that he is also a member of a group. " Man," said Aristotle, " is a political animal." And that means that a man best expresses his personality not in isolated individualism but within the framework of the group. He best finds himself in the company and the service of others.

The good citizen is *active in service*. He is ready for

every work, so long as it is good. The characteristic modern disease is boredom; and boredom is the direct result of selfishness. So long as a man lives on the principle of, " Why should I do it? Let someone else do it," he is bound to be bored. The interest of life lies in service.

The good citizen is *careful in speech*. He must slander no one. No man should say about other people what he would not like other people to say about him. The good citizen will be as careful of the words he speaks as of the deeds he does.

The good citizen is *tolerant*. He is not aggressive. The Greek word is *amachos*, which means *not a fighter*. This does not mean that the good citizen will not stand for the principles which he believes to be right, but it does mean that he will never be so opinionated that he cannot believe that any other way than his own is right. He will allow to others the same right to have their convictions as he claims for himself to have his own.

The good citizen is *kind*. The word is *epieikēs*, which describes the man who does not stand upon the letter of the law. Aristotle said of this word that it denotes " indulgent consideration of human infirmities," that it denotes the ability " to consider not only the letter of the law, but also the mind and intention of the legislator." The man who is *epieikēs* is ever ready to temper justice with mercy, and to avoid the injustice which often lies in being strictly just.

The good citizen is *gentle*. The word is *praus*, which describes the man whose temper is always under complete control. It describes the man who knows when to be angry and when not to be angry, the man who patiently bears wrongs done to himself, but is ever chivalrously ready to spring to the help of others who are wronged or injured.

Qualities like these are only possible for the Christian, for they are only possible for the man in whose heart Christ reigns supreme. The welfare of any community depends on the acceptance by the Christians within it of the duty of demonstrating to all the world the nobility of Christian citizenship.

THE DOUBLE DYNAMIC

Titus 3: 3-7

> For we too were once senseless, disobedient, misguided, slaves to all kinds of desires and pleasures, living in maliciousness and envy, detestable ourselves, and hating each other. But when the goodness and the love to men of God our Saviour appeared, it was not by works wrought in righteousness, which we ourselves had done, but by His own mercy that He saved us. That saving act was made effective to us through that washing, through which there comes to us the rebirth and the renewal which are the work of the Holy Spirit, whom He richly poured out upon us, through Jesus Christ our Saviour. And the aim of all this was that we might be put into a right relationship with God through His grace, and so enter into possession of eternal life, for which we have been taught to hope.

THE dynamic of the Christian life is twofold.

It comes first from the realization that once these converts to Christianity were no better than their heathen neighbours. The Christian goodness does not make a man proud; it makes him supremely grateful. When he looks at others, who are living the heathen and the pagan life, he does not regard them with contempt and with arrogant condemnation; he says, as Whitefield said when he saw the criminal on the way to the gallows: " There but for the grace of God go I."

It comes from the realization of what God has done for men in Jesus Christ. There is perhaps no passage in the New Testament which more summarily, and yet more fully, sets out the work of Christ for men than this passage does. There are seven outstanding facts about the work of Christ for men here.

(i) What Jesus did for us is that He put us into a new relationship with God. Till Jesus came, God was the King before whom men stood in awe, the Judge before whom men cringed in terror, the majestic Potentate whom they could regard only with fear. Jesus came to tell men of the Father whose heart was open and whose hands were stretched out in love. He came to tell men, not of the justice which would pursue them for ever until it caught up with them, but of the love which would never let them go.

(ii) This love and grace of God are gifts which no man could ever have earned or achieved; they can only be accepted in perfect trust and in awakened love. God offers His love to men, not for any deeds of righteousness that men have done, but simply out of the great goodness of His heart. The Christian never thinks of what he has earned; he only thinks of what God has given. The keynote of the Christian life must always be wondering and humble gratitude, and never proud self-satisfaction. The whole process is due to two great qualities of God.

It is due to the *goodness* of God. The word is *chrēstotēs*, and it means *benignity*. It means that spirit which is so kind that it is always ready and eager to give whatever gift may be necessary. It is ready to give forgiveness and blessings as each is required. *Chrēstotēs* is an all-embracing kindliness, which issues not only in a warm, nebulous glow of feeling, but also in generous action at all times.

It is due to God's *love to men*. The word is *philanthrōpia*, and it is defined as *love of man as man*. The Greeks thought much of this beautiful word. They used it for the good man's kindliness to his equals, for a good king's graciousness to his subjects, for a generous man's active pity for those in any kind of trouble or distress, and specially for the compassion which made a man ransom a fellow man when he had fallen into captivity.

At the back of all this is no merit of man; at the back of it there is the benign kindliness and the universal love of humanity which are in the heart of God.

(iii) This love and grace of God are mediated to men through the Church. They come to men through the sacrament of baptism. That is not to say that they can come in no other way. God is not confined within His sacraments; but it is to say that the door to them is ever open through the Church. When we think of baptism in the earliest days of the Church, we must always remember that it was the baptism of grown men and women who were coming direct out of paganism into the Christian Church. It was the deliberate leaving of one way of life to enter upon another and a new way. When Paul writes to the people of Corinth, he says: " Ye are washed, ye are sanctified, ye are justified " (I *Corinthians* 6: 11). In the letter to the Ephesians he says that Jesus Christ took the Church that " He might sanctify and cleanse it with the washing of water by the word " (*Ephesians* 5: 26.) In baptism there came to men the cleansing, re-creating power of God.

In this connection Paul uses two words.

He speaks of *rebirth* (*paliggenesia*). Here is a word which had many associations. When a proselyte was received into the Jewish faith, after he had been baptized, he was treated as if he had been a little child. It was as if he had been reborn and life had begun all over again. The Pythagoreans used the word frequently. They believed in reincarnation; they believed that men came back and back to life in many forms until they were fit to be released from life. Each return was a rebirth. The Stoics used the word. The Stoics believed that every three thousand years the world went up in a great conflagration, and that then there was a universal rebirth of a new world. When people entered the Mystery Religions they were said to be " reborn for eternity." The point is that when a man accepts Christ as Saviour and Lord, life begins all over again. There is a newness about life which can only be likened to a new birth.

He speaks of a *renewing*. It is as if life was worn out and run done; and when a man discovers Christ there is an act of renewal which is not over and done with in one moment of time, but which repeats itself every day.

CAUSE AND EFFECT

Titus 3: 3-7 (*continued*)

(iv) THE grace and love of God are mediated to men within the Church, but the essential power behind it all is the power of the Holy Spirit. All the work of the Church, all the words of the Church, all the sacraments of the Church are powerless and inoperative unless the power of the Holy Spirit is there. However highly a Church be organized, however splendid its ceremonies may be, however beautiful its buildings, and however elaborate its worship, all is ineffective without the power of the Spirit. The more we read the New Testament, the more we come to the conclusion that to the people of the early Church the Spirit and the Risen Christ were one and the same. The lesson is clear. Revival in the Church does not come from increased efficiency in organization; it comes from waiting upon God. It is not that efficiency is not necessary; it is. But no amount of efficiency can breathe life into a body from which the breath of the Spirit has departed.

(v) The effect of all this is threefold. It brings forgiveness for past sins. In His mercy God does not hold our sins against us. Sinners we may be, forgiven sinners we are. Once a man was mourning gloomily to Augustine about his sins. " Man," said Augustine, " look away from your sins and look to God." It is not that a man must not be throughout all his life in repentant sorrow for his sins; but the very memory of his sins moves him to wondering at the forgiving mercy of God.

(vi) But the effect of all this is also present life. Christianity does not confine its offer to blessings which shall be. It offers a man here and now life of a quality which he has never known before. When Christ enters into a man's life, for the first time a man really begins to live.

(vii) And lastly, there enters into life the hope of even greater things. The Christian is a man who lives in hope; he is a man for whom the best is always still to be; he knows that, however wonderful life on earth with Christ may be, the life to come will be even greater yet. The Christian is the man who knows the wonder of past sin forgiven, the thrill of present life lived with Christ, and the hope of the greater life which is yet to be.

THE NECESSITY OF ACTION AND THE DANGER OF DISCUSSION

Titus 3: 8-11

> This is a saying which we are bound to believe—and I want you to keep on affirming these things—that those who have put their faith in God must think and plan how to practise fine deeds. These are fine things and useful to men. But have nothing to do with foolish speculations and genealogies and contentious and legalistic battles, for they are no good to anyone and serve no useful purpose. Avoid a contentious and opinionative man, after giving him a first and a second warning, for you must be well aware that such a man is perverted and stands a self-condemned sinner.

THIS passage stresses the need for Christian action, and the danger of a certain kind of discussion.

The word which we have translated to *practise* fine deeds is the word *proistasthai*, which literally means *to stand in front of,* and it was the word which was used for a shopkeeper standing in front of his shop crying his wares and selling his goods. The whole phrase may mean either of two things. It might be a command to Christians only to engage in respectable and useful trades. There were certain professions which the early Church insisted that a man should quit before he was allowed even to ask for membership of the Christian Church. More probably the phrase has the wider meaning that a Christian must practise good deeds, which are helpful and useful to men.

The second part of the passage warns against useless discussions. The Greek philosophers spent their time on their fine-spun problems. The Jewish Rabbis spent their time building up imaginary and edifying genealogies for the characters of the Old Testament. The Jewish scribes spent endless hours discussing what could and could not be done on the Sabbath, and what was and was not unclean. It has been said that there is a danger that a man may think himself religious because he discusses religious questions. There is a kind of discussion group which argues simply for the sake of arguing. There is a kind of group which will argue for hours about theological questions. It is much easier to discuss theological questions than it is to be kind and considerate and helpful at home, or efficient and diligent and honest at work. There is no virtue in sitting discussing deep theological questions when the simple tasks of the Christian life are waiting to be done. It is indeed true that such discussion can be nothing other than an evasion of Christian duties.

Paul was quite certain that the real task of the Christian lay in Christian action. That is by no means to say that there is no place for Christian discussions; but it is to say that the discussion which does not end in action is very largely wasted time.

It is Paul's advice that the contentious and opinionative man should be avoided. The Authorised Version calls him the *heretic*. The Greek is *hairetikos*. The Greek verb *hairein* means *to choose*; and the Greek word *hairesis* means a party, or a school, or a sect. Originally the word had no bad meaning at all. A *hairesis* was not a heresy; it was simply the party to which a man chose to belong. The bad meaning creeps in when a man erects his private opinion against all the teaching, the agreement and the

303

tradition of the Church. A heretic is simply a man who has decided that he is right and everybody else is wrong. Paul's warning is a warning against the man who has made his own ideas the test and standard of all truth. A man should always be very careful of any opinion which separates him from the fellowship of his fellow believers. True faith does not divide men; it unites them.

FINAL GREETINGS

Titus 3: 12-15

> When I send Artemas or Tychicus to you, do your best to come to me at Nicopolis, for I have decided to spend the winter there.
> Do your best to help Zenas the lawyer and Apollos on their way. See to it that nothing is lacking to them.
> And let our people too learn to practise fine deeds, that they may be able to supply all necessary needs, and that they may not live useless lives.
> All who are with me send you their greetings. Greet those who love us in the faith.
> Grace be with you all. Amen.

As usual Paul ends his letter with personal messages and greetings. Of Artemas we know nothing at all. Tychicus was one of Paul's most trusted messengers. He was the bearer of both the letters to the Colossian and the Ephesian Churches (*Colossians* 4: 7; *Ephesians* 6: 21). Nicopolis was in Epirus, and was the best centre for work in the Roman province of Dalmatia. It is interesting to remember that it was there that Epictetus, the great Stoic philosopher, later had his school.

Apollos was the well-known teacher (*Acts* 18: 24). Of Zenas we know nothing at all. He is here called a *nomikos*. That could mean one of two things. *Nomikos* is the regular word for *a scribe*, and Zenas may have been a converted Jewish Rabbi. It is also the normal Greek for a *lawyer*;

and if that is its meaning, Zenas has the distinction of being the only lawyer mentioned in the New Testament.

Paul's last piece of advice is that the Christian people should practise good deeds, so that they themselves should be independent, and that they should be able to help others who are in need. The Christian workman works not only to have enough for himself, but also to have something to give away.

So there come the final greetings; and then, as in every letter, Paul's last word is grace.

THE LETTER TO PHILEMON

INTRODUCTION

The Unique Letter

IN one thing this little letter to Philemon is unique among Paul's letters. It is the only *private letter* of Paul which we possess. Doubtless Paul must have written many private letters; and doubtless these letters shared the fate of all private letters; doubtless they were destroyed; and of all these private letters only *Philemon* has survived. Apart altogether from the grace and the charm which pervade it, the fact that this is the only private letter written by Paul which we possess gives to this letter a unique interest and significance.

Onesimus, the runaway Slave

There are two possible reconstructions of what happened. The one, the ordinary view, is quite straightforward; the other, connected with the name of E. J. Goodspeed is rather more complicated, and is certainly more romantic and dramatic. Let us take the simple view first.

Onesimus was a runaway slave, and he was very probably a thief into the bargain. " If he has done you any damage," Paul writes, " or, if he owes you anything, put it down to my account—I will repay it " (verses 18 and 19). Somehow the runaway Onesimus had found his way to Rome, to lose himself in the thronging streets of that great city; and somehow he had come into contact with Paul. And somehow Onesimus had become a Christian, the child whom Paul had begotten in his bonds (verse 10).

Then something happened. It was obviously impossible for Paul to go on harbouring a runaway slave, and something happened to bring the problem to a head. Perhaps that happening was the coming of Epaphras. It may be that Epaphras recognized Onesimus as a slave he had seen at Colosse, and that thereupon the whole wretched story came out; or, it maybe that, with the coming of Epaphras, the conscience of Onesimus moved him to make a clean breast of all his discreditable past.

Paul sends Onesimus back

In the time that he had been with him Onesimus had made himself very nearly indispensable to Paul; and Paul would have liked to keep him beside him. " I could have wished to keep him beside myself," Paul writes (verse 12). But Paul will do nothing without the consent of Philemon, Onesimus' master (verse 13). So Paul sends Onesimus back. Now no one knew better than Paul how great a risk he was taking. Remember the position of the slaves. A slave was not a person; he was a living tool. Any master had the right of life and death over his slaves. The master had absolute power over his slaves. " He can box their ears or condemn them to hard labour—making them, for instance, work in chains upon his lands in the country, or in a sort of prison-factory. Or, he may punish them with blows of the rod, the lash or the knot; he can brand them upon the forehead, if they are thieves or runaways, or, in the end, if they prove irreclaimable, he can crucify them." Pliny tells how Vedius Pollio treated a slave. The slave was carrying a tray of crystal goblets into the courtyard; he dropped and broke one; on the instant Pollio ordered the slave to be thrown into the fishpond in the middle of the court, where the savage lampreys tore him to pieces. Juvenal draws the picture of the mistress who will beat her maidservant at her caprice, and the master who " delights in the sound of a cruel flogging, deeming it sweeter than any siren's song," who is never happy " until he has summoned a torturer and he can brand someone with a hot iron for stealing a couple of towels," " who revels in clanking chains." The slave was continually at the mercy of the caprice of a master or a mistress.

What made it worse was that the slaves were deliberately held down. There were in the Roman Empire 60,000,000 slaves. They inevitably formed a constant danger. No doubt they could be crushed, but if they did ever revolt, there would have been serious trouble. A rebellious slave was promptly eliminated. And, if a slave ran away, at best he would be branded with a red-hot iron on the forehead, with the letter F—standing for *fugitivus*, which means *runaway*—and at the worst he would be crucified and would die a torturing death. Paul well knew all this, and he knew that slavery was so ingrained into the ancient world that even to send Onesimus back to the Christian Philemon was a considerable risk.

Paul's Appeal

So Paul gave Onesimus this letter. He puns on Onesimus' name. *Onesimus* in Greek literally means *profitable*. Once Onesimus was a useless fellow, but he is useful now (verse 11). Now, as we might say, he is not only Onesimus by name, he is also Onesimus by nature. Maybe Philemon lost him for a time in order to have him for ever (verse 15). Philemon must take him back, not as a slave, but as a Christian brother (verse 16). He is now Paul's son in the faith, and Philemon must receive him as he would receive Paul himself.

Emancipation

Such, then, was Paul's appeal. Many people have wondered why Paul says nothing in this letter about the whole matter of slavery. He does not condemn slavery; he does not even tell Philemon to set Onesimus free; it is still as a slave that he would have him taken back. There are those who have criticized Paul for not seizing the opportunity to condemn the slavery on which the ancient world was built. Lightfoot says, " The word *emancipation* seems to tremble on his lips, but he never utters it." But there are certain reasons for Paul's silence on this problem.

Slavery was an integral part of the ancient world; the whole of society was built on it. Aristotle held that it was in the nature of things that certain men should be slaves, hewers of wood and drawers of water, to serve the higher classes of men. It may well be that Paul accepted the institution of slavery, because it was almost impossible to imagine ancient society without it. Further, if Christianity had, in fact, given the slaves any encouragement to revolt or to leave their masters, nothing but tragedy and disaster could have followed. Any such revolt would have been savagely crushed; any slave who took his freedom would have been mercilessly punished; and Christianity would itself have been branded as a revolutionary and sub-versionary treason. Given the Christian faith, emancipation was bound to come—but the time was not ripe; and to have encouraged slaves to hope for it, and to seize it, would have done infinitely more harm than good. There are some things which cannot be suddenly achieved, and for which the world must wait, until the leaven works.

The New Relationship

What Christianity did do was to introduce a new relation-ship between man and man, a relationship in which all external differences were abolished because all Christians are in Christ. Christians are one body whether they are Jews or Gentiles, slaves or free men (I *Corinthians* 12: 13) In Christ there is neither Jew nor Greek, slave nor free man, male nor female (*Galatians* 3: 28). In Christ there is neither Greek nor Jew, circumcision nor uncircumcision, barbarian, Scythian, slave or free man (*Colossians* 3: 11). It was as a slave that Onesimus ran away, and it was as a slave that he was coming back, but now he was not only a slave, he was a beloved brother in the Lord. When a relationship like that enters into life, social grades and castes cease to matter The very names, master and slave, become irrelevant. If the master treats the slave as Christ would have treated him, and if the slave serves the master as he would serve Christ, then it does not matter, if you call the one *master* and the other *slave*; their relationship does not depend on any human classification, for they are both in Christ. Christianity in the early days did not attack slavery; it never urged the emancipation of the slaves. To have done so would have been worse than useless; it would have been disastrous. But Christianity introduced a new relationship in which the human grades of society ceased to matter.

It is to be noted that that new relationship never gave the slave the right to be idle and lazy; it did not give him the right to take advantage of this new relationship; it made him a better slave, and a more efficient servant, for now he must do things in such a way that he could offer them to Christ. It did not mean that the master must be soft and easy-going, and willing to accept bad workmanship and inferior service; but it did mean that he no longer treated any servant as a thing, but as a person, and a brother in Christ.

There are two passages in which Paul sets out the duties of slaves and masters—*Ephesians* 6: 5-9 and *Colossians* 3: 22-4: 1. Both these passages were written when Paul was in prison in Rome, and most likely when Onesimus was with him; and it is difficult not to think that they owe much to long talks that Paul had with the runaway slave who had become a Christian.

So, then, on this view *Philemon* is a private letter, sent by Paul to Philemon, when he sent back Onesimus, Philemon's runaway slave; and it was written to urge Philemon to receive back Onesimus, not as a pagan master would, but as a Christian receives a brother, and forgives him.

Archippus

Let us now turn to the other view of what lies behind this letter.

We may begin our study of this view with a consideration of the place of Archippus. Archippus appears in both *Colossians* and *Philemon*. In *Philemon* greetings are sent to Archippus, *our fellow-soldier* (verse 2); and such a description might well mean that Archippus is the minister of the Christian community in question. Archippus is also mentioned in *Colossians* 4: 17: " Say to Archippus, take heed to thy ministry." Now that injunction comes after a whole series of very definite references, not to Colosse, but to *Laodicaea* (*Colossians* 4: 13, 15, 16). It is at least possible to think that Archippus must be at Laodicaea too. He certainly appears among the messages which are sent to

Laodicaea. Why in any event should he get this personal, verbal message? If he was at Colosse, he would hear the letter to Colosse read, as everyone else would. Why has this personal, verbal order to be sent to him? It is surely possible that the answer is that he is not in Colosse at all, but in Laodicaea.

If that is so, it means that Philemon's house is in *Laodicaea*; and it means that Onesimus was a runaway *Laodicaean* slave. This must mean that the letter to Philemon was, in fact, written to *Laodicaea*. And, if that is so, the missing letter to Laodicaea, mentioned in *Colossians* 4: 16 is none other than the letter to Philemon. This indeed solves problems.

Let us remember that in ancient society, with its view of slavery and its treatment of slaves, Paul took a very considerable risk in sending Onesimus back at all. So, it can be argued that *Philemon* is not really only a personal letter at all. It is indeed written to Philemon *and to the Church in his house*. And further it has also to be read at Colosse. What, then, was Paul doing? Knowing the risk that he took in sending Onesimus back, he was mobilising Church opinion both in Laodicaea and in Colosse in his favour. His reception is not to be left to the personal inclination of Philemon; it is one on which the brethren are to get together, and Christian opinion is to be lined up, so that the Christian thing may be done. In other words, the decision about Onesimus is not to be left to Philemon; it is to be the decision of the whole Christian community. It so happens that there is one little, but important linguistic point, which is very much in favour of this view. In verse 12 the Authorized Version makes Paul write that he has *sent back* or *sent again* Onesimus to Philemon. The verb is *anapempein*; this is the regular verb—it is commoner in this sense than in any other—for officially referring a case to someone for decision. And verse 12 should most probably be translated: " I am referring his case to you," that is, not only to Philemon, but also the Church in his house.

There is much to be said for this view. There is only one difficulty about it. In *Colossians* 4: 9 Onesimus is referred to as *one of you*, which certainly looks as if he was a Colossian. But E. J. Goodspeed, who states this view with such scholarship and persuasiveness, argues that Hierapolis, Laodicaea and Colosse were so close together, and so much a single Church, that they could well be regarded as one community, and that, therefore, *one of you* need not mean that Onesimus came from Colosse, but simply that he came from that closely connected group. If we are prepared to accept this, then the last obstacle to this theory is removed.

The Continuation of the Story

But Goodspeed does not stop there. He goes on to reconstruct the history of Onesimus in a most moving way.

In verses 13 and 14 Paul makes it quite clear that he would much have liked to keep Onesimus with him. " I would have wished to keep him beside myself, that he might serve me for you, in the bonds which the gospel has brought to me; but I did not wish to do anything without your consent, so that the boon I desire might not be forcibly extracted but willingly given." He reminds Philemon that Philemon owes him his very soul (verse 19). He says, with charming wit, " Let me make some Christian profit out of you!" (verse 20). He says, " I am writing with confidence, for I know that you will do more than I ask " (verse 21). Is it possible that Philemon could have resisted this appeal? In face of language like that could he do anything else than send Onesimus back to Paul with his blessing? So Goodspeed regards it as certain that Paul got Onesimus back, and that Onesimus became Paul's helper and ally in the work of the gospel.

The Bishop of Ephesus

But now let us move on for about fifty years. Ignatius, one of the great Christian martyrs, is being taken to be executed from Antioch, his Church, to Rome. As he goes, he writes letters—which still survive—to the Churches of Asia Minor. He stops at Smyrna, and he writes to the Church at Ephesus, and in the first chapter of that letter, he has much to say about their wonderful bishop. And what is the bishop's name? It is *Onesimus*; and Ignatius makes exactly the same pun as Paul made—he is Onesimus by name and Onesimus by nature, the profitable one to Christ. It may well be that Onesimus, the runaway slave, had become with the passing years none other than Onesimus, the great bishop of Ephesus.

What Christ did for me

And, if all this is so, we have still another explanation. Why did this little slip of a letter, this single papyrus sheet, survive? How is it that this letter, half-personal, half-official, ever get itself into the collection of the Pauline letters? It deals with no great doctrine; it attacks no great heresy; it is the only one of Paul's undoubted letters written to an individual person. It is practically certain that the first collection of Paul's letters was made at *Ephesus*. There, maybe, about the turn of the century, these letters were collected, edited and published. It was just at that time that Onesimus was bishop of Ephesus. And it may well be that it was Onesimus who insisted that this letter must be included in the collection, little and short and personal as it was, in order that all men might know what the grace of God had done for him. Through it the great bishop tells the world that once he was a runaway slave and thief, and that he owed his life to Paul and to Jesus Christ. Through it the great bishop insists on telling of his own shame that that his very shame might redound to the glory of God.

Did Onesimus come back to Paul with Philemon's blessing? Did he become the great bishop of Ephesus, he who had been the thievish runaway slave? Did he insist that this little letter must be included in the Pauline collection to tell what Christ, through Paul, had done for him? We can never tell for certain; but if that is so, then here is one of the great romances of grace of the early Church. We can never be certain, but it is a lovely story—and we hope that it is true!

THE LETTER TO PHILEMON

A MAN TO WHOM IT WAS EASY TO APPEAL

Philemon 1-7

> This is a letter from Paul, the prisoner of Jesus Christ, and from Timothy, the brother, to Philemon our well-beloved and our fellow-worker; and to Apphia, the sister, and to Archippus, our fellow-soldier, and to the Church in your house. Grace be to you and peace from God, our Father, and from the Lord Jesus Christ.
>
> I always thank my God when I make mention of you in my prayers, for I hear of your love and your faith, which you have to the Lord Jesus, and to all God's dedicated people. I pray that the kindly deeds of charity to which your faith moves you may be powerfully effective to increase your knowledge of every good thing that is in us and that brings us ever closer to Christ. You have brought me much joy and encouragement, because, my brother, the hearts of God's people have been refreshed by you.

THE letter to Philemon is an extraordinary letter, for in it we see the extraordinary sight of Paul asking a favour. No man ever asked fewer favours than Paul did, but in this letter he is asking a favour, not so much for himself, as for Onesimus, who had taken the wrong turning, and whom Paul was helping to find the way back.

The very beginning of the letter is unusual. Paul usually identifies himself as Paul *an apostle;* but on this occasion he is writing as a friend to a friend, and the official title is dropped. He is not writing as Paul *the apostle,* but as Paul *the prisoner of Christ.* Here at the very beginning Paul lays aside all appeal to authority, and makes his appeal to sympathy and to love alone.

We do not know who Apphia and Archippus were, but it has been suggested that Apphia was the wife, and Archippus the son of Philemon, for they, too, would be very much interested in the return of Onesimus, the runaway slave. Certainly Archippus had seen Christian service with Paul, for Paul so asks of him as his fellow-campaigner.

Philemon was clearly a man from whom it was easy to

ask a favour. He was a man whose faith in Christ and whose love to the brethren all men knew, and the story of them had reached even Rome, where Paul was in prison. His house must have been like an oasis in a desert, for, as Paul had it, he had refreshed the hearts of God's people. It is a lovely thing to go down to history as a man in whose house God's people were rested and refreshed.

In this passage there is one verse which is very difficult to translate and about which much has been written. It is the prayer of Paul for Philemon in verse 6. The Authorized Version translation is not very intelligible: " (I pray) that the communication of thy faith may become effectual by the acknowledging of every good thing which is in you in Christ Jesus." The last part of the prayer is a prayer that Philemon may grow in the fuller knowledge of all good things which lead to Christ. The beginning of the verse, the phrase which the Authorized Version translates, *the communication of your faith*, is very difficult. The Greek is *koinōnia pisteōs*. As far as we can see, there are three possible meanings. (*a*) *Koinōnia* can mean *a sharing in*; it can, for instance, mean partnership in a business. So this may mean *your share in the Christian faith*; and it might be a prayer that the faith which Philemon and Paul both share in may lead Philemon deeper and deeper into Christian truth. (*b*) *Koinōnia* can mean fellowship; and this may be a prayer that *Christian felllowship* may lead Philemon ever more deeply into the truth. (*c*) *Koinōnia* can mean the *act of sharing*; it can, therefore, mean Christian charity, Christian giving, Christian generosity in sharing. In that case the verse will mean: " It is my prayer that your way of generously sharing and giving away all that you have will lead you more and more deeply into the knowledge of the good things which lead to Christ."

We think that the third meaning is correct. Obviously Christian generosity and Christian charity were characteristics of Philemon; he had love to God's people and in his home they were rested and refreshed. And now Paul is going to ask the generous man to be still more generous yet. There is a great thought here, if this interpretation is correct. It means that we learn about Christ by giving to others. It means that we receive from Christ by sharing with others. It means that by emptying ourselves we are filled with Christ. It means that the poorer we make ourselves in giving, the richer we are in the gifts of Christ. It means that to be open-handed and generous-hearted is the surest way to learn more and more of the wealth of Christ. The man who knows most of Christ is not the intellectual scholar, not even the saint who shuts himself up and spends his days in prayer, but the man who moves in loving generosity amongst his fellow-men.

THE REQUEST OF LOVE

Philemon 8-17

> I could well be bold in Christ to give you orders as to where your duty lies, but for love's sake I would rather put it in the form of a request, I, Paul, such as I am, an old man now, a prisoner of Christ. My request to you is for my child, whom I begat in my bonds—I mean Onesimus, who was once useless to you, but who is now useful to you and to me. I am sending him back to you, and that is the same as to send you a bit of my own heart. I could have wished to keep him beside myself, that he might serve me for you in the bonds which the gospel has brought to me; but I did not wish to do anything without your approval; so that the boon which I ask might not be forcibly extracted but willingly given. It may be that he was parted from you for a time that you might get him back for ever; and that you might get him back, no longer as a slave, but as more than a slave—a well-beloved brother, most of all to me, and how much more to you, both as a man and a Christian. If you consider me as a partner, receive him as you would receive me.

PAUL, being Paul, could have demanded what he wished from Philemon, but he will only humbly request. A gift to be a gift must be given freely and with good-will; a gift which is coerced out of a man is no gift at all.

In verse 9 Paul describes himself. The Authorized Version translates—and we have retained the translation—Paul *the aged*, and a prisoner of Christ. There is a good number of scholars who wish to substitute another translation for *aged*. It is argued that Paul could not really be described as an old man. He certainly was not sixty years old; he was somewhere between that and fifty-five. But on this ground those who object to the translation *aged* are wrong. The word which Paul uses of himself is *presbutēs*, and Hippocrates, the great Greek medical writer, says that a man is *presbutēs*, from the age of forty-nine to the age of fifty-six. Between these years he is what we might call *senior*; only after that does he become a *gerōn*, which is the Greek for an old man. But what is the other translation which is suggested? There are two words which are very like each other; their spelling is only one letter different; and their pronunciation would be exactly the same. they are the words *presbutēs*, which means *old*, and *presbeutēs*, which means an *ambassador*. It is the verb of this word which Paul uses in *Ephesians* 6:20, when he says, " I am an *ambassador* in bonds." If we think that the word ought to be *presbeutēs*, Paul will be saying, " I am an ambassador, although I am an ambassador in chains." But it is far more likely that we should retain the translation *old*, for in this letter Paul is appealing all the time, not to any office he holds, or to any authority he enjoys, but only to love. It is not the ambassador who is speaking, but the man who has lived hard, and who is now lonely and tired.

Then Paul makes his request in verse 10, and his request is for Onesimus. We notice how he delays pronouncing the name of Onesimus, almost as if he hesitated to do so. Paul does not make any excuses for Onesimus; he freely admits he was a useless and a worthless character; but he makes one claim for him—he is useful now. Christianity, as James Denney used to say, is the power which can make bad men good. It is significant to note that Paul claims that in Christ the useless person has been made useful. The last thing that Christianity is designed to produce is vague, inefficient, dreamy, nebulous people; it produces people who are of use, people who have a grip of things, people who can do a job better than the man who does not know Christ can ever do it. It was said of some one that " he was so heavenly-minded that he was no earthly use." But true Christianity makes a man heavenly-minded and useful upon earth at one and the same time.

Paul calls Onesimus the child whom he has begotten in his bonds. There is a Rabbinic saying which says, " If one teaches the son of his neighbour the law, the Scripture reckons this the same as though he had begotten him." To bring a man to God, to lead a man to Jesus Christ, is as great a thing as to bring him into the world. Happy is the parent who brings his child into life, and who then leads him into life eternal, for then his child will be his child twice over.

As we have noted in the introduction to this letter, there is a double meaning in verse 12. " I am sending him back to you," writes Paul. But the verb *anapempeim* does not only mean *to send back*; it also means *to refer a case to*; and Paul is saying to Philemon: " I am referring this case of Onesimus to you, that you may give a verdict on it that will match the love you ought to have." Onesimus must have become very dear to Paul in these months in prison, for Paul pays him the great tribute of saying that to send Onesimus to Philemon is like sending a bit of his own heart.

Then there comes the appeal. Paul would have liked to keep Onesimus, but he sends him back to Philemon, for he will do nothing without Philemon's consent. Here again is a significant thing. Christianity is not out to help a man to escape his past and to run away from it; it is out to enable a man to face his past and to rise above it. Onesimus had run away. Well, then, he must not be allowed to evade the consequences of his misdeeds. He must go back, and he must face up to the consequences of what he did; and then be must accept the consequences and must rise above them. Christianity is never escape; Christianity is always conquest.

But Onesimus comes back with a difference. He went away as a heathen slave; he comes back as a brother in Christ. It is going to be hard for Philemon to regard a runaway slave as a brother; but that is exactly what Paul demands. " If you agree," says Paul, " that I am your partner in the work of Christ, and that Onesimus is my son in the faith, then you must receive him as you would receive me, myself."

Here again is something very significant. The Christian must always welcome back the man who has made a mistake. Too often we regard the man who has made a mistake and who has taken the wrong turning with suspicion; too often we show that we are never prepared to trust him again. We can believe that God can forgive him; but we, ourselves, find it very difficult to forgive him. It has been said that the most uplifting thing about Jesus Christ is that He trusts us on the very field of our defeat. When a man has made a mistake, the way back can be very hard, and God will not readily forgive the man who, in his self-righteousness or his lack of sympathy, makes it harder.

THE CLOSING APPEAL AND THE CLOSING BLESSING

Philemon 18-25

> If he has done you any damage, or, if he owes you anything, put it down to my account. I, Paul, write with my own hand—I will repay it, not to mention to you that you owe your very self to me. Yes, my brother, let me make some Christian profit out of you! Refresh my heart in Christ. It is with complete confidence in your willingness to listen that I write to you, for I know well that you will do more than I ask.
>
> At the same time get ready a lodging place for me; for I hope that through your prayers it will be granted to you that I should come to you.

Epaphras, my fellow-prisoner in Christ, sends his greetings to you, as do Mark, Aristarchus, Demas and Luke, my fellow-workers.

The grace of the Lord Jesus Christ be with your spirit. Amen.

IT is one of the laws of the Christian life that someone has to pay the price of sin. God can and does forgive, but not even God can free a man from the consequences of what he has done. But it is the glory of the Christian faith that, just as Jesus Christ shouldered the sins of all men, so there are those who in love are prepared to help to pay for the consequences of the sins and the mistakes of those who are dear to them. Christianity never entitled a man to default on his debts. Onesimus must have stolen from Philemon, as well as running away from him. If he had not helped himself to Philemon's money, it is difficult to see how he could ever have covered the long road to Rome. But Paul writes with his own hand that he will be responsible and that he will repay in full.

It is interesting to note that this is an exact instance of a *cheirographon*, the kind of acknowledgment which we were studying in *Colossians* 2: 14. This is *a handwriting against Paul*, an obligation voluntarily accepted and signed.

It is of interest to note that Paul was able and willing to pay Onesimus' debts. Every now and again we get glimpses which show that Paul was not without financial resources. Felix kept him prisoner for he had hopes of a bribe to let him go; Felix must have believed that Paul was well enough off to pay a bribe (*Acts* 24: 26). Paul was able to hire a house during his imprisonment in Rome (*Acts* 28: 30). It may well be that, if Paul had not chosen to live the life of a missionary of Christ, he might have lived a settled life of reasonable ease and comfort on his own resources. This may well have been another of the things which Paul gave up for Christ.

In verse 20 we hear Paul speaking with a flash of humour. " Philemon," he says, " you owe your soul to me, for it was I who brought you to Christ. Won't you let me make some profit out of you now?" With an affectionate smile Paul is saying, " Philemon you got a lot out of me—let me get something out of you now!"

Verse 21 is typical of Paul's dealings with people. It was Paul's rule always to expect the best from others. He never really doubted that Philemon would grant all his request. It is a good rule; to expect the best from others is often to be more than half way to getting the best. If we make it clear that we expect little, we will get little. But if we put a man upon his honour by showing him that we expect much from him, the sleeping chivalry of the human heart will be awakened, and we will get much from him from whom we expect much.

In verse 22 there speaks Paul's optimism. Even in prison he believes it possible that through the prayers of his friends freedom may come again. He has changed his plans now. Before he was imprisoned it had been his intention to go to far off Spain (*Romans* 15: 24, 28). Maybe after the years in prison, two years at Caesarea and other two long years at Rome, Paul felt that he must leave the distant places and the ends of the earth to younger men, and that for him, as he grew near the end, old friends were best.

In verse 23 there is a list of greetings from the same comrades as we met in *Colossians*, and its closing sections, and there we set down all that can be known of them.

And so there comes the blessing, and Philemon and Onesimus alike are commended to the grace of Christ.